Master Gardener

Rolf Margenau

Master Gardener is a work of fiction.
Names, characters, incidents, places, and organizations are the product of the author's imagination or are used fictitiously. Any resemblance to actual persons, living or dead, events, organizations, or locales are entirely coincidental.

Published in the United States by Frogworks Publishing
ISBN: 9780988231115
eBook ISBN-13: 9780988231108

Frogworks Publishing, Tewksbury New Jersey
www.frogworks.com
Typeset by Amnet Systems

By Rolf Margenau

PUBLIC INFORMATION

HIGH ANDES

NATIONAL PARKS

LONGEVITY

PISTILS AND POETRY

THE COMMODE COMPANION

Author's Note

I HAD BUT a hazy awareness of genetic engineering in agriculture until the second month of instruction in Rutgers' Master Gardener training program. The lecturer explained how major chemical companies modified seeds, principally for commercial crops like corn, soybeans and wheat, to enhance their productive qualities and to grow through chemically treated soil inhospitable to weeds.

At the same time, there were newspaper articles about questions raised by numerous scientists concerning the ecological damage both modified seeds and chemical soil treatments caused. Among those reports was a story about the millions of acres of farmland sprayed with chemicals to eradicate weeds – including milkweed. Since monarch butterflies lay their eggs on milkweed and their larvae eat it, that imperils the monarchs. It was suggested that perhaps weeds on farms should be protected.

Having recently visited the monarchs' overwintering grounds in Mexico, that information disturbed me. Since I was involved in a gardening training program anyway, I began to learn more about how seeds are genetically engineered, read the annual reports of major chemical companies, and challenged my non-scientific brain by studying the pros and cons of steps to enhance worldwide agricultural production.

I relied on the knowledge of many gardening friends, on information contained in the University of Maryland Master Gardener Handbook, various gardening websites, and my own experience of trying to grow things. Additional resources were 30 back copies of Garden Gate magazine and Month by Month gardening books. It was impossible to provide advice for gardening throughout the country, so I focused on the East and the fictional state of New Anglia. Given Bitsy's strict sense of probity, she avoided plagiarism in any form.

My story needed a villain. I recalled the characteristics of the few unsavory leaders I came across working with business people, and those traits formed the basis for Dick Geier's persona. As CEO of BIG AG, he could make trouble for my characters.

This book is fiction. No chemical company has ever infiltrated the ranks of Master Gardeners. That would be heresy.

Finally, the national Master Gardener program is a worthwhile and helpful effort to educate the public in the most beneficial aspects of gardening, to foster an awareness of the joy and beauty of growing things, and to preserve the finer aspects of our natural world. My association with the program in my state has provided a splendid continuing gardening education, an opportunity to work with wonderful and selfless people, and a chance to share the joy of nurturing growing things.

Rolf Margenau, Tewksbury NJ -- 2019

Table of Contents

Author's Note	v
Belen	ix
Chapter 1	1
Chapter 2	13
Chapter 3	31
Chapter 4	45
Chapter 5	61
Chapter 6	81
Chapter 7	100
Chapter 8	123
Chapter 9	141
Chapter 10	163
Chapter 11	186
Chapter 12	208
Chapter 13	230
Chapter 14	247
Epilogue	271
Afterword	275

Belen

THE SMALL, BAREFOOT boy flew across the cobblestones of the Belen Market as though pursued by a swarm of hornets. He slipped as a heel contacted stones slick with fish guts and almost slid into a thick post at the curb. A turkey buzzard perched on the lamppost beside the river registered disapproval of this disturbance by ruffling her feathers and craning her pink bald head to one side. That motion was repeated by other birds waiting atop crude streetlights as the boy righted himself, churned down an alley toward the river and disappeared into a ramshackle dwelling precariously resting on stilts rising from the brown water.

One of the buzzards was unwilling to wait until the market closed for the evening when the birds could feast on the scraps and offal swept to the center of the cobblestones. He abandoned his perch, soared on the high from the water's edge, and adjusted his pinions to float effortlessly above the market, searching for available food. Below, the area was divided roughly between small shops floating near the bank of the Amazon River in Iquitos, Peru, and concrete warehouses and substantial buildings pushing against the shoreline. At five o'clock every morning commerce began, with boats laden with the daily needs of the town's people arriving from villages and farms along the river. One warehouse filled with bananas, the next with large bags of charcoal. Melons, nuts, guarana, acai and green and yellow vegetables from jungle farms arrived on the backs of porters, straining against headbands supporting 80-kilo loads.

Firewood was stacked beside walls. Caiman and catfish, fresh and dried, stared from tables wobbling on the stone pavers. Umbrellas opened as the sun rose and the heat and humidity intensified the raucous odors of the market. In back corners, illegal poachers tried to sell baby jungle animals, orphaned when they killed their mothers. Small marmosets, woolly monkeys, anteaters, capybaras, red-faced monkeys, sloths, parrots and macaws strained against rattan cages. Children poked sticks at them.

At first light, shamans from the villages arrived, selling loose tobacco, cigarettes and potions designed to cure almost all known ailments. Numerous shops sold 120 proof seven-herbs liquor; if the herbs didn't work, the alcohol did, in most cases. In one three-block section, hawkers displayed medicinal items from the jungle. Red, brown, yellow and black bark from jungle trees filled bins along the sidewalk. Vendors would press heat-producing bark powders into shoppers' hands to demonstrate the power of their products. In fact, potent pharmaceutical products had been derived from some of these jungle trees. In the area devoted to fresh produce, sellers extolled the quality of mangos, avocados and plantains. Seeds of all sorts in plastic envelopes were stacked on shelves. Household goods, plastic pails and basins, children's clothing, work shirts and the latest styles of blue jeans were piled on tables, threatening to spill onto cobblestones moist from humidity.

Belen is one of the largest and most colorful markets in South America.

The bazaar appealed mainly to the town's people, who found almost all their daily needs there. Tourists were not encouraged, and petty theft was rampant. However, hardy souls from docked tour boats, or coming and going from various jungle lodges along the river, occasionally visited – cameras at the ready and passports and money tucked in wallets sequestered about their midsections. Many of them tired of the noise and smells before completely navigating the thirty-block area, and some of them did have unfortunate interactions with petty thieves.

The buzzard spotted the body of a lizard decapitated by a house cat on a wooden boardwalk next to one of the shacks along the river and swooped down to collect that tidbit. As it happened, that was the shack the small boy had entered so hastily. He was a scrawny seven-year-old called Edson Montechristo Gonzales-Moro. His mother was convinced that someday he would grow into his name. Breathlessly, the boy stood before his mother and offered her the silver trinket he clutched in his small brown hand, a worn lady's Timex watch with a slender silver band. He claimed he had discovered it lying beside one of the market booths. Edson, unfortunately, had a reputation for finding things that were not actually lost, and his mother challenged his story. Well, he admitted, it might have slipped off the wrist of one of the gringas wandering through the market but, he said brightly, he believed his mother had a greater need for it than the old, red-faced woman did. His mother sighed. My boy, she thought, may God protect you, for I am not sure I can!

Anne Proctor probably would have bridled at being called an old, red-faced woman. Yes, recent exposure to sun while riding in canoes and small boats on tributaries to the great river had enhanced her natural color, but she was in her mid-forties – not old. She was spending her last day in Iquitos before returning to the United States, soaking up local color and photographing the sights of the market to share with her garden club in Middletown. The exotic sights and colors of the market excited her, and she was not as attentive as she might have been while reaching out to feel the texture of a strange green fruit with odd bumps. At that moment, Edson Montechristo Gonzales-Moro's slender hand dislodged her watch from her wrist. He vanished before she even realized it was gone. Well, she thought, I was warned by the guide, so I guess it's my fault. She was determined not to let the small theft spoil her last day on this jungle adventure.

Moving along the stone path between the concrete buildings and the river, she noticed several stands displaying large and attractive fresh vegetables that surpassed in color, quality and size anything she was able to grow in her garden in the Northeastern United States. There were lima and string beans, cucumbers, corn, cabbage, okra and sheaves of grain that seemed to burst with internal energy. On a dusty shelf behind one of the stalls, she noticed a handful of seed packets arranged in plastic sleeves. In her fractured Spanish, she inquired about them and was assured they would, no question about it, germinate and grow in her home garden. The shop owner, a woman of her own age, personally guaranteed it. And what plants were the seeds for? Mainly beans, but some melons, wheat and corn – maybe a few others. They were all she had.

Anne offered the few soles remaining in her purse and collected the seeds, considering them a wonderful souvenir of her visit. After all, she usually found seeds for her garden on other vacation visits, though never from so exotic a place as the Belen market. She knew the seeds would not take up much space in her carry on and were certainly easy to ease past customs back in the States.

Anne gave a farewell glance to the broad green expanse of the Amazon River. The little glassine packets of seeds crackled in her hand and reflected waning sunlight. However, in the rush of activities upon her return to Middletown, the seeds were forgotten. They remained in a zippered compartment of her suitcase for many years. Their later rediscovery and use far from the great river would affect world agriculture and, unfortunately, imperil Anne Proctor.

Chapter 1

MARCH

Middletown Courier-Times

Mastering your Garden

By Elizabeth Pendleton Crangle

Since gardening is America's number one hobby, Marc Graddis, our editor, asked me to write a monthly column about all the things that need doing in the home garden. As a long-time member of the Middletown Garden Club and a New Anglia Master Gardener for the past eight years, I am happy to pass along information to make gardening fun and productive. This is my first attempt.

Unfortunately, there are so many plant categories, ranging from houseplants and fruits to shrubs and vegetables, there is no way I can cover them all in the column inches Marc has allowed, so I'm going to focus on the vegetable and flower garden this month, and say a few words about your lawn.

What a winter we had! Record-breaking snow falls and an ice storm that cut off our power for almost a week. Not good for shrubs, which broke under the ice (get those pruning shears ready!), but the plants should be fine after that nice white insulation. Now is the time to check and divide bulbs and tubers you wintered over and toss out the soft and mushy ones. Pot up your begonias and cannas and make sure they get lots of sun.

About the only flower you can plant from seed outside this month is the annual poppy. Just toss the seed in a meadow area and rake lightly. Many flower seeds can be started indoors early this month: dianthus, snapdragons, dusty millers, petunias and impatiens are a few of the popular seeds. You can also prepare a new bed by covering it with a piece of old carpet or used exterior plywood pieces this month. Anchor them with rocks. No grass or weeds in May!

Remember to plant peas on Saint Patty's day but be sure to give them something to climb on. My sugar snaps grew over six feet last year. After you get those peas in the ground, you can plant onions (from seeds or sets), spinach and potatoes. On potatoes, be sure each piece has two or three eyes, and use a lot of organic matter in the soil. This is also a good time to make up your vegetable garden plan and start your warm season seeds like peppers, tomatoes and eggplants. Don't forget to rotate your crops (like all good gardeners) and move nitrogen-fixing veggies, like beans, around each year. It's especially important to rotate veggies in the nightshade family, like tomatoes, peppers, eggplants and potatoes.

For fun, plan to include some of the more exotic veggies you saw in all those seed catalogs that showed up during the first part of the year. Remember all the things that show up in the supermarket during the summer and plant something else. Your neighbors will be impressed.

Serious lawn renovations should be done in September, but you can do spring seeding this month. If you haven't had it checked for a while, get a pH soil test kit from the county Ag center to see whether you need to lime your lawn. Don't waste your money on expensive fertilizer, just make sure it has low or no phosphorous, and be sure to follow the label and NOT add too much nitrogen. That does nasty things to our water supply!

Marc says no more than 500 words – and I'm over that already. Time to plant some seeds with Hubby. You can ask me questions at Bitsy@cranglehouse.com or call/visit your Master Gardener helpline in the Middletown Municipal Hall.

Blissful gardening - Bitsy

Wylie

The young Weimaraner sat quietly beside the bed, gazing curiously at her master's face. Attracted by the sputtering snores from his bedroom, she had left her place in the hallway and settled on the hooked rug next to his bed, fascinated by his fluttering lips, the grunts and whistles. He lay on his left side, his head on a pillow, facing her. His lips were on a level plane, inches away from her nose. She released the pink tip of her tongue to sample the lips. They tasted of the essence of her beloved master, and she decided to expand her exploration and began licking his lips as though chasing a tick between her legs. The experience was pure delight.

Wylie remained in deep slumber, but the novel sensation of tongue on lips intruded on the parts of the brain that conjure dreams. The middle brain's split-second encyclopedic reference to Wylie's experiences and sensations drew a blank. At a loss, electric synapses scurried to invent a scenario appropriate to the intense rubbing on his lips, and he experienced the sensation of rough waves abrading his skin. Dissatisfied, the brain reconsidered as he began to waken and substituted the erotic pulse of a passionate kiss during lovemaking.

As he opened his eyes, Wylie remained under the influence of his dream and briefly enjoyed a mild tumescence. He then recognized Emma's eager eyes and realized she was licking his lips. He pulled his face away and spat involuntarily, then rubbed his mouth with the back of his hand. Emma responded with a soulful look and licked her large russet nose.

"Dammit, big girl, get outta here!" he exclaimed.

The dog sat down next to the bed, waiting for a more serious order. He made no move to punish or strike her. His long association with dogs allowed him to recognize she was simply doing her thing. Punishment would only confuse her, and it certainly would not make him feel better. He yawned and reached out to scratch her behind a long gray ear, then patted her head. She moved as he swung his legs from the bed, searching for slippers with his toes.

Linda had left her side of the bed not long before. Her pillow was indented and smelled of the cream she applied nightly, and he sensed retained warmth under the covers beside him. Slippers secured, he raised himself upright, supported by the bedpost, and began his morning ritual with halting steps toward the bathroom. As usual, he felt phantom pain at the side of his left foot where his little toe was so brutally amputated. Emma padded behind him. Wylie counted three trips to the bathroom since retiring for bed. For years, his prostate had denied uninterrupted sleep. He sat to urinate and began to recall his plans for the day ahead. Sunlight spilled through the bathroom window. That was a good sign.

He rubbed the stubble on his chin and decided to wait until the next day to shave. His perennially dry left eye stung a bit and resisted opening, so he splashed warm water on his face and flushed the eye until it felt almost normal and the cloudy mucus covering dissolved. With restored vision, he examined his face in the mirror, wondering at the deep furrows on cheeks and forehead and the wisps of hair struggling from his scalp. Wryly he repeated his customary morning thought. Well, you old fart, you're still here, but you continue to look about thirty years older than you feel. The furrows deepened as a smile appeared. Well, you still have all your teeth.

As Wylie walked into the kitchen, Linda was stirring an omelet over the flames of the gas grille in the center island. She was dressed in a fuzzy pink bathrobe that had loosened, displaying ample décolletage as she leaned over the pan. Wylie was about to encircle her with his arms and give an affectionate squeeze to her breasts when he noticed Portia, his granddaughter, snuggled in a corner of the breakfast nook, holding a cup of coffee, watching a pair of blue jays attacking the bird feeder. They shone a brilliant blue and black against the light dusting of snow on the little yard behind his condominium.

Wylie postponed his plans for the frontal attack on Linda and moved to the coffee pot on the kitchen counter.

"So, Porrie, what excitement have you planned for today?" he asked as he poured his first cup of coffee.

"Not very exciting. Second semester constitutional law with Professor Arnold, insurance and preparation for a moot court argument Friday night. Think you might want to see me in action? A few tips from an old… I can't believe I said that! I mean 'seasoned' litigator would be appreciated."

"Friday night is doable, right, Linda? We have nothing else planned?"

Linda pretended to consult an imaginary smart phone in her left hand as she deftly turned the omelet and slid it onto Wylie's plate.

"Nothing except that dinner at the governor's mansion," she joked.

She knew Wylie detested the governor and enjoyed his scowl as he reacted to her comment.

He joined Portia at the breakfast table by the window and sipped his coffee. Linda had arranged his morning pills next to his plate: omeprazole for recurring heartburn probably caused by his hiatus hernia, and simvastatin for elevated cholesterol that no form of dieting seemed to help. Relying on medications pained him. He recalled seeing his mother and father dole out little cairns of pills at each meal and resolved then he would never do that. So demeaning! The pills slid down his throat assisted by a gulp of orange juice, and he attacked the omelet.

The two women in his kitchen exchanged banter and teased him about his recent designation as a "certified" Master Gardener, as reported in the Courier-Times. He accepted their comments with good nature.

Two years ago, Wylie had tired of the practice of law. He specialized in international legal work, principally involved in the buying and selling of businesses. The constant travel, time changes and stresses of negotiating took their toll, and Wylie bequeathed his clients to younger members of his firm. As he withdrew from active practice, he found pleasure in tending his little garden and relearning the botany he studied in college. At a gardening center, he learned of the county Master Gardener program.

Washington State University Cooperative Extension in the Seattle area founded the prototype of the program in the early seventies. The curriculum provided extensive training to volunteers who, in exchange, would provide gardening information to the public. Since then, land grant universities in all fifty states, through their cooperative extension services, created similar programs. The one in Marlborough County, where Middletown was located, was quite active.

Wylie eagerly responded to the county agriculture agent's notice of openings in the Master Gardener program and diligently pursued seven months of training followed by one hundred and fifty hours of indentured servitude to the state university's agricultural extension program. He particularly enjoyed working at the state experimental farm located on 150 rolling acres a few miles south of Middletown. The Van Poppen family had bequeathed the farm to the University for agricultural use.

The family made its fortune supplying artillery shells to the military during World War I. In the early twenties, the munitions factory area was converted into a large horse farm with substantial acreage devoted to corn, hay and soybeans. In 1952, the Van Poppen descendants lost interest in the farm and decided to deed the farm to the university, taking a substantial charitable deduction.

In the seventies, a plume of improperly disposed of factory waste was discovered and the university had to take remedial action under new regulations promulgated by the Environmental Protection Agency. Fortunately, a grant from the Bemis International Group, Agricultural Chemicals Division ("BIG AG") provided the necessary funds. BIG AG enjoyed a long and prosperous relationship with the university.

In addition to working at the Van Poppen farm, Wylie happily participated in the Master Gardener help line, providing gardening information to the public. He drove from his home to their office in the basement of the county seat by the Middletown square two mornings a week, met with other Master Gardeners and fielded questions from the public. The "MGs," as they called themselves, were a very congenial group. Though they were not replacements for his old cronies, he made new friends who shared his interest in growing things. Upon completing the hours needed for certification, Wylie was awarded a plastic badge on which his name was engraved – and proper notice appeared in the local paper. His pinochle-playing friends had observed it as well.

The three friends in his weekly pinochle group provided pointed taunting about his new status the evening before. They were Wylie's best friends in Middletown – Sy Wiser, an oral surgeon who had salvaged Wylie's gums; Arnie Brackett, judge of the appellate court, who was Wylie's classmate in law school; and Billy Clarke, a self-identified fishmonger who owned a large chain of fish and chips restaurants in New Anglia and seven nearby states.

"So," demanded Billy, "that mean you're not a shyster anymore? Diggin' in the dirt instead of slinging mud?" As usual, he laughed at his own witticism.

"One of my patients recently presented me with a certified Virginia ham. And I sometimes get certified letters. A certified public accountant does my taxes. So, who is the great certifier that decides you are now authorized to garden? I may need to see him before I prune my roses," Sy added in his dry fashion.

Arnie simply rolled his eyes and concentrated on his cards. He was proud of his friend and looked forward to Wylie's help in his own, rather sorry, flower garden. Consequently, he refrained from serious taunting, but did mumble about Wylie's well-known black thumb.

Tired of teasing Wylie, Portia shared with Linda details of a date she had with her recently acquired boyfriend. He presented her with a bag of chalk and introduced her to rock climbing at an abandoned quarry in the northern part of the state. She was exhilarated by the experience and rather impressed by her "new" young man. Linda expressed her concern about the potential danger involved in the sport, causing Portia to emphasize the thrill of swinging from a thin rope over a seventy-foot abyss.

Wylie sipped his third cup of coffee and observed these two women in his life with unalloyed pleasure. At twenty-five, Porrie was his oldest grandchild, his daughter Mercy's daughter, well favored both with good looks and an active intelligence. She graduated cum laude two years before from Wesleyan University and was now in her second year of law school at the state university – located in the long valley north of town. After one term in the musty and overcrowded dormitory at law school, a significant downgrade from her lodgings at Wesleyan, she approached her grandfather about staying in the three-bedroom condominium with him – in exchange for light housekeeping and passionate arguments.

Wylie readily agreed, and Portia soon arrived in her somewhat battered Prius festooned with Planned Parenthood and Hillary bumper stickers. She had lived with Wylie for almost a year and he already worried about what his life would be like when she graduated from law school.

His gaze and thoughts turned toward Linda, still standing over the range in the kitchen and in animated conversation with Portia. Linda was twelve years younger than Wylie, a very attractive blonde woman given to a slight excess of flesh. For many years, she was head nurse at the intensive care unit of the Goucher memorial wing of Middletown's hospital. But, after becoming a grandmother, she decided to make herself more available to help her daughter, and joined the local Visiting Nurse Association, working thirty hours a week. The VNA assigned her to provide support to Wylie at home, as he recovered from back surgery.

Wylie was immediately attracted to Linda. She satisfied latent maternal needs and provided medications that eased sciatic pain still coursing down both legs. Yet, she insisted he exercise and move about his home and offered no pity or sympathy when he attempted to malinger. Over the weeks of treatment, he improved steadily – with her help – and he looked forward to her visits so he could show her his progress. She was warm, caring, and funny, yet he sensed resiliency, a firmness of character. She was steel inside bunny slippers, the silk glove over the mailed fist.

Linda was happy to engage in short-term romantic alliances over the years, but a bitter experience with her former husband discouraged her from any permanent liaisons. Consequently, she was surprised, after a few weeks of frequent visits with Wylie, that she began to entertain domestic fantasies about life with an older man. She found him debonair, charming and obviously well off. Although a scruffy comb-over barely disguised his scalp and attested to a certain degree of vanity, he was fit, had an encyclopedic memory for jokes and made her feel respected. She was extremely comfortable in his presence and felt, for the first time in her life, that this was a man who could care for her, emotionally and financially.

As this stage of their relationship, Linda slept over two or three nights a week and her domestic fantasies became real, at least on a part-time basis. She enjoyed accommodating herself to Wylie's needs, whether it was preparing meals or joining him in bed. As a dedicated caregiver, she was able to raise Wylie's sexual enjoyment to a level he had not enjoyed since he was in his forties. In return, he provided simple but continuing affection: the morning hug, a kiss on her neck, small presents and an unhusbandly talent for discussion. Wylie understood, based on years of deal making and negotiation, that it was not his role to solve problems or act, but to listen.

Portia knew her grandfather was a happy man and credited Linda with their harmonious relationship. She liked Linda better than she liked grandmother Mavis. She never understood why Mavis chose to move so near Wylie's condominium a few years ago. Her grandmother claimed it was to be near the members of her bridge club. Portia, however, suspected it was so she would be near Wylie. That way he would be freely available for her complaints that he was not doing enough to assist their middle-aged children.

Wylie began began his mandatory service on the Master Gardener help line. For three hours, he and other volunteers in the Master Gardener office responded to telephone calls and walk-ins needing answers to gardening questions. The basic categories were plants, pests, lawns and other. Wylie responded well to "other" questions. He found them more varied and challenging. On his second day with the helpline, Anne Proctor and Bitsy Crangle joined him. He knew Anne from the two times they had established seedbeds together at the experimental station's greenhouse. Tall and slender with aquiline features, she stood beside him as they added potting soil to trays and carefully inserted seeds destined to become flowers, herbs and vegetables that would be sold at the annual fundraiser in May. Some of the seeds would become produce for various experimental gardens. Wylie watched as Anne tapped seeds from ancient-looking glassine envelopes on to her three personal trays in the greenhouse. She told him the seeds were just discovered in one of her suitcases and probably were too old to germinate.

"They came from this funky native market along the Amazon River years ago. I am just curious to see if they grow at all."

Wylie noted that Anne enjoyed traveling to odd places.

Bitsy Crangle was short, round and well versed in all matters relating to gardening and the Master Gardener program. She printed the list of expected gardening questions and answers for that month on the white board on the wall of the office and coordinated help line activities with the county agent responsible for volunteer activities. Based on her manner, Wylie suspected she must have had authority over recalcitrant youngsters; he soon learned she had been a sixth-grade teacher. Since, at that time, Wylie was an "intern," Bitsy reviewed in detail the proper procedures for filling out paperwork, exactly what written materials could be mailed to callers, and her personal dress code. Shorts and dungarees were frowned upon. She pulled Wylie to the "pesticides book" and explained why only limited information about chemicals could be provided.

"The powers that be don't want it to seem as though we are endorsing any particular product," she said. "So, we don't ever call it Roundup or Klobber, we tell them to use 'glyphosate,' the generic term. They are afraid we might be sued or something."

As their shift ended, Wylie escorted Anne to her car after their time in the office and reopened the subject of her travel experiences. Where, for example did she enjoy traveling most?

"Well," she said, "that place where I got those silly seeds on the Amazon River in Peru was great. The densest jungle I have ever seen. We stayed at a primitive jungle lodge for about a week. There were more varieties of birds and plants than I could count, and the trips on the river were sublime. I love the solitude, the beauty and the wonderful animals. They were…but how I'm going on! Too Much Information, I'm sure."

Wylie disagreed. He invited her for a sandwich at the deli across the square from the office, and they shared a long discussion of places they had visited. Anne was a single woman, never married, and resigned herself to paying the extra charge for traveling alone. It was not during that lunch, but over the course of the next two months, that Wylie tried to recruit Anne as a traveling companion. His major selling point was one of economics. He had so many frequent flyer miles, he would be glad to share them with her.

After a couple of months, Anne could resist no longer. She agreed to go with Wylie on a weeklong trip to Barcelona and Madrid. They had a pleasant and chaste time together.

Linda was not overjoyed with this turn of events, but she understood Wylie's need to roam the world and knew he was faithful to her. His relationship with Anne in no way changed his behavior toward Linda after he returned from Spain. Considering the many hard times she experienced during her life, the one she was in now was very agreeable. She decided not to complain about Wylie's vacation with Anne Proctor, at least for the time being.

Portia pulled a Wesleyan sweater over her blouse and shrugged the backpack with law books and computer to her shoulder. She returned to the kitchen to plant a kiss on Wylie's bald spot and gave Linda a little hug. There was no sound as she left the garage. The Prius purred as she sped toward her first class.

Linda rose to go upstairs and dress. She was planning to spend time with her little granddaughter and hoped to visit the Middletown mall to select her Easter outfit. Wylie was about to scan the front pages of the Wall Street Journal and New York Times when he became aware of a gray presence beside him. Emma had waited patiently near the door as her master dallied with the women. With Portia's departure and Linda's going upstairs, the Weimaraner silently inched toward Wylie, sure he would take notice. She was preparing to use her most persuasive trick, resting her chin lightly on his knee and gazing at him with soulful eyes, when he glanced her way.

"All right, Emma," he said. "I got the message."

She followed him gleefully as he took down her leash from the hook by the back door, pulled on his jacket and opened the door. She waited for him to attach leash to collar and walked with him into the brisk morning, both their breaths clouding the air.

Emma had almost mastered heeling. She strode at Wylie's left side, trying not to pull on the leash and match her pace to his. All went well until she spied her first squirrel. Her tug almost unsettled Wylie, who was musing about the women in his life. He applied a correcting pull on the leash and Emma settled – until the next squirrel or deer, Wylie knew.

Yes, women in his life. He had a distant but loving relationship with his two daughters and was deeply enamored of Portia, who served as a conduit to a new generation. Mavis was an irritant and a reminder of the bitter years they stayed together "for the children," now a questionable reason for lengthening baleful cohabitation. Linda rejuvenated him. Then, of course, Anne Proctor. What a delightful person and excellent traveling companion.

As he and Emma succeeded in matching their strides and settled into a relaxing pace, Wylie let his mind wander. As often happened, his thoughts turned to his first love, the lovely Amelia, the light of his young life when he served, so long ago, as a soldier in Korea. As always, the abruptness of her loss saddened him. Emma tugged at the leash again as a wild turkey scampered across a stone fence.

Upon their return, Emma nosed into the kitchen and stood in front of the cabinet door where her treats were kept. He obliged with two T-bone shaped snacks. Emma was soon asleep. He watched her front paws twitch as she dreamt of wild turkeys, squirrels, and deer.

Wylie relaxed in the easy chair in his little office. He had time to review both of his newspapers before cleaning some of the winter debris from the side and back gardens of his home. Then he intended to meet Arnie Brackett for a light lunch before exercise and a swim at the health club. He would have no trouble, he believed, in filling the rest of his day.

Yet, as he looked into the mirror while starting his car, he experienced a pang of restlessness. He compared the way he filled his days now with a more active period of his life when he served his clients with diligence and fervor. This retirement thing seemed so easy, so fluid, so agreeable. It was easy to slip effortlessly into simple tasks and small challenges, letting his days dissolve like morning fog on a June morning. His time passed with deceptive simplicity. He had difficulty recalling what he accomplished the day, the week, the month before. He admitted to himself that he had not felt intellectually challenged for over a year. The feeling of restlessness changed. A stabbing pang of guilt added to his discomfort. His desire to enjoy a gracious retirement contradicted his engrained work ethic that demanded he be productive – even now. Of course, service as a Master Gardener was productive, but in a facile way. He did not care to feel so conflicted in his eighth decade. It was not what he expected.

He nicked the side of a trash barrel with his rear fender as he backed out.

Chapter 2

April

Middletown Courier-Times

Mastering your Garden

By Elizabeth Pendleton Crangle

Thanks so much for your encouraging e-mails, and I'm sorry that a couple of you thought I was being superficial and obvious. I can only respond with what the carrot said to the rabbit – "Bite me!" But, seriously, I hear you and will spend some time this month on roses.

Roses, of course, require pruning beginning April Fool's Day if not sooner, and so do any of those unruly foundation plantings. If your shrubs aren't looking the way you want, consider pulling them out and replacing some with ornamental grasses to add winter interest. Remember to sterilize your pruning shears with alcohol or a mild chlorine solution to avoid transferring diseases among plants. And, let this finally be the year you purchase rose gauntlets, so your arms don't look like pin cushions in June.

Don't prune climbing roses; they bloom on last year's growth. Deal with them after they bloom. Cut out the dead canes and prune back to an outside bud on your hybrids and knockout roses and, if new stock arrives, be sure to save their little metal tags and secure them to 10-penny nails so you won't forget what you planted. The nails rust but stay in the garden forever. Use a granular fertilizer to feed the roses, all the better if slow release. If you've been bothered with black spot and other fungal diseases, be sure that all winter debris and leaves are removed.

In case you need a reminder when to prune roses, watch for forsythia to bloom. That time triggers several gardening chores: pruning roses and other shrubs, getting crabgrass under control with pre-emergent chemicals, going after other weeds and sowing cool season seeds in the veggie garden.

Cut back gaura, lavender, perovskia, buddleia, spirea, and Montauk Daisies when you start to see bud break.

I'll be looking across a field of daffodils this month and wish there were more. I will snap a few photos on the cell phone to tell where they were next fall so as not to overplant. The same with tulips.

Fall blooming perennials can be divided this month – mums, asters, false dragonhead and perennial sunflowers are among them. Now is the time to start other perennials from seed. I encourage planting yellow and orange asclepias (milkweed), which the Monarch butterflies love, false indigo (which comes in yellow as well as blue) and hyssop. I can't get enough of the scent of the anise variety. Like licorice braids!

If you are planting perennials this month, DON'T toss a handful of fertilizer in the hole. The roots will burn. Use a water-soluble fertilizer instead. And, of course, water, water, water – unless there's a deluge like last year.

It's a busy month – but you should not forget to examine your trees for scale. If needed, apply dormant oil to deter scale and aphids. Almost all trees in our area will benefit from this treatment. Toward the end of the month look for tent caterpillars in cherry and plum trees – and don't go after them with flaming torches the way our grandparents did. There are benign sprays, instead.

Well, I'm over the word limit, again, and haven't talked about lawns or annuals. Next month! Got to go anyway. Hubby needs to be fed.

Blissful Gardening – Bitsy

Bitsy

The light from the fluorescent grow lamps stabbing the sky above the greenhouse/office was a beacon for Bitsy as she placed the carefully folded article from the New York Times in her purse and locked the car door. Lavender dusk brushed the far hills in the west, but the fields of the Van Poppen farm were dark, lit only by security lights in the barns and the lamps glowing in some of the greenhouses. Though she had once been to Winston's office in daylight, she was glad for the light leading her to his office. Nevertheless, stumbling on the gravel path beside the barn would have been awkward, so lighted her way with the LED from her cell phone.

Winston told her three others would be joining their meeting, and she looked forward with interest and a bit of concern to meeting them. What she and Winston had in mind was unconventional, to say the least, and she hoped he had selected future "partners" carefully. Bitsy had difficulty relinquishing control to anyone else, even in the smallest matters.

As he held the door open for her, his face was illuminated from below by creamy slits of light escaping from ventilating slots above the seed trays. His Asian features took on an ominous glint, a portly Fu Man Chu villain from movies in her childhood. But, in the bright overhead light of the office, he returned to Winston Wu, Ph.D. biologist and associate professor in the agricultural school of the state university. He greeted her warmly and directed her to the plastic conference table, along the north wall where two other men occupied upholstered card table chairs of questionable parentage.

The older of the two stood as she turned toward them, while the younger man continued to lounge on the chair, apparently twisting the tip of his long ponytail and fluffing its end under his large nose. She saw he wore a green N.A.Ag baseball cap slightly askew, from which the ponytail protruded. He was introduced as "Freddy C." She was never to learn his actual last name.

"Myron Ng," said the other man as he reached his hand toward her. "I was in the MG class that graduated after yours. We did the helpline together for a couple years."

"Yes, of course, of course. Nice to see you again. You've been at most of the monthly meetings. What are you doing these days?" she asked.

"Aside from what I do for a living, I volunteer mainly to work here at the farm. I help with analysis of turf environments and input some of the data of the hybridizing programs."

They chatted on for a few more minutes until it became obvious that Winston was becoming impatient and Freddy C. bored.

"I don't know why Jerome isn't here yet," said Winston, "but, it's my pleasure to introduce Freddy as our savant. He can program our computer the way Keith Jarrett plays the piano. What we have accomplished in the past two years probably would have taken a decade without his help. He's a virtuoso at genetic programming."

Freddy rose to take a little bow, displaying a Grateful Dead T-shirt and artfully torn dungarees above bare feet. As he moved into the light, Bitsy saw he was no teenager, but a rather spindly forty-something.

As their friendship developed over the next few months, Bitsy learned that Freddy had been a promising but neurotic physics student at M.I.T. who suffered a "nervous breakdown" in his junior year. Lithium, marijuana and other controlled substances alleviated his psychological problems, but he somehow never found the time or inclination to further his formal studies. After two false starts, he was employed by a computer game company near Boston, where he developed the last thirty minutes of "Bitch Blasters on Mars," the most popular computer game for teenage boys ever created. After designing four sequels to the game, involving other planets, he was a wealthy man. He was retained as a consultant to the game company and had ample free time to follow other paths, one of which led him to Winston Wu.

"Man, count me in...sounds bitchin'," said Freddy after Winston explained the clandestine project he was pursuing.

"I like it that we're gonna stick it to the man," he added.

That was two years ago. During that time, Freddy became more deeply involved in the venture and was eager to meet the newly recruited member, Bitsy, the needed woman.

Myron volunteered to help Winston on a university aquaponics project at Van Poppen farm. Winston believed Myron to be a kindred soul and confided his extracurricular project to him. Myron loved the ecological boldness of Winston's concept and began helping with the laboratory work and fed data to Freddy. They met on evenings and weekends in the office where they were now gathered, looking forward to a time in early fall when their efforts would result in success.

Bitsy had come to Winston's attention only a few weeks ago. He had wandered to the Master Gardeners' break room for a fresh cup of coffee and observed a portly, white haired woman expounding to others on a New York Times Science article smoothed out on the table in front of her.

"It's right here, clear as can be," she said. "Farmers are planting genetically modified corn and soybeans in the Midwest and spraying Roundup on the fields to eradicate weeds. So, corn and soybeans grow, and weeds don't. The thing is, they're killing milkweed and other plants that provide habitat for butterflies and other beneficial insects."

The others nodded in agreement.

"Take the monarch butterfly," she added. "It survives on milkweed. This article claims milkweed has disappeared from at least 100 million acres, which partially accounts for a significant decline in their populations. I LOVE monarch butterflies, and engineered crops are destroying them. That really frosts me!"

The others were similarly frosted. Observations about the effects of Roundup ricocheted around the table.

"They say it leaves the soil in a week, but I don't believe it. Nothing that kills everything could disappear that fast."

"Kills dill. I grow dill to feed swallowtail caterpillars. Kills dill."

"I won't use it. Those chemists, they're the same ones what did the D.D.T. thing. Killed bald eagles – our national bird, for heaven's sake."

"Armageddon. Armageddon for biodiversity. Absolute Armageddon.

"I shall never let a genetically modified thing pass my lips."

"Well, I'm arthritic, you know. It's much easier for me to spray it and get rid of weeds."

Stony silence.

"Armageddon. Absolute Armageddon."

The Master Gardeners had spoken, but Bitsy furrowed her brow. This was not resolved. Blowing off steam was fine, but it didn't help the monarch butterfly. She loved the monarch and agreed with the entomologist who called the monarch "the Bambi of the insect world." Was there anything one could do to save Bambi?

In the following weeks, Winston made excuses to be nearby whenever Bitsy arrived for volunteer service at Van Poppen farm. He interested her in his aquaponics experiments and gradually assessed her potential interest and participation in the other matter that took all his spare time and effort. He wished to recruit a woman for the project, someone who appeared harmless and unthreatening.

That would be a valuable attribute should certain authorities become aware of his group's objectives. Not one to make snap decisions, Bitsy considered the venture for a few days, prayed on it, and told Winston she would be a willing participant.

As she nodded toward Freddy in acknowledgement of his little bow, the gravel outside the door crunched loudly as a motorcycle came to rest, the kickstand was lowered, and leather boots crunched the pebbles. The door pushed open and a burly, bearded man wearing a leather jacket entered, removing a helmet that might have been found atop a German infantryman.

"Evening, everybody," said Jerome Hastings, clasping Winston's hand in a complicated maneuver that ended knuckles to knuckles. "Sorry to be late. Couldn't find the damn key to the hog. Cat had it in his bed."

He removed the leather jacket, becoming slightly less burly, a strong man in his early sixties.

About my age and very self-assured, thought Bitsy.

Jerome repeated the fancy hand salute with Myron and Freddy and took Bitsy's hand as though to kiss it, thought better of it, and offered a gentle squeeze.

"Bitsy Crangle," she said.

"Jerome," he offered, "delighted to meet you."

They seated themselves around the plastic table, looking toward Winston for the expected update on the project's progress. He spoke in general terms about recent tests determining the plant's resistance to herbicide, addressed a new protocol in gathering data about the genetically altered material to conform with Freddy's brilliant new algorithm for tweaking the DNA, and thanked them for their contributions to date. Much of the scientific jargon eluded Bitsy, though she certainly understood the impact of the project.

"Are we still on target for early fall to begin dissemination?" asked Myron.

"You bet!" Freddy piped up. "Done deal, guys."

"Hot damn," cried Jerome. "Roundup and Klobber resistant milkweed seeds. Tens of millions of them. Next year will be good for monarchs, the little beauties."

Would it really? hoped Bitsy. Would it really?

Bitsy's involvement with Winston's group was uncharacteristic. Hers had been an ordered life, following the rules, playing the game, trusting authority. She had an exemplary career as a sixth-grade teacher in the Middletown school system and was fondly remembered in the town by her former pupils.

Little favors came her way. A parking ticket cancelled by the patrolman she guided through beginning algebra; forgiveness of overdraft charges when her paycheck was deposited late; and eager assistance with carrying her grocery bags to her car. She felt respected in Middletown.

Her husband, Fred, had worked for the Middletown Public Works Department, an outside job that he enjoyed. They were unable to have children, but numerous hobbies and vacations in the travel trailer Fred hauled behind their pickup provided an interesting and fulfilled life together. Only when it became clear that Fred suffered from dementia did Bitsy's belief in the infallibility of local institutions begin to waver.

For almost two years after becoming ill, Fred enjoyed helping in her garden, following her directions, moving heavy bags of compost, raking and weeding. Although he could not explain his feelings, Bitsy knew he was, if not happy, at least content. There came a time, two and a half years ago, when Fred required professional treatment in a long-term care treatment facility because Bitsy simply could not care for him alone. She visited him regularly, always saddened that he no longer recognized her.

On her final visit, she was informed that Fred had "passed on."

Although she was told that he had succumbed to natural causes, she wanted to know how her husband had died and demanded an autopsy. The pathologist confirmed that Fred's brain was ravaged by Alzheimer's disease, but his complete examination pointed up some irregularities. An investigation ensued, and certain inconsistencies in medical records ultimately disclosed a fatal error.

Whether it was a poorly written prescription, inattentive nursing care or an unfortunate combination of both, an injection of Temazepam for Fred's agitation, a dose ten times the required amount, induced a coma from which he never recovered.

Such egregious malpractice challenged her normally trusting and accepting persona. Indignation and anger rose, especially since the care facility had tried to pass off the error as a natural occurrence. Such underhanded effrontery! Such … such…mean people! It stung particularly that they had attempted to conceal it as she grieved for her husband.

About a week after the investigation confirmed the details of Fred's death, she outfitted herself in her most flattering navy-blue dress, had her hair done, and marched into the offices of one of her favorite sixth graders, the Honorable Clem Gatz, Esquire. Now many years past the sixth grade, Clem avoided representing the interests of those involved in Middletown's medical establishment, thereby eliminating potential conflicts of interests with those he might be called upon to take to court. Since other attorneys in town had not been so foresighted, Clem Gatz held the Middletown monopoly in representing those injured by the medical profession.

Once Bitsy disclosed the findings regarding Fred's death, the attorney outlined the customary procedure for pursuing litigation.

"Missus Crangle," he said, "ninety-six percent of all cases are settled before any court appearance, but it usually takes a year and a half of legal wrangling before settlement Of course, no amount of money could make up for your loss, but the care facility would certainly be more cautious in the future. Your bold action could well be saving other lives."

As he proceeded, it became clear that Bitsy would prevail if the case was brought to trial, and discussions between Clem and the insurance company's attorney simply involved the amount of settlement.

When Clem delivered the settlement check to her Bitsy felt that she had vindicated Fred's death, but that did not make his departure more bearable. But the belief that she was controlling a foreign legal process, that she was in charge, emboldened her.

After receiving the substantial settlement, Bitsy made changes to what she now considered her dowdy appearance. She joined a gym and concentrated on shedding some weight – nothing extravagant, just enough to drop one dress size. She visited her hairdresser weekly and changed her hairstyle and color. Again, nothing overstated, but a slightly more youthful look with more pepper than salt in her hair. She purchased the first pair of jeans she had owned since her teenage years.

The injustice of what happened to Fred radicalized her. She began reading newspaper editorials very carefully and expanded her interests beyond happenings in Middletown. Women at her gym discussed feminist issues, and she pondered how it was that a group of white men in Washington felt empowered to tell women how to manage their bodies. That led to twinges of doubt about how well that same group of men was managing the country. She attended a rally in support of a young woman running for congress in her district, not even concerned that she was a Democrat.

Her Master Gardener program offered monthly lectures of interest to all gardeners, and one lecturer, an earnest woman from the agricultural program of an adjoining state, discussed basic elements of genetic engineering of plants and the use of glyphosate to eradicate weeds. She pointed out that some scientists were unsure about how long the toxins that suppressed plant growth remained in the soil, or their long-term environmental effects.

Bitsy reviewed the unintended consequences of many man-made environmental exercises – like D.D.T., dams that caused rivers no longer to reach oceans, attempts to drain Florida, kudzu, salmon ladders, and mountain top mining. She read articles and scientific journals about the pros and cons of genetic engineering and the use of chemical suppressants. However, there were so many positive and negative aspects to the research that she was unable to decide which side to favor. In addition, she recognized that much of the material she reviewed contained academic jargon that she was unable to decipher. She did note, however, that articles subsidized by chemical companies extolled the positive aspects, while articles prepared by academics were either noncommittal or raised concern about unknown or unreported effects.

So, when she discovered the New York Times story about the decline of monarch butterflies, she was instantly enthralled. This was clear-cut, unambiguous and definitive. Saving the butterflies was a cause she could and would embrace. If it meant doing battle with an establishment business, so be it.

The coincidence of Winston Wu's gentle introduction to his "project" at Van Poppen farm seemed to her like divine intervention. One day she discovered a cause that truly excited her, and the next an opportunity arose to act on it. Surely, this was meant to happen. She felt empowered. It was irreverent and important to work with Winston's group. That, along with the monthly column she wrote for the Courier-Times, provided newfound feelings of self-worth.

Bitsy Crangle was on the move.

The young woman held forth the branch of red twig dogwood like an accusing finger.

"Please look at this," she requested. "See these little bumps all along it. They weren't there last year. See, see there, those dark spots. This can't be good, right?"

The young woman had been waiting with her crusty branch as Wylie and two other Master Gardener volunteers arrived at their helpline office. As they opened the office, Wylie ushered the woman to the long, high counter near the door and began to examine the branch with a magnifying glass. Tips of leaves were beginning to show, and little orange-brown hummocks paraded along the branches. As always during such examinations, Wylie tried to look very serious and thoughtful. He found it helpful on the occasions where he had no idea what the horticultural problem was.

In this case, however, he knew exactly what was wrong.

"Scale," he offered, confidently.

"Scale? Like a bathroom scale?"

"No. It's an insect that lives under each of those little bumps. The hard cover protects it as it sucks nourishment from the plant. Then the baby insects come out and do more damage unless wasps or other predators stop them. But you can stop them now."

The young woman appeared relieved. In the year and a half Wylie had been offering advice to the public, he learned that almost everyone who visited the office with plant material was primarily concerned with one simple question. Was whatever it was going to kill my plant? So, his first act was to determine the nature of the problem and, if possible, offer assurance that no, this was not going to kill your plant.

"Thoroughly dose the dogwood with an oil spray and, since it is a bit late in the season, keep watch for the arrival of tiny insects," he said. "If they show up, kill them with pesticide."

She accepted a fact sheet that clearly described the procedure Wylie had outlined and thanked him. He tossed the offending branch in the office waste bin, feeling pleased with himself.

In the age of the internet, potential clients of the Master Gardener program might be excused for thinking the volunteers could diagnose any problem based on a telephone conversation. On occasion, such conversations tended toward the surreal. Wylie engaged in one that morning.

"Yeah, listen, something is eating the little leaves on this bush in back of the house," said the low-pitched voice.

"Do you know what kind of bush it is?"

"It has berries."

"Are there berries on it now? What color are they?"

"It has little green ones that go orange in the fall."

"I see. And can you see what is eating the leaves?"

"No. If I could see it, I wouldn't be calling you."

"Would it be possible to bring in one of the branches for us to look at?"

"No, I live over in the next county."

"Well, perhaps you could call their helpline, then."

"I did, but I didn't like their answer."

"Which was?"

"None of your business."

"I see. I'll do what I can to help. Now, what makes you think something is eating the plant?"

"Man, the little leaves have holes in them."

"What size are the holes."

"They are average."

"Well, are they as big as a dime?"

"No, smaller."

"Okay, I really need to see that plant."

"Here's another thing. Whatever is eating them is leaving its poop on the leaves. The poop is real small and round and about the size of, like, a pinhead. And it's sort of a greeny black color. You could check that out for me, right?"

"So, you want me to tell by its feces what is eating your plant?"

"Sure."

A dozen rejoinders raced through his mind, most with scatological implications. He resisted the urge and remembered his training.

"I am very sorry, but I won't be able to help you," said Wylie.

"Shit."

The caller hung up.

That conversation was the highlight of the morning. Wylie and the two other volunteers rose to respond to several questions about what the late frost might be doing to the vibrant green shoots of daffodil and narcissus bulbs, and how serious it was to have sap leaking from trees adorned with machine gun holes created by yellow-bellied sapsuckers. Would pre-emergent weed killers affect the birds searching for succulent spring worms?

This morning there were only minor concerns, readily resolved. During slow moments, the volunteers researched other questions, chatted about family matters and searched out personal questions in the small library of reference materials. The three-hour shift was soon over, and Wylie started his car to begin the short ride to his condominium.

His thoughts turned to the young woman with the red twig dogwood. He recalled the time, during the first months of Master Gardener instruction, when he was overwhelmed by the sheer magnitude of all the things, pests, diseases, soil conditions, sun, shade, rain and drought that nature designed to thwart both the gardener and plants he intended to grow. Then, after a tumbler or two of Glen Morangie, his favorite whiskey, he related negative forces of nature to pernicious conspiracies to destroy socially or financially positive efforts of his clients.

There was moral scale. He had long ago determined this was not a Panglossian universe, that it was not the best of all possible worlds. But, throughout his career, he tried to maintain his innate optimism and, if not strive for the best possible world, at least work to thwart those who would bring it down. When, as often happened in the complicated international business deals he managed, greed, mendacity and discrimination raised their ugly heads, he did his best to resist --especially if such demands worked against his client's interest. He was good at it, as his client list and fees indicated.

Driving home, he considered the orange bumps on the red twig dogwood. Certainly, it was not evil incarnate, but it was a darker side of nature, trying to destroy the good and the beautiful. Even in the humble role of Master Gardener, he could thwart malevolence. Yet, compared with his former practice of managing large financial combinations and complicated international business arrangements, those orange bumps lost significance. A familiar uneasy feeling asserted itself. How significant was he now? Would he continue to feel less potent as his years wore on?

The gray BMW turned hard left in front of him at the intersection and he narrowly avoided decapitating its left rear light array. He calmed down. Where was he going with all this anyway? He had his share of conflict, crisis, danger and disappointment over his last half century. He was retired. He deserved to stay on his current, simple, pragmatic path. Like Candide, he should be content to cultivate his garden. Yet, it was inevitable that he would continue to encounter scale. He knew he could not ignore it. But, could he defeat it? Would it matter?

Portia moved across the kitchen as though struggling through chest-high water and settled gingerly on the chair at the breakfast table. Involuntarily, she grimaced.

With her practiced nursing eye, Linda considered two alternatives: a night of energetic lovemaking or unaccustomed and excessive exercise. Considering Portia's doleful look, she ruled out sex. Linda handed her a cup of coffee.

"Toast?"

"That would involve chewing. I'm not sure my jaw muscles are up to it. How about some juice? I'm pretty sure I can lift a juice glass."

"So, you were with Grover yesterday. Is he responsible for your condition…. or did you get hit by a truck?"

Linda opened the refrigerator door and found the cranberry/guava juice.

"Pretty much it's Grover's fault," said Portia. "But I can blame myself, too. No way was I going to let him beat me."

"Oh, tell me it isn't so. You are competitive?"

The glass with rosy liquid arrived in front of Portia.

"Okay. Okay," she said. "Imagine that – a competitive law student."

Linda sat on to the little bench across from Portia and peered inquisitively at the young woman. Peoria reported her adventure with Grover Merson, the "new" boyfriend, as she slowly chewed buttered toast.

"So, yesterday, Sunday, was a rare day without classes or other commitments. I explained to Grover on our last date that I was not crazy about squeezing through wet, mossy openings in bat-infested caves, which is one of his favorite things—called 'caving."

Portia managed to lift her cup pf coffee and continued.

"Grover asked if I would like to use one of his bicycles and join him for a day of cycling through farming villages over by the Allasquash Mountains. I used to love riding my lovely, fat white-wheeled bicycle with streamers flowing from handgrips, and I thought that would be fine. It was going to be a fine spring day, so I said yes."

Grover had arrived with two slender bicycles mounted atop his SUV, and they drove about fifteen miles to park the car and take down the cycles. Portia was surprised at how little they weighed. He adjusted the seat for her.

"That's a bike I've had for a while. It's a Cannondale Quick Carbon road bike, really good for cruising. I got it used but loaded for less than two thousand."

"Dollars?" she asked.

"Yeh. That's not so much for a bike these days. I have a friend who added Shimano's Di2 electronic shifting system to his Trek bike. He's got over sixteen thousand in it, and that's before getting a custom-made saddle."

Portia decided not to pursue the subject as he handed down his bicycle. She saw the "Pinarello" name emblazoned in bold relief on the frame and assumed it must be pricy because it sounded Italian. She began to wonder about Grover's financial status. Where was the money for these fancy toys coming from?

She knew that Grover worked for Congresswoman Pert Pewtree in some sort of executive political position and spent part of his time in the District of Columbia and the rest at her local office in Middletown. She did not know that he was heir to the Merson estate – the Merson who patented the device that attaches the end of toilet paper to the rest of the roll. The fraction of a cent royalty on each roll contributed to a tidy fortune Grover shared with two siblings.

They started up a hill toward a red barn perched on a knoll surrounded by fields of bright green shoots of hay. Portia soon realized it would take some effort to become accustomed to the slender bicycle seat and learn how to shift through the twenty-seven gears. Grover was solicitous toward her, which she interpreted as condescending. She would prove how fit she was. She would climb these damn hills no matter what!

The odometer read 22.3 miles when Grover suggested they return to the car. A peculiar tightness ran from the back of her thighs to her calves, and there was soreness just below her rib cage. They paused to drink water and coasted down (thank God!) the long hill to the car. With the bikes stowed, Grover suggested a quick meal of crab cakes and beer.

The kiss she gave Grover at her doorstep was in appreciation for the excursion and in relief that it had ended. Encouraged, Grover suggested that they engage in a less active date next weekend– dinner and a movie. Portia readily agreed. She was attracted to him – and curious about his background. She confirmed her acceptance with a longer kiss and briefly pressed herself close.

She waited on the steps as he drove away, taking inventory of fresh notes of discomfort in unusual places on her body. This is going to hurt tomorrow, she thought. Unfortunately, her expectations were met.

The black letters on the cell phone confirmed another call from Mavis. He let her last two calls slide into voicemail. Now, her less than dulcet tones demanded he pick up.

"You're doing something for Brooks on his birthday, aren't you?"

Mavis ignored the niceties of social intercourse and plunged into whatever it was she needed Wylie to do at that moment. That, among numerous other quirks, had precipitated Wylie's desire to continue his life without her. If only, he thought.

Brooks was their oldest, currently married to his third wife. Until recently, Brooks earned a comfortable living as an investment banker with Global Strategies Limited. The great recession of '08 highlighted certain of the firm's financial practices. They were so egregious that even a Republican administration could not tolerate them. Brooks departed the now-defunct firm with dim prospects for future employment, but he managed to find work as a professional golf instructor, benefitting from a misspent youth. Mavis now used every opportunity to support her first born in his hours of need. As always, Wylie was her lender of first resort.

"I was planning to have a nice lunch with him next week."

"You know you should help him out with money. Deena needs braces."

Deena was Brooks' twenty-two-year-old daughter, three years younger than her cousin Portia. She had a slight overbite, which Wylie found charming.

"Is that so?" Wylie asked

"Yes, you cheap bastard, that's so!"

"Was there anything else?" he asked, his finger poised above the red cutoff button.

"Listen, I know you can afford to help your own kid. He's going through a tough time. And don't give me that crap about self-inflicted injuries! So he made a few bad bets for G.S.L. So did a lot of the others. You should do something nice for him on his birthday."

"All right, I'll see what I can do to help out with Deena."

"The least you could do!"

"As I said, I'll see what I can do."

"I know what you do," she said accusingly. "You spend your money on that blonde floozy. Don't deny it. Everyone knows about it. You spend your money on her and neglect your own family. Wylie, you should be ashamed."

"So nice to hear from you."

He pushed the red button, almost cracking the phone's glass cover, resisting the impulse to throw it into the nearest bush.

The greenhouse at Van Poppen farm lived up to its name that April day. Sunlight gleamed through frosted glass coverings, lighting the long rows of seedlings sitting on wooden benches that stretched along the length of the building. Apple, lime, yellow, blue, frosty: every possible shade of growing green shone atop the benches. Shoots of all varieties popped from the black plastic seed trays, stretching toward the brilliant light above.

It was ten in the morning, and eight Master Gardener volunteers worked their way along the rows of young plants, pinching off extra shoots and checking the condition of the plants. Many of them would be for sale at their annual fundraiser, some would be for experimental use at the farm, and a few were for personal use.

Wylie and Anne Proctor worked their way, side by side, down one of the rows. They tossed pinched stalks into plastic buckets for future recycling into compost. They had been doing this long enough to settle into a steady, almost trance-like. rhythm. Anne broke their reverie.

"Well, look at this! These are the flats I used to plant those odd seeds and, my gosh, they are doing so well."

Wylie examined the seedlings Anne indicated. As far as he could tell, they were for soy and green beans, corn, wheat, sorghum and a couple of other monocots he could not identify. He was surprised he had not noticed their abundant growth as they worked their way down the line. Not only were they a third taller than similar varieties in the greenhouse, they were thicker and a deeper green than their peers. In addition, where similar plants indicated a need for prompt watering, Anne's seedlings stood in moist potting soil. There was also no indication of damping off, the fungus that affected a few of the other seedlings in the nursery.

"No question, "he said. "These are robust seedlings."

"So they are," said Anne. "I never even thought they were viable. I'm very proud of my seeds. I'm going to see if we can add them to our experimental crops this year." .

Anne lingered over her super seedlings for a few more moments, and then she and Wylie continued down the row to check the young plants until noontime when their "shift" was over. Anne spotted Dan Frimmel (Ph.D.), the experimental farm director, as they prepared to leave. Dan was hard to miss. He wore blue jeans with wide fire engine red clip-on suspenders. A starched white shirt was his concession to a graduate degree, and a string tie announced that he originated in the Southwest. Black and white tennis shoes completed his sartorial ensemble. He affected a droopy mustache to contrast with his bald head. The volunteers were fond of Dan, and he of them. Their labor was even cheaper than that of graduate students.

Anne told him she had some seedlings she would like to grow in one of the experimental garden rows. Dan readily agreed, so long as she coordinated with Bruno Gladstetter, the greenhouse overseer, and kept accurate records for the university program.

"That would be just fine," she said.

Chapter 3

May

Middletown Courier-Times

Mastering your Garden

By Elizabeth Pendleton Crangle

No, Hubby is my Maine Coon cat. My husband, Fred, passed away two years ago from Alzheimer's. He enjoyed weeding until the end, though. Thanks for asking. And to tulipmaven@yahoo.com and anyone else who loves tulips, I'd recommend Keukenhof Gardens in the Netherlands.

There's not much to say about lawns this month. If you don't mind exuberant growth, feed it with a slow-release fertilizer. Grass clippings should be left on the lawn. They are a source of nitrogen. If you collect clippings, add them to your compost pile. If you don't have a compost pile, start one!

When it comes to annuals, we need to remember two simple rules: mass plantings of a single color (not necessarily the same plants) look best from a distance, while beds you see close up may be multicolored. Taller plants go to the back of the bed (or to the middle if viewed from all sides). When organizing the flower garden put that ruler away! Think in terms of complimentary splashes of color, like yellow and blue, red and white, etc.

Work with variations of height. Some gardeners think in terms of aroma as well, and others focus on flowers and shrubs that attract butterflies and birds. There are endless varieties of choices, but the goal is pleasing symmetry that allows the eye to move back and forth, up and down, and rewards the gardener with a feeling of calm and restfulness.

I think there might be too much emphasis on the idea of trying to create formal gardens in our area. It is certainly nice to try for English, French, Japanese or other exotic gardens, but what's wrong with establishing an American garden? We can use native plants, shrubs and trees to create wonderful native areas that take advantage of our natural habitats. People in the Capitol complain about too many immigrants. We should follow their thinking about non-native plants as well!

Which leads us to pests. Cutworms and aphids are out this month. For cutworms I like to put a crumpled-up aluminum collar around the base of young plants. For aphids, I carry a spray bottle filled with soapy water. That usually does the trick. Weeds are also pests, and most can be controlled by pre-emergent chemical control. But then you can't expect volunteer plants from last year's seeds. Like many gardening issues, it's a mixed bag.

All gardeners should be familiar with the idea of I.P.M. (integrated pest management) that is promoted by our state agricultural college. The idea is to use all available techniques to reduce pest problems – and not immediately reach for the latest pesticide or herbicide. I worry about all those chemists, anyway. They're the ones who invented DDT and napalm. Not to be trusted!

Probably the best home fruits in our area are blueberries and raspberries. They're easy to grow, not too much work and give bountiful harvests. Keep them well watered this month and feed the blueberries during bloom. If the soil isn't acid enough, add garden Sulphur – not aluminum sulphate. Who wants berries that taste like aluminum? Don't forget to consider blueberries as living hedges that feed you and the birds. They need less pruning than privet and look splendid in bloom and in the fall.

That's it, except that I need to point out that gardening is as much art as science. The artist in me is entitled to her own opinion! And I don't need any e-mails from chemists.

Blissful gardening - Bitsy

Myron

The weather in Scottsdale remained pleasantly warm. The one hundred degree plus days would not arrive for a month or so. Myron's special friends always invited him for a stay in late spring, past the high season. He had not decided whether that was because of parsimony or tact. He really did not care. He and his wife looked forward to these five-day vacations at the Phoenician resort. She loved the view of Camelback Mountain from their room, the delicious spa treatments, and the opportunity to get an early tan by the pool.

He rose early to play eighteen holes of golf each morning and enjoyed driving into the desert at day's end, searching for unfamiliar plants. He was especially interested in desert plants unknown in New Anglia and captured them in photographs for later identification. The couple agreed that the vacation always ended too soon.

Etta Sporelli hailed Myron from the little bar nestled among palms near the pool. As an inducement, she held up her vodka martini so it caught the slanting light of midafternoon and indicated there was one waiting for him. Myron understood his little chats with Etta were necessary to keep invitations to resorts like the Phoenician coming, but he was uncomfortable during their meetings. What intimidated him most was her height. Etta was middle aged, well turned out, very stylish and six feet one inch tall, without her heels, which she wore in defiance of accepted convention.

Myron believed that she reported directly to Dick Geier, so she certainly had a very responsible position with Bemis. Her business card indicated she was director of corporate affiliates, but his Google search confirmed that Etta had retired from the Army as a Lieutenant Colonel of Military Police. She certainly showed the distinctive bearing of a person accustomed to authority, but it was mainly her height that unsettled the five-foot-half-inch Myron. He walked quickly to her table, glad that she did not stand, clasped her hand and sat stiffly in the chair opposite her.

"They make an excellent vodka martini here – some secret Russian stuff not usually available in this country. Try one?" she asked.

"Yes. That would be very nice."

Pause.

"Enjoying your stay?"

"Very much. My wife loves it. We really appreciate the opportunity to come here. Bemis has been very generous."

"We have a reputation for taking care of our friends."

"Yes," Myron agreed.

The martini arrived. Myron sipped what turned out to be a potion of distilled lightning. He coughed.

"So, Myron, now that the niceties are out of the way, shall we discuss what might be of interest with the New Anglia agricultural program and what's going on at the Van Poppen farm?"

Myron managed to swallow another sip of liquid lightening without coughing.

"Well, basically, you know, on the experimental farm side, there isn't much going on. We're just monitoring rows of seedlings and watching the early planting of soybean and corn. Tomatoes need the warmer soil, so they won't be going in till the end of this month. I am paying special attention to the seeds Bemis wants us to monitor and your new nutrient management system with low potassium. And there have been no new people with special projects or anything... and no stuff from any of your competitors that I could discover. It looks like almost the whole farm is dedicated to the university or Bemis projects."

"O.K. good, Myron. So, what about that other thing – that thing Doctor Wu is working on in his spare time?"

"You mean that milkweed stuff?"

"Exactly."

"Well, we are about at the end of the hybridizing process and are all excited about actually isolating seeds that will grow through glyphosate. Looks like the proof of that will come in a month or so. Winston is planning to test the seeds in the open by the end of the summer. They figure there will be sufficient growth then to establish resistant fields south of here for next year. That's about it."

Etta favored Myron with a quizzical look, as though anticipating more, as though wondering why she was being lied to,

"But they haven't actually tried to germinate seeds in glyphosate-impregnated soil?"

"Well, yes, I guess they have. It looks like some of the seeds, at least, grow up through it. But I don't know whether they will die out later. They are worried about that."

"Well, if you think they are that close I'd better arrange to keep in closer touch with you this summer."

Myron offered Etta a wan smile that in no way concealed that Myron did not find that prospect appealing.

Etta was not sure how to construe this news about the milkweed project. She would report its current status, which was unclear. She guessed that the amateurs engaged in the project would not be able to defeat the stout chemical onslaught of Bemis' glyphosate, and that the existing milkweed seedlings would wither and die. Furthermore, what were the risks of having milkweed seeds that resisted the herbicide? She had no idea how that could affect her company financially. Most likely, all those MBA types running around the seventh floor at headquarters might figure it a financial disincentive. That was above her pay grade.

However, there was something threatening about a bunch of amateurs fooling around to thwart the carefully designed properties of their highly profitable chemical. That's the sort of thing that would really piss off Dick Geier – if it ever came to his attention.

Myron politely refused another martini, saying he needed to get back to his wife. Etta signaled for a third as Myron departed. Among her many sterling virtues, she could hold her liquor.

During her employment with the company, Etta Sporelli learned that BIG AG carefully maintained good relations with faculty and staff at all the land-grant colleges and universities established under the Morrill Acts of 1862 and 1890. Many, such as Cornell University and the Massachusetts Institute of Technology, remained private institutions, while others became renowned state universities. What they all had in common was teaching, experimentation and research in the field of agriculture, and BIG AG had a serious business stake in encouraging and sponsoring new developments and the testing of their own products, whether hybrid seeds, chemicals or soil amendments.

Until about the middle of the twentieth century, the company's relationship with the educational institutions was limited to academic pursuits. However, BIG AG representatives sometimes felt their university associates were overly constrained by ethical considerations. For example, the academics tended to withhold information about their tests and research until they were certain that any papers they wrote would be reasonably safe from serious challenges and that their results could be easily duplicated. Consequently, there were many delays in providing information about ongoing research. Those delays upset Bemis' top managers. If, say, preliminary research indicated that the latest hybrid corn seed could out-produce the competitor's, the two or three year wait while the academics confirmed those results meant unacceptable delays in bringing their product to market and losing significant profits.

Etta knew that BIG AG's own large staff of farmers, researchers and technicians was continually engaged in company-sponsored entrepreneurial endeavors. Given the competitive nature of the industry and the significant bonuses offered for "first to market" products, it was understood there could be the occasional misstep. But the unfortunate incident of unexpected toxicity in hybrid cattle corn seeds that euthanized a third of the calves born in Kansas one year demanded greater circumspection. Consequently, whether they liked it or not, BIG AG's managers were obliged to rely on and wait for the guaranteed reliability of careful academic research.

Patience came hard to the managers and, in the mid-sixties, they decided to find other ways to discover what was going on in university programs. During the height of the cold war, industrial espionage seemed to be the proper American thing to do. And in the nineties the program expanded to include university Master Gardener programs throughout the country. The person in charge of what BIG AG now called "affiliate intelligence" observed the influx of Master Gardener volunteers at many of the institutions where they had contacts, contracts or grants. A program was initiated to befriend some of the volunteers and glean whatever nuggets of information about ongoing projects might be obtained. Over time, certain blandishments beyond the occasional lunch or sports tickets were provided to those who offered valued information.

The upshot of these many clandestine business arrangements was that management of BIG AG's "affiliate intelligence" department expanded. The Vice President reported directly to the President and CEO, Dick Geier, and had four directors reporting to him. One of these was Etta Sporelli. Under customary practices, a director of affiliate intelligence would have let a subordinate engage in direct contact with someone like Myron Ng, but Etta enjoyed fieldwork and selected a few "clients" for her personal supervision. She was amused at Myron's discomfort in her presence.

Bitsy and Myron peered at the little green spears protruding from the dark brown soil in the potting trays. Much of what was occurring in Winston's laboratory was new and foreign to Bitsy, but Myron had participated almost from the beginning of the project and understood all its aspects. Although he was an avid gardener, he had not been educated as a biologist or trained in any of the plant sciences. He earned his living as a CPA employed by the Middletown branch office of a national accounting firm.

His parents, Myron, a brother and sister had escaped from South Vietnam in the late seventies and joined the migration of boat people fleeing their devastated country. By the time they made their way to a refugee camp in Thailand, his tiny sister had mysteriously disappeared. All attempts to locate her failed. Despite this tragedy, his family was among the fortunate ones permitted to enter the United States, sponsored by a group from the Middletown Methodist Church.

Like many Vietnamese immigrants, his parents intuitively recognized the importance of a good education as a step toward achieving upward mobility in America. Sacrifices were made within the little Vietnamese community to assure the best available education for their children. the elders worked two, even three, jobs and pooled their resources. Funds for education were a priority but, as time went by, money to open a restaurant, a dog-grooming parlor, and a franchised fast food emporium became available.

Within a year or so after their arrival, his parents began calling him "Myron," an anglicized version of his Vietnamese name. When he turned fourteen, he matriculated in a Catholic high school and, four years later, began studies at the main campus of New Anglia University. With a natural flair for numbers, studied accounting. and earned good wages upon graduation.

Myron slowly rose in his chosen profession, married, but had no children. In his early forties he indulged his passion for gardening by becoming a Master Gardener. He truly enjoyed working at the Van Poppen farm. While there, he was befriended by one of the Bemis employees working with the University to test a multi-purpose commercial apple orchard spray. She introduced him to Etta Sporelli. Etta introduced him to certain perquisites enjoyed by special friends of BIG AG. Once he became a special friend, it was extremely difficult to alter that status. Etta, in her own fashion, made that clear to him. So, here he was: a rising talent within his chosen profession, a respected Master Gardener with a gold badge for five years of volunteer work, and a Bemis "mole." It was scary and exciting, like his recollection of the exodus from Vietnam.

"The seedlings look quite healthy," said Bitsy. "At this stage, each seed is coming through the glyphosate-saturated soil. And, see over there, in the plat with ninety-six containers, Asclepias (milkweed) has been growing for forty-six days and only seven have succumbed to glyphosate. I'm beginning to think we are just about there."

Winston's smile was broader than they had ever seen before.

Myron shared the moment and then excused himself. He was scheduled to help at the peach orchard, reducing the number of buds to enhance future growth. Bitsy took the opportunity to speak with Winston.

"Winston, I've been reading those articles you recommended, but I don't really get it. I mean, all this stuff about gene splicing and all. Is there an easier way of explaining how you managed to create these wonderful new milkweeds?"

Winston motioned her to the metal chair beside his desk and moved his hands rapidly over the desktop as he talked.

"About two years ago I had a couple of graduate students look for milkweed plants that grew in fields of hybridized canola plants that had been sprayed with a concentration of glyphosate. They found a handful of plants that seemed to have a natural resistance to the stuff. We cross-pollinated those few plants and tested the offspring for their herbicide-resistant traits. With the most resistant ones, we repeated the process until we developed some sturdy plants that seemed to sneer at glyphosate."

"Are those the ones here?" she asked.

"No. These guys are the result of recombinant DNA, what they call 'gene splicing'."

"Okay, now you're talking way over my head. I had a hard enough time explaining the double helix and DNA stuff to my sixth graders."

"Right. I won't go into the intimate details of the process," Winston said. "But I do have to swear you to secrecy because the next steps we took are just a bit questionable."

"You have all my attention."

"Well, with Freddy C. took a careful look at the herbicide-resistant genes in some of the corn plants we are testing here, managed to extract that gene, and hooked it on to a bacterium. We then infected the milkweed plant cell with the gene-carrying germ and, lo and behold, we had a transgenic plant, a weed highly resistant to the herbicide. That is what you are looking at right now. We will have tens of thousands of seeds from that plant and its peers this fall!"

"I don't quite follow all that, but I understand the result. My, my...tens of thousands of seeds. That's exciting."

Winston paused.

"There's one other piece to this little project that I haven't mentioned yet."

He motioned Bitsy to a far corner of the greenhouse where mature milkweed plants set in a six-by-six-foot plat were growing. They looked quite ordinary, as did the herbicide-resistant plants in the other part of the greenhouse.

"Many scientists are worried that herbicide-resistant traits of plants with altered genes will escape into the ecosystem through hybridization," he said. "In other words, corn plants that have been tweaked through gene splicing might send their genetic information to unaltered plants in distant fields in the legs of bees or other insects. They are concerned about the unintended consequences of that kind of breeding. It's not as though monster plants would rise up and eat Kansas, but no one is certain what might happen."

Bitsy drew back as that sank in.

"So, all the work the chemical companies have done to change the plants might be transferred to plants they don't control?"

"Yes."

"My, that's got to scare you a little bit!"

"Perhaps, but we are looking for benefits for our project. As we developed our own herbicide-resistant milkweeds, Myron and I set up another test program outdoors where we planted ordinary milkweeds far away from our hybridized ones, provided proper nutrients and waited to see whether simple cross-fertilization by insects would affect their offspring."

"And?"

"The ones you're looking at," said Winston, "are first generation and they are over twenty per cent herbicide resistant! It's an amazing result."

"Do you mean that as time goes by their resistance could be increased?"

"Not sure, but it looks as though there will be a profound ripple effect from the milkweed seeds we intend to sow this fall. Things are looking very good for the monarch!"

Bitsy lit up. Now we're getting somewhere, she thought.

As they returned to the office corner of the building, Winston gestured toward some corn seedlings growing in trays nearby.

"You know, Bitsy, when we were borrowing herbicide-resistant genes, we discovered another aspect of that BIG AG corn, something I hadn't known about before. Their corn contained a terminator gene, a toxin harmless to the growing plant that affects its developing seeds and makes them sterile".

She frowned. "That sounds pretty dangerous."

"Not really, the corn grows fine, but farmers who save seed for the following year are out of luck."

"They're sterile, right?"

"Yes," he said. "BIG AG wants to keep on selling new seeds year after year."

"What about the poor farmers in developing countries?"

"Good question."

Billy held his cards close to his chest and looked at Wylie.

"So, Mavis told my Lillian that you are such a cheap bastard that you won't pay for your granddaughter's braces."

Wylie suspected that Billy had been waiting for a quiet pause in the game to initiate a subject that promised to enliven the lackluster evening. Sy and Arnie waited for the repartee.

Wylie drew a card and said, "How nice that Mavis and Lillian are speaking again, especially after that kerfuffle where Mavis lobbied so hard against her becoming president of the book club."

"Yeah, they decided to have lunch a while ago and made up," said Billy. "Women, I guess, are more forgiving than men are. As for me, I'm saving a fine bottle of wine to pour over the grave of Ted Simpson, that mangy prick who sets up his fish and chips shacks across from all my places. Of course, I'm planning to pass it through my kidneys first."

The other card players had not heard that one before and collapsed in generous laughter.

"Anyway, whatever her faults, Mavis continues to be an excellent source of local gossip – or so Lillian tells me. Anyway, what's with your granddaughter's braces, Wylie?"

"Oh, it's just another way Mavis continues to dig in her claws. She wants to be sure our kids get what she thinks they are entitled to before I spend it on myself or my friends."

"This damn false sense of entitlement plagues the younger generation," noted Arnie. "Your kids might be after her to make demands on you."

"It's possible," said Wylie dubiously, thinking of his daughter, Mercy, who was a giver, not a taker."

Billy adjusted the cards in his hand and frowned.

"It's the women. Like the guy says, we're from Mars and they are from God knows where."

"Venus" Sy said.

"Whatever. I guess my point is it's kind of amazing we get along with them at all."

Sy, now widowed for four years, enjoyed the banter. Usually circumspect, he decided to join the conversation. His cards were lousy, anyway.

"I offer for your education an epiphany that occurred some years ago. I was in the city, on my way to the Union League Club and fell in behind two salesmen on Seventh Avenue. I overheard their conversation about a mutual customer who was a good friend to them both. They kept agreeing about what a wonderful guy he was, like one of the family. Then one of the guys paused and said – Yeah, he's the kind of person you don't lie to unnecessarily."

"That's an epiphany?"

"I thought we were talking about women."

"We still are," Sy said. "Think about it. We lie to each other all the time. One way or another – little white lies, exaggerations, hyperbole, boldfaced whoppers and weasel words to escape blame."

"Okay. I'll grant you that. But, women?"

"When dealing with my wife particularly, and, now, with other women," said Sy, "I give momentary but careful consideration to the necessary lie. Sometimes, if I give a matter enough thought, I can avoid saying anything. The other party moves on."

"I see where you are going," said Billy. "Honesty can get you in trouble. Like, Lillian could ask if the dress makes her look fat. You lie and say of course not, she's happy."

Arnie pursed his lips, an indication that an objection was coming.

"I don't think you can be quite that cavalier about it. For example, if I glibly say she looks great, that's opening a challenge to my sincerity. That could mean sliding down the slippery slope of explaining exactly how it is that she looks great, as compared with, say, the outfit she wore on Tuesday, and you have no idea what it was. No, the quick lie can really bite you in the ass!"

"I like Sy's approach," said Wylie. "I think it would be wise to deliberate about lying as long as possible. I would rather she be exasperated than really pissed."

"That's a very delicate distinction without a difference," suggested Arnie.

"Well, in any case, it has been enlightening, Sy," said Wylie. "Any other epiphanies you wish to reveal?"

"No, you sarcastic a-hole."

"Such talk! Are we still playing cards?"

They were. Billy stared at his hand. Who dealt this crap, he wondered?

The seeds sowed by the Master Gardeners earlier in the year had germinated and were striving toward the sunlit roof panes of the large greenhouse. Bitsy had organized a group to simulate breezes above the growing plants. They fanned cardboard squares above them and watched as the little green stalks stirred in response to the moving air. It was the latest thing. Breezes in nature toughen up the plants and stimulate growth. There would be no hothouse queens on Bitsy's watch. They would all become assertive, just as she had. She brushed her hand gently over the top of a row of corn seedlings.

Uniformity among the varieties of seedlings was expected, and there were few exceptions. Much care had been given to creating consistent potting mixes and providing just the correct amount of moisture and temperature variation. Nature provided the correct cues when it came to available sunlight. To the practiced eyes of the Master Gardener caretakers, everything was proceeding agreeably. However, there was one patch of green in the southeast corner of the large growing area that was different.

Wylie stood next to Anne as she examined the stocky plants protruding from one of her personal plats.

"Look at that," Wylie. "These are from those ancient seeds that I thought probably wouldn't be viable any longer. Seems every one of them germinated and is growing like mad."

Wylie agreed. He identified two types of corn, soybeans, beans and wheat. There was a grassy, lighter green plant he did not know, but Anne was able to categorize it as rice – a crop never grown in New Anglia. In the next plat there were large, circular cucurbit leaves forming on fat stems. Wylie guessed they would have to wait to see what members of the gourd family were forming. He hoped they would be melons of some sort.

What interested them both was the robust character of these plants. Their root systems channeled through the walls of the peat pots trying to contain them, and their stalks grew thicker and higher than similar varieties around them. They also had a deeper green color than their peers, and the leaves had an unusual luster – as though lightly sprinkled with fine golden pollen.

"These guys will need to be potted up for transplanting very soon," said Wylie.

"Yes, like tomorrow," Anne agreed.

Although they had not planned to return to Van Poppen farm for a few days, Wylie checked his calendar and promised to help Anne for a few hours the following day. Then they continued to examine the seedlings, looking for pests and malformations. They found none.

Myron Ng was helping Bitsy's group create the slight wind to stimulate seedling growth. He noticed Anne and Wylie fussing with the batch of seedlings in the southeast corner. They do look interesting, he thought.

Chapter 4

JUNE

Middletown Courier-Times

Mastering your Garden

By Elizabeth Pendleton Crangle

"Oh, my love is like a red, red rose, that's newly sprung in June" says the poet, Bobby Burns, and how right he is! We can look forward to abundant rose buds early this month undisturbed by Japanese beetles (they'll be here soon, though). To extend their life indoors, re-cut stems with a sharp knife at an angle under water and place them in a deep container of warm water and floral preservative. You'll get at least two more days of wilt-free bloom.

While thinking about watering, collect some two-liter soda bottles and buy soaker tips to water your container plants this summer.

If there are still bare spots in your flower garden, it's not too late to plant seeds for flowers that germinate and grow quickly. Portulaca, zinnias, cosmos, cleome (spider flower) and sunflowers can be planted now. For a spectacular corner of your garden, plant short, medium and tall sunflowers in staggered rows. By early August, you'll have a wall of sunny faces attracting bees – and birds feeding in September. Keep an eye on your mum plants and pinch them back as soon as they look leggy. While you're at it, your marigolds, zinnias and petunias would benefit from pinching to encourage lateral growth.

This month blueberries should be fed again. If you have peaches, thin them so there are four fingers between each fruit. The same for Asian pears, which I favor, since they are resistant to brown rot later in the season. Cherries have a short harvest time and the sweet ones are ripe before the tart. If you pit them and add syrup before freezing them, they will make excellent winter desserts.

This is the time to remove all the stalks from your spring flowering bulbs that have faded. Some people (I won't call them gardeners) trim or weave their daffodil leaves or tie them with rubber bands, I guess because they are crazy neat. Don't do that! The leaves need to ripen and convert sunlight into energy to replenish the bulbs so they can flower next year! Wait until tulip leaves have turned yellow before trimming them back – for the same reason as for the daffodils.

Perennials will certainly be popping this month. Enjoy all the columbines, Baptisia, lupines, yarrow, gaillardia, lily-of-the-valley, lavender and peonies that brighten your garden and your day. But, you know, any garden is but a work in progress, so visit other gardens and arrange trades with your friends when the right time comes to divide plants. Take notes and pictures and keep them handy when the catalogs come next winter and garden centers open next spring.

You should never visit a garden center without a well-thought-out shopping list. Otherwise, you're going to succumb to buying the plant some crafty horticulturist has forced to bloom early or some colorful exotic which grows well in the Philippines but not so well in our soil.

As far as veggies go, pick the beans and peas and the caterpillars and bugs. Look for egg masses under leaves and destroy them. And, watch out for the brown marmorated stink bug (which arrived from Pennsylvania a few years ago), the same one you probably found in your house last winter. They are nibbling on fruit, tomatoes and other commercial crops – and they could be partial to your garden. Sounds silly, but I go after them with a portable hand vacuum.

That's not a pleasant note to leave on, so I'll just add thanks to all of you who agreed about chemists and DDT! There are a lot of you.

Blissful gardening - Bitsy

Pierre

The after-effects of a recently replaced knee kept the senior senator from Louisiana from putting both alligator leather-encased feet on the corner of his massive desk. He resolved the issue by leaning farther back in the leather chair and stretching out both legs. He was able to rest his left foot atop the lower drawer thoughtfully pulled forward by an aide. Thus settled, he reviewed material in a blue folder he selected from an end table in his large office.

"Energy, energy!" he exclaimed. "Ever damn time they want to solve all our economic problems by frackin', drillin' or suckin' oil out of some place closer to our earth's core, they want me to co-sponsor the damn bill. I know energy – been close to it for years. Made a bundle on energy. And I know that is not necessarily the answer to whatever the damn question is."

The two aides in the room tried to forget how many times they had heard this litany before as the senator continued to pour over the pages in the folder. They watched as a stubby finger slid down each page. Occasionally it paused to tap an offensive or revealing word. A look of exasperation crossed his face as he completed reading the document.

"Tell you what," he began, addressing the closest aide. "You take this memo to Senator Boggle's aide and politely suggest it requires revision. Basically, they've got to wring the horseshit out of it, but I'm sure you can find a better way of expressin' that."

As his aide reached for the document, the luminous pad on his communicating device (he had been informed it was too sophisticated to be called a telephone) glowed yellow/green and Zelda Barnickle's disembodied voice filled that part of the office.

"Mr. Wylie Cypher is on the line."

Zelda knew that Wylie was one of the senator's oldest friends. and he always answered his calls.

"Wylie, Wylie, Wylie, what's going on, man?"

Senator Pierre Rowe came from very humble beginnings. Orphaned in his early teens, he avoided the intercessions of social workers, truant officers and well-meaning relatives, and squatted on a few swampy acres in a parish outside Baton Rouge. He fished, hunted alligators, ferried tourists through bald cypress forests in a flat-bottomed boat and managed to survive reasonably well. For all his avoidance of meddling officialdom, his name still appeared on the rolls for the national draft. A notice from the Selective Service System found its way to the rural post office that was in a country store that Pierre occasionally frequented, mainly to get cigarettes, dog biscuits and pints of moonshine from the back of the store.

He had been selected, the notice said, for military service and was required to present himself for recruitment at the Saint James parish offices on a "date certain," a few days after he unsealed the notice. He had on occasion thought about military service. Even in the remote bayou, young men were aware they were subject to the draft. He had seen many World War II movies: Back to Bataan, Thirty Seconds over Tokyo, Sahara, Wing and a Prayer, the Story of G.I. Joe and Command Decision. They all seemed splendid, the warriors noble and the action exciting. He was a little put off by the dying part, but, at the age of eighteen, he believed that only happened to other people. He was vaguely aware of the "cold war" and something involving United Nations troops near Japan but, if it wasn't displayed in headlines or on the covers of Life, Colliers or the Saturday Evening Post, he generally ignored the "news." The immediate concerns of the bayou always took precedence.

The crabby Creole woman tending the store recognized the letter and told him he would be courting hellish trouble should he fail to appear as demanded.

"Service do you good," she explained. "Didn't hurt my Beauregard none."

He prepared to go. The only loose end was Blue, his hound, but the woman at the store agreed to keep him, on the understanding that he was one hell of a damn good ratter. Blue would earn his keep.

Pierre Rowe became a member of the United States Army and completed his basic and advanced infantry training without major mishap. He shipped out to Korea in late 1950, and, again in early 1953. He became one of the many privileged to engage in two tours of duty in the Land of the Morning Calm during the height of combat. He remained a private during his early years of service and reenlisted once for the bonus and because he enjoyed being a soldier. He was an expert jeep driver and miraculously escaped being wounded on the many occasions others around him succumbed to enemy fire.

Without the burdens of a lengthy formal education, Pierre was unaware that beginning most of his utterances with "Shit, Dad" might be inappropriate. Fortunately, he was in the military, where his linguistic quirk was a source of amusement and inspiration. In any case, within days of his arrival in a combat battalion fighting its way north against Chinese volunteer forces, he was known as "Shit Dad" and his comrades in arms respected him for it.

Of course, the nickname was forgotten after he left the Army, except by his best friend in Korea, Wylie Cypher who, on occasion, forgetfully called him that when he was distracted. The Senator always forgave him.

A child of the bayou, Pete did his best to remain as independent as possible under military rule. He managed to avoid most military strictures, flaunted regulations (by getting married to a Korean girl) and enjoyed his position as low man on the Army totem pole. Wylie managed to extricate him from self-inflicted military messes and encouraged him to begin proper soldiering.

Pete finally followed Wylie's advice, with satisfying results. He believed Wylie rescued him from himself and a dire future in Korea and the Army.

Pete returned to Louisiana in 1955 a very different person from the one drafted in 1950. He now had a Korean wife and two children, Kim Pierre and Ah Sung. He discovered that being "squared away" in the Army was more rewarding than being a "slovenly screw-up," and returned to the United States as a Corporal, with extra financial benefits for having a wife and children. He arrived in Fort Polk with his family and served out the remaining months of his enlistment as an NCO training southern recruits. The family was housed in rudimentary family barracks, but Sunhee was extremely happy with running water, constant electricity and a Laundromat to clean toddlers' clothing. Her idyll was short lived, however, since Pete decided to return to the bayou to earn his living when his enlistment ended. His old ways, however, could not support his new family and he moved with them to the town of Houma on the coast, intending to get a job on a shrimp boat or oilrig.

There, he was hired as a mechanic and helper on a shrimp boat that ferried supplies to Deepwater oilrigs beyond the horizon. Within a few months, Pete demonstrated a natural talent for seafaring, and became a mate on the shrimp boat and a captain soon after that. He let Sunhee handle family finances, and she proved both frugal and canny.

Pete worked hard ferrying supplies to the various offshore rigs within navigation distance of the Louisiana shore. Sunhee saw to the children, kept their little apartment spotless and practiced English by watching soap operas on their grainy black and white television set. This was heady stuff for a young woman who, a year before, lived in the hut of a small farmstead on a hilly slope in the outskirts of Tongduchon-ni, Korea, five miles from the Demilitarized Zone.

Their savings grew, and soon Pete was able to finance his own boat, which he dedicated to supplying oil rigs in the gulf. His Senate web site told the rest of his story. It chronicled the building of his fleet of delivery boats, investments in several of the rigs he supplied and ventures in oil and gas along the Louisiana coast and beyond. As a Cajun versed in rites of survival, he naturally gravitated toward the political elite as his fortunes grew. Sunhee agreed that political contributions made to the shakers and movers of the bayou were good investments.

Eventually, as Pete's children graduated from college and began new lives of their own, he decided to run for government office. His folksy ways and unvarnished manner of speech reminded Louisianans of the fabled Kingfisher, Huey Long. Pete ran for senate and won – four times. Sunhee and Pierre managed his business interests, and he became a political alchemist. He more than doubled the amount of money returned to his state by the federal government, compared with the funds received from Louisiana's taxpayers. There was no doubt that Pete's senate seat would be secure for some time.

Wylie returned to Princeton after his military service. He received a degree in Economics and went on to Harvard Law School. In 1961, he obtained his law degree, joined the New York City law firm of Biddle and Ofstrosky, and married a recent graduate of Radcliffe College. He had literally bumped into Mavis in Harvard Yard. Their courtship began as he helped her recover books and papers he dislodged from her arms. He was sure she was the sweetest, most loving person he had ever met. He continued in that belief for about a dozen years.

Though the two men lost touch for a few years after they left the service, Pete located Wylie as his business empire grew and employed him as counsel on many occasions, especially for complicated deals involving Persian Gulf oil. Their friendship strengthened and grew. As the years wore on, they talked once or twice a week, whether business was afoot or not. Zelda Barnickle was aware of their relationship as good, well-trusted, old friends. The Senator shoed his assistants from the office as he settled in his chair and listened to Wylie.

Their telephone conversation continued.

"Not much old man. Just touching base. I need to know how long it'll be after your knee surgery before you'll be wrestling alligators again."

"I'd be doin' it now, but for Sunhee. She holds me back, man. Holds me back."

"Well, thank her for me and give her my best. The kids, too. They're O.K., I assume."

"Happy as a little boy with two peckers. You all right?"

"Sure. I hear you're getting involved with that legislation being proposed to reduce corporate welfare for energy companies."

"And it's a damn good thing I am."

Wylie knew he would hit a nerve with that comment. Pete believed in a balanced and nuanced use of tax legislation to foster desired financial and social behavior. He was incensed by bumper sticker descriptions, like "corporate welfare," which attempted to reduce complex issues to the lowest common denominator understandable by the ignorant and uninformed. So, for the next ten minutes he lectured Wylie about the complexity of the issues and how difficult it would be to resolve the pros and cons.

When he thought Pete was about to wind down, Wylie asked

"Well, are you for it or against it?"

He bit.

"Has what I've been saying gone completely over your head? Have I been wastin' my breath explaining the issues to you? Are you just…"

The Senator realized Wylie was pulling his leg.

"Got me again, you sum'bitch."

He laughed.

"Wylie, I do miss you so. When can you get down here again?"

"I love the capitol in June, before the heat and humidity roll across Foggy Bottom. Maybe in a week or so. It always makes me feel good to see you again."

"Do it, man."

Senator Pierre Rowe lowered his leg gingerly and cursed the four-footed aluminum cane leaning against his desk. He needed to head for the subway and board the shuttle to the chamber. With the aid of his cane, he walked slowly to the door of his suite and shuffled down the corridor to the large atrium of the Hart Senate Office Building, which contained Calder's massive mountains and clouds sculpture. Pete was confused by modern sculpture, since he was never sure whether the artist was laughing all the way to the bank. He was particularly uncertain about the massive black forms in the atrium. As he was fond of telling his aides, all it meant to him was there were always dark clouds on the horizon. He cast a sidelong glance at the huge, jagged mountain peaks and made his way to the elevator.

Across the mall, in the Rayburn House Office Building, Grover Merson sat at one of the desks squeezed into the back room of Representative Pert Pewtree's three-room suite. He watched information scrolling across the screen of his laptop, making occasional notes in the pull-down rectangle near the top of the screen. His assignment, as explained by Ms. Pewtree, was to review the protest lodged by a group of environmentalists against a proposed grant by the National Institute of Food and Agriculture (NIFA) to New Anglia University's Biotechnology and Genomics Department.

"NIFA is an agency of the United States Department of Agriculture (USDA), and the department requesting the grant is in my district," said the congresswoman.

"I don't know who makes up this crazy alphabet soup of acronyms, but, as you know, Grover, there wasn't a whole lot of agriculture where I grew up in New Bushwick. However, I learned that there are seventeen USDA agencies, and the USDA shares responsibilities with the FDA in numerous areas, not one of which I understand. I don't even know what the heck "genomics" are. Or is it 'is.'. But you've got to figure out whether I want to oppose this grant or whether I will be helping hand over the grant check for the benefit of newspaper photographers."

The bulk of Grover's farming experience occurred in the fourth grade when he watched a bean seed germinate in a plastic cup. Nevertheless, he was an excellent researcher, and he tackled this problem with customary curiosity and skill.

He discovered, by drilling down through the USDA agencies to their programs, sub-programs and focus areas, that NIFA was vitally interested in "advancing knowledge for agriculture, the environment, human health and well-being." And, he guessed, they were also in favor of motherhood and apple pie.

NIFA was particularly interested in "supporting research, education and extension programs in the Land-Grant University System and other partner organizations." Plant breeding, genetics and genomics were high on their preferred programs list. What rings their chimes, discovered Grover, were items like completing the assembly of the soybean genetic code and unlocking the secrets of the rice gene.

The controversy was over a three-million-dollar grant for research into the genetic secrets of quinoa, an ancient grain favored by the Incas of South America. Quinoa had the interesting quality of containing a complete protein, meaning that it included all nine essential amino acids. Good stuff, thought Grover. What could be wrong here?

Green Pieces, an amalgamated group of related environmental activists, thought there was a lot wrong with granting that much money to study quinoa. Their first objection was that the grant money would be shared with BIG AG, a perennial research partner. The environmental group sarcastically asked why the multi-billion-dollar second largest chemical company in the United States needed hard working taxpayers to fund their part of the research.

The second objection was that the grant did not require the results of the research to be made public for at least five years. And their third objection was that the program included no protections against the inadvertent cross-pollination with other grains, such as the rice and wheat so favored by the Biotechnology and Genomics Program. There were also gratuitous comments about what a boondoggle the government ethanol program was, and questions about when the USDA was planning to stop paying farmers not to plant certain crops.

This is a stinker, thought Grover. While it would be very desirable to have his employer receive credit for pumping three million dollars into her district, alienating Green Pieces would be politically stupid. On top of that, the issue reeked of moral ambiguity. Representative Pewtree was no fan of moral ambiguity. If only there was a way of relying on benign neglect. He went to the congresswoman's notes to see who raised the issue. Was it someone who could be put off or ignored? He would see.

Anne and Wylie stood near the southwest corner of the largest outdoor experimental plot at Van Poppen farm. At three in the afternoon, the sun warmed their shoulders and cast strong light over the expanse of ordered rows containing many varieties of plants. Corn, soybeans, tomatoes, canola, sunflowers and various grain crops filled their field of view. Anne was interested in the rows directly in front of her. Cryptic markings on a white card stapled to a stake read "APX – Var. 5/17." From his time working at the farm, Wylie readily translated – "Anne Proctor, experimental, more than one variety, transplanted May 17th."

During the previous month, when all risk of late frost was gone, Anne was preparing to take some of her seedlings from the greenhouse to her home vegetable garden. As she began to work on the transfer, the prolific plants caught the attention of Bruno Gladstetter, Van Poppen's green house and experimental turf overseer.

"Very strong, very nice. I love the corn. I love those cancador fillet beans," he said admiring the plants.

Anne was impressed. She had no idea she was holding fillet bean plants.

Bruno noted the large number and variety of Anne's plants, and compared them instinctively to the run of seedlings ready to be transplanted. Anne had a superabundance of plants, and Bruno recalled Anne's earlier suggestion that they add some of her seedlings to the new experimental plant rows. So, a month later, she and Wylie stood by those experimental rows. She had an idea of what they would find – if they were like the super plants crowding her home garden.

Wylie kneeled before a row of corn. He confirmed with Anne that it was sweet corn.

"Listen, I'm no corn expert, but there are six baby ears coming off this stalk and they already have silk growing from them. And, look, it's the same with the others in the row. With regular corn plants, if it's more than two ears, the extra ones are stunted and need to be pulled off. We'll see how these guys turn out."

He stood and shifted his view to the regimented rows flowing from their position. He sensed he was missing something, and then realized what it was – weeds. In adjacent rows, clusters of green invaders sprang toward the bases of young stalks. The earth under Anne's plants remained pristine, brown and crumbly and slightly moist. The contrast was remarkable.

"Check out the soil under your plants."

Anne did. It was as though tiny hands had plucked all vagrant weed seedlings from beneath her vegetables and slightly churned the soil.

"Yes. It's much the same in my backyard garden. I thought it might be the late frost, but maybe there is something about the plants."

They looked at the vigorous plants in her rows. All were blockier and taller than similar ones in the experimental garden area and had the same gold-dusted look as when they were seedlings. They were abundant and thriving in the good earth of New Anglia.

"Maybe there is something about the plants," he agreed.

Grover and his employer, Representative Pert Pewtree, sat side by side at the conference table. Papers were spread out around them, and they both worked with their laptops. A large TV screen across the room showed highly lacquered and botoxed young women pontificating on the day's events, and rows of letters and numbers scrolled on the chyron. The sound was muted.

Grover was one of her principal advisors. Though only in his late twenties, he conveyed an uncommon maturity and steadfastness. He never jumped to conclusions and never rested until he had discovered, understood and analyzed all aspects of the issue at hand.

The congresswoman did not understand his desire to fling himself into every challenging athletic opportunity that presented itself, but she was appreciative and grateful for the many times, in the past three years, he had navigated her away from potential political disaster. He was a wise counselor and, she believed, a young person with a promising future, political or otherwise.

Pert's correct name was Priscilla, but her father nicknamed her "Pert" as a baby and it stuck. Her parents moved from the gritty city of New Bushwick to Middletown when she was thirteen. She involved herself in politics since high school. Her political outlook was moderate, leaning ever so slightly to the left, which, in the dark red political atmosphere of the northwestern rural part of her district, branded her as a socialist. The urban parts of her district, however, favored her leanings and appreciated her dedication to public service. Her congressional elections were close, but she won.

Pert was a mother of two and worked until her election to Congress as a very successful realtor. She had been married for twenty-six years to Tom, a pediatrician with a practice in Middletown. She was one of the more attractive members of Congress, with a Pilates-toned body and a dark bob of hair above startling green eyes.

Now, she and Grover were completing their review of constituents' requests. Visits to the Capitol; recommendations for appointments to the military academies; problems with the social security administration; e-mails, pro and con, about her position in favor of including the yellow crowned night heron under the endangered species act; and what businesses in her district should be considered favorably for government funding. That was the routine stuff. Grover then turned to the Green Pieces protest of the NIFA grant for genomics research to her hometown university. He mentioned the involvement of BIG AG.

"They seem to have their fingers in many pies," she said. "I understand the choice may be between alienating Green Pieces and passing on a needed infusion of cash to greater Middletown. What sort of support has BIG AG provided for my campaign?"

"Just a token amount during your first run, but about twenty-five thousand last time. However, representatives in other states, especially in the mid-west, take in much more from BIG AG and its executives."

"So, what if we suggest BIG AG simply waive their interest in the grant – get them to take their name off the grant entirely?" she asked.

"Might be doable, and it would certainly mollify the Green Pieces executive director. She could take credit for a very successful lobbying effort."

"Grover, try that approach."

"I'll deal with it today. I have a contact in their general counsel's office. But, you know, it will give them a chip to call in down the line."

Pert slightly hunched her shoulders and tilted her head in acknowledgement. She picked up a phantom chip from the desk and tossed it over her shoulder toward the large but invisible incoming chip bin perched on a corner of her desk.

"We'll just add it to the others," she sighed.

Grover smiled. He was concerned that the two phantom chip bins, incoming and outgoing, could threaten inequality. In his view, it was like a trade imbalance. If the incoming political debts overwhelmed the political capital, it boded ill for his employer. Elections were one thing, but the support of the powerful was quite another.

Pert turned to make telephone calls, and Grover left for his desk in another room. He was eager to complete today's tasks, as he planned to return to Middletown late that evening and meet tomorrow with Portia. He was hoping she would join him in kite surfing on the big lake not far from his apartment.

Myron joined the group of Master Gardener volunteers congregating at that part of the experimental farm where Anne Proctor planted her seeds from Peru. The loud buzzing of bees was overwhelmed by the sonorous clamor of volunteers exclaiming at the size and seeming perfection of the plants reaching maturity in the long days of June. In the week or so since Wylie and Anne inspected the plants for pests and disease, they had added height and girth. While normal expectations for corn were "knee high by the fourth of July," the three varieties before them were closer to "elephant eye high" and robust little ears peeked from the leaves on the stalks. The other plants were similarly blessed, together combining into a green monument in that corner of the experimental rows.

Myron mingled with the others. No doubt about it, this was unique, interesting. He thought about reviewing it with Etta but reconsidered. Too soon, he thought.

What tipped Mavis over the edge was the sight of Wylie cruising down the block in front of her condominium in his new Mazda Miata two-seater. Linda was laughing at his side, her blonde hair caught in the slipstream of the car's wake, streaming over the red deck like an unfurled flag. They were, of course, oblivious of Mavis who peered from the bay window where she sat holding her cat, Studly, on her lap.

Wylie had been extremely generous in the financial settlement of their divorce, and Mavis believed she had extracted the maximum from her former spouse. She hoped she had reduced him to a permanent state of penury. The sight of her ex cruising down the street with his blonde floozy in a shiny new toy was simply too much. That cheap bastard can afford a fancy new car, but he won't spare a few dollars for his granddaughter's braces, she told Studly, who seemed to agree. His opalescent eyes turned toward her knowingly. That cheap bastard, he seemed to echo.

The situation was intolerable. She considered appropriate punishment for the wayward former spouse and ruled out, on grounds of self-preservation, outright murder. The technicalities of maiming or dismembering him and/or his paramour proved too onerous and taxing to her imagination. Yet, as she gazed at Studly, she realized there was something dear to Wylie she could attack. That stupid Weimaraner dog that he walked every day. How fitting it would be to get rid of her. She probably cost a lot to feed anyway.

Mavis considered for a few days the appropriateness of her planned caninicide. She concluded it was thoroughly justified.

Since Middletown retained the character of a farming community, it was unremarkable that she added a box of rat poison to her purchase of household items at the local hardware store. It encouraged homey banter from the clerk.

"Yeah, they'll be coming out about now. Norway rat or wood rat?"

She flushed, uncertain.

"You know, one of those gray ones with the long tail."

She had seen one in the basement of their old house one time.

"Yeah. That'd be the Norway. Don't worry. This stuff will do him in. Rats are smart. They just nibble a little bit at first and wait to see if it might hurt them. When they think it's pkey, they scarf it all down. This stuff has a delayed effect. You don't want to know what it does to them."

True. She did not want to know.

He smiled as he rang up the sale.

Mavis was not a dog person, favoring the arrogance and independence of cats. She was sure, however, that ground chuck would be palatable to any young Weimaraner and purchased a half pound of the organic variety. She also purchased some doggy pita pockets, designed for discriminating canines whose owners prepared meals for them.

She pulverized the garish green rat pellets in a small metal dish with the heel of a spoon and added a few ounces of ground beef. What remained would be added later to a small meatloaf. She looked at the pink slurry with green bits and stuffed it carefully into the puppy pita pocket. She dropped the Trojan treat into a freezer bag and placed in the refrigerator. She rinsed the bowl carefully in very hot water, put it in the dishwasher and set the rubber gloves aside, to be discarded later.

Mavis knew that Wylie walked with his dog just after breakfast each morning. Her plan was to get up at four in the morning, walk to his condominium and put the fatal pita pocket near the bottom of the steps to the back door where the dog would consume it when the walk began.

She did the next morning.

About a half hour after the poisoned puppy pita pocket was distributed, the male leader of the raccoon family that customarily foraged through the condominium area for breakfast treats discovered that delectable item. Had it been his female counterpart, she would have taken it immediately to the condominium swimming pool to be washed before sharing it with her two offspring. However, he greedily bit into the morsel and immediately recognized something was amiss. Perhaps a quick wash would improve its taste.

He carried it to the edge of the swimming pool and used both black paws to swish it through the water. The material disintegrated almost immediately, and, in the moonlight, he looked wistfully at the soggy bits sinking to the bottom of the pool. They were sucked into the filter and disappeared. But a bit of the poison was enough to cause stomach pains and discomfort to the raccoon for a few days.

Studly awoke early that morning and felt peckish. He wandered to the kitchen and executed a flawless high jump to the counter by the edge of the sink. He encountered the rubber gloves Mavis left to be cleaned. Morsels of ground chuck and molecular remnants of rat poison clung to the gloves. Studly concentrated on the aromatic beef, his favorite, and tenderly licked up what goodness he could discover on the gloves. The onset of intestinal difficulty was delayed, but still sudden and severe. He moaned slightly and stood on tiptoe on the new white damask couch he chose as his resting place. When the eruptions from both ends of his chubby body ceased, he felt better. He would not return to the couch, however.

Myron pushed the sealed plastic bags containing green materials across the table in the booth of the coffee shop to Etta.

"The one marked 'A' holds flower buds, leaves and part of the stalk of the milkweed plants Dr. Wu developed. They are all growing well in a corner of the experimental farm, and we are going to harvest the seeds at the end of summer. The way they proliferate, there's going to be a whole lot of them."

"And what's in this bigger bag marked 'B?'"

"Those are samples of these robust plants growing in an experimental plot started by one of our Master Gardeners, Anne Proctor. Everybody is excited about them. Never seen anything like them here".

"Do you know where they came from?"

"No."

Seeing the dangerous look in Etta's eyes, he added, "But I'll do my best to find out."

Etta examined the contents of the larger bag, opened it and held a corn leaf in her fingers.

"That looks like a really large leaf. I've never seen a corn leaf covered with these little specks of gold. I'll let the lab guys check this out."

Myron seemed eager to leave.

"Come on. Sit down," she said. "Have something to eat. Let's talk about what's going on in your life."

As Myron made uncomfortable small talk with Etta, he felt a hurtful twinge of conscience. Passing on those plants, was crossing a line into perfidy. Disclosing information that was just gossip was bad enough, but to remove actual plants and offer them to BIG AG was, he now believed, dangerous. It was like feeding a voracious beast. Never sated, it would keep coming back for more and more.

As Etta babbled on, he wished he could take it all back. That was not to be. BIG AG had the plants. It had him. Myron was about to enter a very dark time in his life.

He had not listened to Etta's question and picked a noncommittal response.

"I'm sure you are right."

Chapter 5

July

Middletown Courier-Times

Mastering your Garden

By Elizabeth Pendleton Crangle

The Farmers' Almanac says this may be one of the hottest months on record, so prepare yourselves to water, water, water. Do it deeply at least once a week. Early mornings are best and try to keep moisture off rose leaves. Wetness promotes black spot. Cannas are especially thirsty, and they attract Japanese beetles (which are probably feasting on roses as well). It is best to hand pick them and drop them into a jar of foamy, soapy water. They succumb quickly.

If you find little bulbs on Asiatic lily stalks, they can be replanted to increase your lily bed. Unlike some other lilies, they will be exact duplicates of the parent plants.

You will have more blueberries this month, and raspberries will become abundant in July. Watch for ants on the raspberries and use water spray to discourage them. The fruits need plenty of water as well. If you have enjoyed strawberries earlier in the season, watch the runners – which will set this month and bear fruit next year. Pull out the mature plants and tidy up the rows. You'll thank yourself next spring.

Sawfly larvae are active early this month. They are wasp larvae but look like caterpillars. They attack pines, roses and dogwoods and are extremely damaging. You can go up to a mugo pine this month and see what looks like little black headed needles waving. They are sawflies and need to be eliminated – like

Japanese beetles or with oil or insecticidal soap sprays. I suppose you could use insecticide labeled to control them, but who knows what else it might attack or how long it will reside in the environment.

Speaking of pests, those nice little white moths that look like butterflies are cabbage moths and they are laying their eggs on cabbage family plants. The larvae are green, so they look like the leaves – into which they bore large holes. Pick them off by hand or try Bt (Bacillus thurengiensis), a naturally occurring bacterium that releases a toxin that does the picking for you. Since they are freely found in nature, I'm willing to let them do their thing.

Tomatoes will be ripening this month, and I think there is nothing finer than eating a warm, ripe tomato just picked from the vine. I carry a little packet of salt with me to enhance the flavor! If your tomatoes have black end rot, it usually means they have a calcium deficiency. Pep up the soil with a tomato fertilizer with calcium. If there is a little end rot or the tomatoes are split, cut out the bad parts and eat the rest. As you all know, don't refrigerate tomatoes; it spoils the flavor. Finally, don't those tomato hornworms look fierce? Hunt for them at night with a flashlight – and wear gloves!

It is never a good idea to fertilize when the temperature is over 85 degrees – which could be the whole month – so use water-soluble plant food if your perennials need a boost. Pruning is not needed this month except to cut out damaged materials AND to cut back dried lilac and buddleia flowers. The lilacs need all their energy to grow, and the buddleia will produce more flowers if the dead ones are cut off.

Hummingbirds should be active around your flowers this month, especially Monarda (bee balm), buddleia, columbine, hollyhock and Rose of Sharon. All these plants grow easily in our area. Note that, although red flowers seem to attract these little birds, they will drink from almost anything with abundant nectar. We always place a hummingbird feeder by the kitchen window. It is such a treat to watch the babies feeding this month.

My editor, Marc Graddis, says I'm too long-winded, but still makes room for the extra words! Enjoy summer gardening and stay cool.

Blissful gardening – Bitsy

Dick

The numbers for the second quarter were slightly below forecast. That, in Dick Geier's view, was enough cause to treat those responsible to the judicious application of burning cigarettes on the soft flesh of their bodies or, at least, water boarding. In fact, it would even be instructive if those not responsible were included.

Geier's marketing vice president, Manfred Balducci, explained to the members of the weekly staff meeting what happened.

"Our market share is growing, but Plow AgroSciences, our closest competitor after Monsanto, matched our share. We didn't think Plow could do that well and projected a greater share of the growing segment in the plan approved last year."

Geier was notorious for his apoplexy. While members of his management team suspected his explosive rants were carefully orchestrated, they were scary, nonetheless. The team watched his face turn purplish red, highlighting his close-cropped white hair, and the veins on forehead and neck throb alarmingly. He craned his glowing head from side to side as he sucked mightily from his ever-present cigarette and spat out words and smoke at the same time.

"Competitors! Competition! Listen, Manny, you tell those peckerheads you call salesmen and marketing experts that they better become ninja competitors, fierce competitors or they will be out on the street."

"O.K. Dick. It will be done."

Geier looked at Manfred through narrowed eyes. He had the distinct feeling he was being patronized.

"Listen, asshole, do you even know what a fierce competitor is?"

"Sure, Dick," said Manfred, eying the conference room door as a primary escape route, "that's...."

Geier thrust his glowing face toward Manfred.

"I'll tell you what a fierce competitor is!"

He took another mighty drag on his cigarette and swished it through the air, sending little fireflies of ash onto the conference table.

"That's the guy who comes in first and second in a masturbating contest! Did you get that? Did you get that?"

"Got it," said the strained executives around the table.

"O.K. Shove a hot poker up their asses and make sure we are on target for the third quarter."

The President, Chairman and Chief Executive Officer of Bemis International Group lit a fresh cigarette and turned to the others arranged around the large walnut conference table situated in the north side of his office. Seven of his top managers sat around the table. Lavitra Gascoigne, Human Resources; George Stirrup, Operations; and Frank Edger, Public relations, had their "turn in the barrel" just before Manfred Balducci. Of those four, Stirrup and Edger were friends and cronies from Geier's days in the capitol.

When he was recruited for Bemis' top position in 2001, he asked them to join him and help manage the company. Simon Targle, his General Counsel, was a recent hire, but he came highly recommended as an assistant Attorney General in Washington. Targle had found novel legal approaches to condone harsh treatment of foreign combatants so long as they did not result in outright death. He joined Bemis just after receiving a grant of immunity from prosecution from the Attorney General's office.

Armin Haak was Geier's Vice President for corporate development. He rose and gathered his skeletal frame to report on various potential acquisitions of smaller chemical companies and agreed to meet with Targle later to review the possibility that any might be subject to challenges of antitrust either from the Justice Department or under the Robinson-Patman Act. The final report came from Randi Fochik, Geier's Vice President for research and development. The CEO was particularly interested in what Fochik had to say today.

Geier, a chemistry major at the University of Wyoming at Laramie, took his first job with Chevron in La Barge. Native management skills fostered swift growth within the oil company, and he soon moved to the headquarters office in Denver. There he met his first wife, who remained so for about thirty months. There were irreconcilable differences centered mainly on her unwillingness to understand that the diverse aspects of his persona required the attention of different women.

As he rose within the Chevron ranks, he was exposed to the political aspects of running an oil business. The basic objective was to keep politicians convinced that the oil business was financially risky and physically dangerous and that it would be un-American to deny them extraordinary tax deductions and depreciation credits that had almost no relation to their actual business. Geier enjoyed entertaining local and national politicians with influence over the oil business. He became not only well known, but quite friendly with many of them.

When he was thirty-eight, he ran for Congress and was elected for four terms. As a reward for his dedicated and thoughtful public service, he was asked to join the George H. W. Bush administration as assistant secretary of Defense, a position he held with distinction for almost three years before joining other neo-cons at the Heritage Foundation.

He was recruited from that organization to become the leader of Bemis, at a handsome pay package. The recruiter confided to members of the Bemis board that Geier was just the man for the job. According to the headhunter, he was really smart and mean as cat shit.

As Geier began his tenure at Bemis, Monsanto's U.S. patent for glyphosate expired. That permitted other chemical companies to produce the most widely used herbicide in the country. Geier noted that over two hundred million pounds of the stuff were consumed annually in the United States alone. Randi Fochik and his research teams were working on genetically engineered seeds resistant to glyphosate – called Roundup® by Monsanto. The industry knew that Roundup had different effects than glyphosate alone. Other substances were added.

Bemis quickly began production and registered the trade name Klobber® for its brand of glyphosate. Operations followed the development group's recipe and added surfactants plus caffeine to the glyphosate.

There was no obvious reason for adding caffeine other than, according to Randi Fochik, to fuck with their reverse engineering competitors who would waste many man-hours attempting to decipher the reason for adding the substance. Geier complimented Fochik on his creative perversity.

After two years of intensive marketing, sales of Klobber began to accelerate. Geier helped by asking his government contacts to convince the CIA to purchase highly concentrated versions of Klobber to spray on and eradicate illegal coca fields in Colombia – under a good neighbor program. Unfortunately, those attempts resulted in the development of herbicide-resistant strains of coca known as Boliviana negra. That variety was larger and higher yielding than the original strains of the plant and seemed to thrive on applications of Klobber. Geier's international foray failed.

Nevertheless, production of Klobber increased and Geier pleased the Bemis board by taking advantage of his political influence to resolve unpleasant allegations raised by the EPA. He also skirted around a potential FDA finding that Klobber could not be considered GRAS (Generally Recognized as Safe).

Balducci's marketing team enthusiastically advertised that Klobber was biodegradable, cleaning the soil after being applied. Tangle's predecessor mistakenly approved the copy (which hastened his departure from Bemis) and numerous consumer lawsuits ensued, challenging the advertising as false and misleading.

The EPA rejected the claims of an obscure independent testing laboratory that Klobber was virtually clear of side effects. The study indicated that the laboratory took specimens from the uteruses of male guinea pigs.

Geier used his influence to assure that relevant functionaries at the government agency diverted their attention to more pressing matters. The lawsuits dwindled away.

The FDA matter required more astute handling. An independent panel decided, six to three, to rule Klobber unsafe in some instances because two unique tests by scientists in university laboratories showed that constant exposure to the herbicide caused little holes to appear in mouse brains. To the surprise of some, the FDA section leader overruled the panel's recommendation, as was his right, and no further stigma attached to the Bemis product. That section leader soon left the FDA for a high-paying job in research with Standofi LTD, one of Bemis' subsidiary companies.

Thus, during his decade-long tenure at Bemis, Dick Geier won the admiration, if not the affection, of his board of directors.

Randi Fochik loved offering his Power Point presentations at weekly staff meetings. He had raised the act of presentation to an art form. The design of each slide and its complimentary color scheme, along with appropriate fonts and scientific dingbats, were rendered with the precise eye of an artist. His greatest challenge was to meet Geier's demand to "boil it down to twelve minutes, dammit." Consequently, he moved more rapidly through his superior slides than he intended, churning out commentary in his Bangalore-accented English. His captive audience listened intently, afraid of missing something Dick Geier might consider important. Randi described progress in ongoing research areas before turning to "new business."

A multi-colored graph containing numerous little boxes appeared on the large screen next to the conference table.

"As we all know," began Randi," there is a long-established program of information gathering directed toward the university programs we sponsor. Occasionally, substance of a non-trivial nature comes our way. That occurred recently regarding our outreach to certain programs at the Van Poppen farm at the University of New Anglia. Actually, we received samples of two unique plant forms that attracted our interest."

Lavitra Gascoigne was eager to leave the meeting and confer with the au pair monitoring her two children. She made "hurry up" hand motions in his direction However, Randi droned on about how the samples were obtained and the intricate tests his team performed. The slide on the screen, he intoned, documented the similarities between certain of BIG AG's genetically altered plants and the samples obtained from Van Poppen farm.

The slide was replaced by photographs of desiccated plant samples, followed by a picture of Anne Proctor's super plants bursting from the experimental plot at the farm, courtesy of Myron Ng.

"We consider these plants true mysteries," Randi said. "There is no evidence that any of them succumbed to genetic engineering, yet they are more vigorous and productive than anything we have created so far. Further, there is nothing extraordinary in their genetic and molecular structure that differentiates them from normal vegetable plants found anywhere in our database. Yet, and this is the truly inexplicable part, when subject to high magnification under the electron microscope, there are hints of gold color found on the interstitial molecular bonds. And, as we all know, color is not decipherable under high magnification. There is also evidence that the plants secrete a toxin that destroys the growth characteristics of known invasives. We are continuing to investigate. Now, turning to…"

Before Randi could pontificate on the second sample under consideration, Geier interrupted.

"Let me get this straight. You've screwed around with these plants for a couple months and can't say for sure that they've been altered."

Two thin strands of smoke escaped from his nostrils.

"On the other hand, you didn't find anything to indicate they have not been subject to genetic alteration. There's something about this gold crap, right?"

Randi agreed.

"O.K. That is the great thing about demanding evidence that something didn't happen. If ever these plants should threaten our business, we can affirm they violate our various plant patents. We would keep those peckerheads off our backs for years as they struggle through federal court. Right, Simon?"

His General Counsel considered amending Geier's statement, thought better of it, and nodded his head in confirmation.

A photograph of Asclepias syriaca, common milkweed, appeared on the screen.

"Now, here, we were able to be more definitive. A little group of well-meaning but deluded eco-terrorists operating out of Van Poppen farm is fixated on the way Klobber prohibits the development of weeds and invasives that support insect life. They seem to be particularly interested in the Monarch butterfly, which thrives on milkweed. Here is a mature plant that is indeed highly resistant to Klobber's beneficial effects. The plant almost seems to thrive in concentrations of the material. Klobber's caffeine content may have something to do with it…we are not certain."

"Why should we give a rat's fart about this? There's no money in milkweed," Geier interjected.

"Well, we were intrigued that a little group of amateurs could so quickly replicate techniques we considered as industrial property rights, especially the intensive computer capabilities involved in sequencing the plant genomes. We suspected they might have hacked our computers and stolen information. As it turns out, they had not, though we discovered numerous attacks from addresses in China and Russia."

"You're seriously boring me, Randi. Get to the point."

"The point is that we discovered hints of our own genetic code in the milkweed plants. We can't be sure, but we suspect they skipped a few steps by "borrowing" from us."

Geier paused to light another cigarette from the tip of the one hanging from his lips.

"That's a non-starter. I don't see how this could be a problem for us. If those commie eco-terrorists get in our hair, we'll just turn them in to the feds. There's always the department of Homeland Security. What else you got?"

Randi had strayed well beyond his allotted time limit. There was nothing else.

Grover added some wine to Portia's glass and leaned back from their table. He skipped strenuous sporting activity during the day in hopes of a different form of activity after their meal. They were dining at one of Middletown's best restaurants, The Olde Congerie.

She smiled at Grover to acknowledge the fresh dollop of Cabernet, sipped and said, "It's corny, but a penny for your thoughts."

The line of thought he pursued at that moment was not ready for public or private consumption. He and Portia had now been lovers for almost four weeks, matching each other in passion and inventiveness. He was unable to gaze at her without seeing her as she was in her best moments. Laughing giddily as she rappelled down the side of a granite quarry wall; feigning exhaustion just before challenging him to a race to the top of a long, winding hill; opening her towel to reveal her rosy flesh as she stepped from the shower; or resting her head in the crook of his arm after love-making.

"Oh, nothing. I was just wondering how your summer job was going."

In May, at the end of her second law school year, Portia considered two summer employment opportunities: working as a research assistant at the local law firm of Clem Gatz and Associates or working as a volunteer with the College's Legal Aid Society. The local bar association and Court of First Instance relaxed certain rules to allow Legal Aid volunteers to handle small matters in court, if they were under the direct supervision of an attorney. Portia chose the more active role offered by the Legal Aid Society program and was enjoying her interactions with clients from the less desirable addresses in Middletown.

"Well, it's a little dispiriting trying to help people with serious financial problems, which many of our clients have. People on the lower rungs of the social system seem to pay more for basic needs, whether it is for groceries or for loans."

"Sounds like you're turning into a bleeding-heart liberal," said another bleeding-heart liberal.

"That's possible. Let's face it: I've led a cosseted life and haven't rubbed shoulders much with disadvantaged folks. But it is infuriating and frustrating to see how badly they are taken in."

She went on to report instances where her clients served jail time for inattention or ignorance – where no harm to the fabric of society occurred.

"We almost had a "LWP" rubber stamp made to mark some of the files."

"LWP?"

"Yes, Living While Poor."

Grover smiled, but then suggested that was rather flippant.

"O.K. That's a bad joke," she said. "And maybe I am just reacting to an incident this afternoon when a woman charged up to my cubicle. She heard I was helping defend a boy falsely accused of menacing her daughter with a knife and was truly pissed. She threatened me and was still cursing me out when security dragged her from the office. I may be having second thoughts about my chosen profession."

"I'm sure that's just a response to a bad day."

Grover took her hand across the table.

"I've heard what a good job you are doing there. I have no doubt you will become a great litigator, teacher, judge or, if times get hard, someone's excellent wife."

Grover's inopportune comment, whose origin even he did not understand, immediately dampened the conversation. Worse, Portia needed to go back to Wylie's condominium directly after dinner. She had work to do before tomorrow.

Emma was certain she saw a rabbit munching on tall summer grass on the shoulder of the lane, just yards from her place between Wylie and Linda. She stiffened and her left paw left the ground. She posed as a pointing hunting dog, an involuntary ancestral aspiration coded into every canine DNA. Wylie had given up on requiring her to walk at his left side whenever he persuaded Linda to walk with them. Emma felt she could be a more effective guardian from a place between the two people she loved the most.

Wylie observed her new attitude and searched the side of the road. Rabbits indeed! It was time for Emma to have a good run, so he slipped the leash and stepped aside. She bounded forward. At the last moment, the rabbit took flight into a thicket of floribunda roses and disappeared. Emma stood motionless, listening. Then she made a joyful leap and pounced into the tall grass. A highly confused vole took its last look at the surrounding landscape before she playfully shook it to eternal sleep. Her catch now inert, she made a final survey of the meadow beside the road and trotted back to Wylie and Linda. Yes, yes, yes, it is a good day.

Even though it was just after eight in the morning, the heat of a mid-July day pressed on them. Linda was glad she followed Wylie's advice to put on shorts. The two of them, with creamy white legs protruding from dark shorts, marched along the narrow road half a mile from the condominiums. With no cars in sight, Wylie let Emma explore the exciting shoulders of the road, squatting occasionally to release a few drops of urine. She had no intention of depleting her reservoir unnecessarily. After all, she had no idea how long the walk would last.

There had been little conversation during their walk. While Portia was on her date with Grover, the older couple engaged in lovemaking which, for Wylie, continued to be a delightful revelation. Linda, as well, was pleased with Wylie's dogged stamina. Once his little pill took effect, he refused to leave the field of battle until ripples of contentment coursed through Linda's body. So, it seemed to Wylie, the afterglow of the previous evening's entertainment made idle chatter superfluous. He was unprepared when Linda furrowed her brow and turned to speak with him.

"I've been thinking that maybe I'll spend more time in my own apartment. I want to be with the grandchildren a bit more, and the hospital has been after me to help retrain the nurses they just hired from the Philippines. You know how difficult it is to find good hospital staff these days, and they are offering me flexible part-time hours and quite a lot of money."

"Well, if it's a matter of money…"

"Don't go there! Basically, it's an issue of self-worth. I just don't feel as though anything is happening in our relationship. It's all very comfortable and easy, and I love being with Portia but, at the end of the day, I just feel I need more space."

As a practiced negotiator, Wylie recognized Linda was advising him she needed more from their liaison. He correctly suspected his involvement with Anne Proctor was sub-text to Linda's announcement. He also believed that women usually needed to talk about their concerns before taking definitive action. He had some time.

He thought quickly about the tack to take in reaching what he hoped would be a reasonable compromise – whatever that might be. Now, caution was required.

"Well, my dear, I understand your feelings. You have always been such a wonderful caregiver, and important work at the hospital is probably quite tempting."

"Yes, yes, it is."

That was not the response Linda expected.

"Of course, it's hard to see how taking on more work and spending more time with the grands fits together. But I'm sure that is something you could work out."

Dammit, thought Linda, I should have phrased the whole thing better. When is he going to stop being a lawyer?

"Yes, I suppose there is that. I wasn't planning to rush into it, anyway. I just wanted you to know what was on my mind."

"You know I always appreciate that."

Wylie was pleased with himself. He had demonstrated his sensitivity and willingness to listen to his partner. He reached an arm around her shoulder and squeezed lightly – his love squeeze he called it. Linda shrugged and his arm fell away. Emma saw they were turning back toward home and bounded back to the place between them.

Bitsy had flown on commercial aircraft over the years, but this was the first time she found herself in the co-pilot's seat of a single engine plane – a certified antique at that. Jerome Hastings occupied the pilot's seat. He pointed to the array of gauges, knobs, toggle switches and displays crowding the cockpit, explaining their functions in basic terms. Bitsy absorbed some of it but put her trust in the man sitting next to her.

Jerome was an engineer and inventor. In the seventies, he created a weighing/filling machine that became standard equipment for the dairy processing industry. He gathered royalties from users for some time and astutely sold the remaining years of his patents for a substantial lump sum to a venture capital company a year or two before, as he anticipated, they became obsolete.

Financially secure, he tinkered with numerous ideas for mechanical improvements, from bicycle gears to fuel injection devices. Though his new inventions did not generate the level of income his early patents provided, the annual royalties and their management required a staff of seven. He now tinkered mainly with ideas for software programs.

Financially, he could do whatever he wanted. That included dedicated bachelorhood and the resurrection of antique mechanisms, preferable those that went fast. His motorcycle was a 1940 Indian Chief model with fat fender skirts and leather saddlebags that he had found covered with layers of dust and chicken manure in a barn outside of Springfield, Massachusetts. Restoring it occupied him for more than a year.

Of his many autos, his favorite was a 1937 Mercedes-Benz 540 K Cabriolet B, which its former owner prudently stored it in a warehouse as World War II began. It remained there for many years after the owner died until it was brought to auction in Scottsdale, Arizona. Even in its unrestored condition, it was a major find, and Jerome bid over a million dollars for it. Half again that much more brought it into showroom condition. Jerome loved driving it along winding roads in the farmlands still surrounding Middletown. He thought the auto felt at home in that bucolic setting.

At sixty, Jerome decided it was time to learn to fly light airplanes, an excellent excuse to expand his collection of antique vehicles. He tempered his affection for antiques by considering safety issues associated with old airplanes. If the Benz or the Indian broke down, he could simply call for help and walk away. Failure of a light plane at altitude was another matter. However, as he familiarized himself with all the mandated inspection requirements and began to experience flight itself, he was reassured.

He found a 1955 Cessna 170 B, fixed wing, single engine, painted sky blue and white for sale at the Middletown Aerodrome the year before. The craft was sound, but Jerome replaced the leather seats, engine, and wing tips anyway. He used it to commute, with friends, to a trout-fishing site in upstate New York and to visit friends and family as far away as Minneapolis. He was an excellent pilot.

"She's an oldie but a goodie," he explained to Bitsy. "She is well balanced and responsive with some extra pep now that she has a new engine. I've put over 200 hours on her since she was overhauled and she's like an old friend now. I look forward to her being part of our milkweed program!"

The idea was that, in early fall, they would harvest all the genetically engineered seeds with their pods and pack them in cartons. They would fill the back seats and cargo areas of the Cessna with seeds to be dispersed from the passenger side window at about seven thousand feet. Freddy C. calculated that was the optimum altitude for seed dispersion. He also concluded that would affect plant ecology over at least five states that were in the flight path of monarchs making their way to Mexican over-wintering grounds.

Not one to leave matters to chance, Jerome suggested a test run, and Bitsy was the first to volunteer. As the Cessna took flight, there were two cardboard cartons filled with perlite, substituting for seeds, on the back seat. Bitsy planned to experiment with dispersing this light material from the airplane once they were at seven thousand feet.

They both wore headphones and microphones. Bitsy had not expected so much noise from the plane's engine. Jerome winked at her and explained she need not shout into the microphone. He could hear her just fine. She relaxed, watching the fat clouds ahead and the receding towns and waterways below. The thrumming of the engine and the whistle of air across the side windows was not so bothersome. She and Jerome chatted about family matters until he noted that they had just passed seven thousand feet. She should try dispensing the perlite.

She slid the passenger window forward, creating a seven-inch opening on her right side. Bitsy fished a carton from the back, opened one of its flaps and scooped out a handful of perlite, which she raised to the opening. Gusts of wind blew the perlite back into the cabin. It filled with little white specks like a wintry scene in a snow globe. Both had perlite bits clinging to moist lips and eyelids. Bitsy began to panic, but Jerome was unflustered and maintained the Cessna on course.

"Looks like we need a plan B," he said.

While spitting out bits of perlite, Bitsy agreed.

Jerome understood aerodynamics and began to think about the shape of forms moving through air. He concluded that Bitsy diverted the airflow as she reached toward the window, making it push instead of pull, creating a perlite shower.

There was a length of dryer vent hose that Jerome used to divert exhaust gases during engine during wedged beside one of the back seats. He asked Bitsy to collect it and wedge one end into the side window opening while holding the other end over the box of perlite. To Bitsy's amazement, the perlite was quickly sucked into the atmosphere. She craned her neck to see the little white pieces disappearing behind the Cessna. Jerome was a genius! Her admiration of him expanded. She hugged his arm.

He laughed.

"O.K. I think we got that covered. The idea works. I'll improve on the design when we get back. Go Mariposas!"

Go, indeed, thought Bitsy, as she looked at her companion. She wondered why her face was so warm.

Anne Proctor had the reticence of the well-bred, and the continuing attention being paid to what were now called "super plants" bothered her. She understood the publicity surrounding the clearly superior plants in her patch of the experimental garden was good for the entire Master Gardener program and the University. However, she preferred to be left out of it, thank you. So far, the only one she had told of the seeds' provenance was Wylie. They agreed that the less said about where they were obtained the better. Wylie explained the potential liability of importing foreign seeds through customs. The risk was slight, but any involvement with federal bureaucracy had the potential for unpleasantness. Anne appreciated his advice and turned to Wylie when additional forebodings occurred.

Now they were standing together at the border of the Van Poppen experimental fields and she was speaking with him about the request by a reporter from USA Today for an interview.

"First of all," she said, "I don't know how she even got my name."

"That's easy. The paper has stringers who report on all sorts of interesting local events. It was hard to miss that picture of Bruno Gladstetter in the Courier-Times looking up at your corn plants. He's over six feet tall and he's looking up. And he wanted to give you credit so he mentioned you by name."

"She called them 'super plants' and suggested there were important 'implications.' I really don't want to talk with her, but then she might suspect I'm hiding something. Wylie, what if she asks me where I got the seeds?"

"Well, part of effective misdirection is to tell the absolute truth, but not all of it," Wylie advised. "Let's see…how about not mentioning at all where you found them but say they were in your luggage when it was sent through an airport X-Ray machine by TSA. Then you look pensive."

"So, you hope she will start thinking about irradiating seeds?"

"That's the idea."

"But what if she asks where the seeds came from?"

"Down south?"

"You really think that will work?"

"I do, as long as you are comfortable with answering that way. Modern journalism seems to be focused on extremes. Give her a potentially sensational angle and other facts become irrelevant and get pushed aside. 'Irradiated seeds produce bountiful crop.' Nice headline."

Anne did as Wylie suggested. The headline did not mention irradiated seeds, but the story did. It also included speculation about the "super plants" by two noted scientists, a biologist and botanist. Neither believed that "normal" seeds could be so productive.

The pinochle game was at Sy Wiser's home that week. The conversation included speculation about which teams would be in the series that fall, ribbing Billy Clarke about the huge Cadillac SUV he had purchased to travel among his expanding group of restaurants, and comments about all the women in Wylie's life.

Wylie lingered as Arnie and Billy walked to their cars.

"Sy, got a minute? I want to talk with you about a medical matter. You are my guru when it comes to that stuff."

Of course, he had a minute. Wylie returned to the dining room table and sat down across from his friend.

Wylie, never at a loss for words, hesitated.

"It's a water works question," he began feebly.

"Is it to do with getting up frequently at night? We all have that problem at our age."

"Yes, but lately nothing seems to want to come out. I have to think hard about pissing and then, finally there's sort of a burning sensation and the stuff comes out."

"Is there any discoloration of the urine? Is it orange or brown?'

"Not that I can tell."

"Well, it could be a lot of things. The prostate enlarges as we reach our sixties, no matter what we do. Have you had a prostate exam lately?"

"Not for a while."

Sy reached for the prescription pad that he always carried in a pocket, even at home.

"This is the name of my urologist. He's very good and his offices are in my building. It's probably nothing, but I think you should see him – soon."

Sy scribbled the name of Harrison Oliver. Wylie would see him – soon.

The two old friends exchanged goodbyes. Sy thought it unwise to tell Wylie that, at his age, he had a one in twelve chance of being diagnosed with prostate cancer. Also, he had not bothered to tell his friend about his own very slow growing prostate cancer he had been monitoring for the past two years.

The weekly staff meeting ended and Geier signaled Frank Edger and George Stirrup to remain in the meeting room. They were friends and associates from his days in the capitol. Frank was a lobbyist who provided valuable assistance in drafting legislation and funding his campaigns. Well suited to handling public relations for Bemis, his talents ran to finding silver linings in even the darkest news clouds. George Stirrup was a friend from Chevron and the brother of

Geier's third wife, long since divorced. The two men retained their friendship, and Stirrup proved to be a capable manager. Geier hired him to be his detail man, his manager of operations who saw to it that all manufacturing plants in the Bemis panoply ran well and profitably. As red-blooded American entrepreneurs, both men shared Geier's no holds barred approach to business.

"You both see Manny's memo about how the Home Warehouse chain was making noises about requiring second sourcing for Klobber?" asked Geier.

They both had. Frank Edger spoke.

"Well, they're surely gun shy on that subject. They got burned badly last year when the FDA cracked down on their private label fertilizer for containing too many heavy metals. Their supplier couldn't fix it, and Scotts was really pissed off at them for supplementing their products with an off-label competitor. They showed them no mercy when that supplier went belly up. Scotts hosed them pretty good on pricing for replacement product. And Home Warehouse had to eat their entire inventory, which was extra expensive because they had to dispose of toxic material. HW is not about to give on the second sourcing issue any time soon."

The tip of Geier's ever-present cigarette glowed as he inhaled and focused his steely eyes on the two men.

"O.K. In this situation we would normally identify another supplier acceptable to HW and license them technology and industrial property rights for an upfront fee and continuing royalty, right?

Both agreed. Stirrup said, "Sure that's the traditional way it's handled. The customer is willing to pay a little more for assurance there will be a second supplier if there's a disaster or whatever."

Geier exhaled a malformed smoke ring.

"Now suppose," he said, "that the three of us created our own company to act as second supplier. I know people who would be willing to act as proxy -- retired businessmen who would enjoy an extra stipend. We would set up a warehouse for a supply center and George could deliver bags of privately labeled Klobber there. Legitimate operators would handle warehousing, shipping and accounting, and Bemis would be paid the same as if a third-party vendor was involved. We would enjoy the spread between the cost of private labeled Klobber and WH's purchase price. We'd make a buck or two on every bag, give or take, depending on taxes. That would add up."

As successful businessmen, George and Frank were familiar with dodgy practices in their industry and had participated in them over the years. The bold move Geier suggested went beyond the norm, but certainly seemed plausible. They calculated the risks involved and believed they were containable. With proper management and the placement of reliable workers, the creation of a sham operation to line their pockets could work very well. WH's demand seemed designed for their exploitation.

The three discussed the details of making Geier's proposal work. Plans and people were evaluated. As highly placed executives at Bemis, there seemed little risk the program could be discovered or challenged. In any case, it was a straightforward business opportunity. They were simply taking on the role of second source suppliers to satisfy the needs of a valued customer. Bemis would be receiving approximately the same reward as if it involved third persons. That the arrangement would divert potential licensing profits due to their pockets was ignored. Why worry over petty issues. They agreed to move forward.

Geier received annual remuneration, combining salary, performance bonus, stock options and guaranteed retirement benefits, of more than thirteen million dollars. Edger and Stirrup, as reported in Bemis' annual shareholders report, received almost three million dollars per year each.

An economist might wonder what motivation there might be to accumulate even more through such questionable means. It was simple. Greed was at its base, but the great American competitive spirit, to go higher, faster, score more, have more than anyone else was the driving force. In their world, the winning number on the scoreboard of life was denominated in dollars. The more you had, the better you were. You always needed more. And no one seemed to give a shit how the game was played.

The office building for the Middletown Aerodrome was a rather dingy Quonset hut, a World War II surplus building that reminded the civilian pilots who congregated there of earlier times, with dashing airmen, aerial adventures and the romance of the skies. At least that was the argument when suggestions were made to raise funds for a modern office.

The young office manager responsible for confirming pilots' logs, billing, assigning parking locations and light maintenance looked up from the paperback novel he was reading to welcome the peculiarly dressed man who pushed open the door. He wore cowboy boots, faded jeans and a plaid short-sleeved shirt secured with a tiger-eye stone bolo tie. He wiped a bandana handkerchief across his forehead, collecting droplets of sweat formed as he strode across the tarmac. He walked to the low partition that separated him from the young man.

Wordlessly, he pulled a leather wallet from the jeans and displayed his gold and blue badge and identity card. He was a Federal Air Marshal with the Transportation Security Administration. The TSA letters were displayed in bold relief on the badge. He was there, he said, to review flight logs from the previous month. It was a security matter.

The young man knew the request was out of the ordinary. Usually, routine reports from the flight logs gathered dust awaiting FAA review. He retrieved logbooks and placed them on the counter. The Marshall carried them over to a desk and began turning pages, pausing from time to time to lick his thumb and make notes in a folder he carried with him. Soon he returned the books to the counter.

"Now, this Jerry Hastings, the one with the old Cessna. You expect him in any time soon?"

Chapter 6

August

Middletown Courier-Times

Mastering your Garden

By Elizabeth Pendleton Crangle

Let's start this column with a quiz: why are the "dog days of summer" associated with the month of August? The answer appears in the last paragraph.

Hundred-degree days and Japanese beetles don't go well together, but, as mentioned in last month's column, you should go after the bugs and drop them in soapy water. If that's unappetizing, I give you permission to use an appropriate insecticide on them – but be careful. In this heat plants may succumb more readily to insecti-side effects.

If you are growing fruit, keep up with your spray programs. Wet as it's been in July, black rot is a serious problem for grapes. There are several organic fungicides available to thwart the rot but be sure to follow the labels. Use a little extra nitrogen when fertilizing those new strawberry runners this month. This will help the buds set and produce an abundant crop next summer.

Now is the time to order bulbs and peony roots for fall planting. But, remember how much work it was to plant the 250 daffodils you ordered last year? Get your significant other to help with an auger attached to a power drill!

If your mums set flower buds early this month you might want to pinch them off to encourage a fuller flower display in September. This is also the time to divide and replant your daylilies. Look at the pictures you took while they were in bloom to see how you might change the color mixes for a different look next summer. Irises may also be divided later this month. If you cut them with a sharp knife to separate the rhizomes, set them aside for a few days before replanting to give the cuts a chance to scab over.

Now is the time to inspect your lawn to see whether it needs reseeding or renovation. Late August through early fall is the time for these tasks. By spreading cool grass seeds now, you give them two seasons to grow strong before next summer's heat wave. While looking at the lawn, check for white grub damage. Early August, when the grubs are closest to the surface, is the best time to control them. As always, use a dedicated grub killer and follow the label carefully. There are benign insects in your grass that should not be slaughtered.

Just before Labor Day is a good time to plant or transplant needle type evergreens. They will benefit from cooler temperatures and fall rains before sleeping during the winter. And, of course, now is the time to harvest the produce in your vegetable garden and plant cool weather crops. Everyone will have too many tomatoes, but dedicated gardeners will freeze or can them. One friend tosses whole tomatoes in the blender, lets the slurry stand, pours off the yellow liquid on top and pours the remainder into ice cube trays for freezing. He claims they make great soup stock and Bloody Mary ice cubes!

Finally, late August is the right time to divide your hellebores (Lenten roses) so you will have those wonderful early flowers that bloom even under the snow in January. Wear gloves and be careful. Every part of the plant is poisonous. There is research that indicates hellebores contain wild yeasts that break down sugars stored in the plant to generate heat, so they can pop up through snow. Who knew?

The answer to the "dog days" question is that it refers to the night skies of late July and August when Sirius, the Dog Star, can be seen just before sunrise. And I always thought it was the weather.

Blissful gardening - Bitsy

Winston

All the windows in the green house were open wide, and fans at each end of the building moved humid air above the empty tables. It was a few minutes before seven in the evening, when the milkweed project group would meet. Winston Wu bustled into the large room and headed for the corner designated as his office. The battered conference table and metal chairs were set up, and a cooler of refrigerated water purred in a corner near his desk. He placed his faded denim book bag on the desk and removed some papers, collecting thoughts and data for the evening's meeting. Matters were rapidly coming to what he hoped would be a successful conclusion.

Winston was excited about the culmination of almost three-year's planning and clandestine work. He originated the project because of his deeply felt belief that human intervention was necessary to thwart the environmental damage caused by human intervention. Nature alone, in his view, would not be able to respond to or correct the accelerating risks of environmental disaster.

As a scientist, he was incredulous that there were groups who doubted that humankind was directly responsible for the atmospheric pollution that was raising the earth's temperature. He was particularly incensed with zealots who used divine inspiration and complete ignorance of scientific matters to proclaim that global warming was a hoax. Peculiarly, those same people felt threatened by genetically engineered plants.

Winston's parents emigrated from Taiwan in the early seventies, when Winston was an infant. They originally settled in New Jersey, where his father, a physicist, worked on the development of laser technology for Bell Labs. His mother was trained as a medical doctor, but her credentials were not immediately accepted in the United States. She cared for Winston and his two sisters when the children were young. Winston developed an early fascination with growing things and joined a local 4H program where he grew sunflowers and learned about hybridization. He graduated cum laude from Rutgers and moved to Middletown for graduate studies at the University.

It was there he met Hazel Chen, who he married when he was offered an assistant professorship at the University and began a family, a son formally named David, but nicknamed "urchin." When David was a few months past his second birthday, and his mother was pushing him in his stroller by a nearby park, a car driven by a septuagenarian suffering a stroke jumped the curb, neatly separated Hazel from David, and pinned her to a tree. She died instantly.

For the past three years Winston submerged his grief and raised his son as a single father. It was not easy, but he delighted in being with his son as often as possible. He settled into an ordered and predictable routine, relying on a cadre of housekeepers and babysitters to help with David's care. He had no thoughts about remarrying. The memory of his wife was too poignant.

Myron and Freddy C. arrived together, arguing about a recent football game. As they greeted Winston, a motorcycle roared to a stop outside. The door to the room banged open, revealing Jerome and Bitsy, both pulling off their helmets. Jerome was dressed in denim, with worn leather chaps, and Bitsy sported a black leather jacket with sequins showing an eagle in flight.

There was little to report about developments in the plants themselves. They were thriving in remote spots in the environmental plots of Van Poppen farm. Now, the second week of August, some were beginning to split their pods and disgorge silky seeds. The team harvested them and stored them in hemp bags in one of the barns. They believed all available seeds would be collected by mid-September and could be released soon after.

Jerome reported on their first abortive attempt to dispense the perlite seed substitute. He explained that they had taken two subsequent flights to test Jerome's invention, a contraption of wires, canvas and PVC pipes that worked wonderfully on the second try.

They agreed on a tentative date in late September to release the seeds, and the meeting adjourned amid mutual words of congratulation. Bitsy climbed onto the back seat as Jerome revved the Indian, and they disappeared down the country road leading from Van Poppen farm, their bodies silhouetted against the orange ball of the setting sun.

As Wylie entered the helpline office, Sue Flack, a member of his class, was writing monthly reminders on the white board behind the counter. "Drought and heat stress, grubs, stink bugs, rot=blight, cabbage worms" appeared in bright red printing. Wylie thought of her as "sunny Sue," as she always had a smile and friendly word for him whenever they met on Master Gardener business. This morning was no exception. She favored Wylie with a bright smile and asked how his weekend had been.

There had been some perturbing moments. Linda and Portia both were in grumblesome moods -- Portia because of an altercation with Grover about some silly nonsense Wylie could not remember, and Linda still chewing the bone of contention between them about her unmet expectations. On Saturday, Wylie invited Linda to dinner at The Olde Congerie, which mollified her somewhat. They consumed a bottle of wine with dinner, which calmed her further, but her unspoken and, perhaps, poorly understood resentment lingered. That night she claimed the wine gave her a headache.

Even the round of golf he played with Arnie Brackett and two others on Sunday morning was unsatisfying. Temperatures hovered near one hundred degrees that afternoon, and they quit the game after the thirteenth hole.

"Just fine. How about you?" Wylie responded.

Sue also was just fine. Before she could expand on the degree of fineness, the third volunteer for the morning arrived. Six-foot-tall Tawny Belcher, former professional tennis star, entered the office under full steam. Wearing Bermuda shorts, she was in violation of Bitsy Crangle's dress code, but the expected heat of the day allowed forgiveness. With a friendly wave, she placed her daypack on the table and extracted a one-liter water bottle with a pop off top. They were ready for visitors and telephone calls.

The telephone calls were mostly about the effects of the current heat wave. Callers were assured that, yes, their grass would become green again with fall rains and cooler temperatures. Various fungi were opportunistic and attacked heat stressed plants and shrubs. We just have to wait and see. A man brought in a freshly dug patch of sod that showed clear signs of grub damage. Yes, this was the best time to apply grub insecticide, but be very careful to follow the directions on the package. The heat, you know.

At midmorning, Wylie greeted a well-dressed woman who entered the office carrying a Prada shopping bag. She extracted two damaged tomatoes from the bag. He examined them with professional care. They were bereft of large chunks of pulp and held teeth marks, smaller than a person's, larger than a fox or skunk. She wanted to know what the Master Gardeners could suggest to protect her tomatoes. Wylie examined them more carefully.

"Clearly, some animal is attacking your tomatoes, which appear to be Ramapos."

"Oh, really? I thought they were tomatoes."

"No," Wylie added, "Ramapos are locally hybridized tomatoes."

"I see – well, then, probably it's Roland."

"Roland?"

"Who is biting the tomatoes. He is my chocolate lab."

Very interested in where this was going, Wylie asked, "And Roland likes tomatoes?"

"Oh, yes, he does. Very much. Ever since he was a puppy."

"It is unusual for a dog to like tomatoes."

"Not for Roland. He sometimes eats so much that he gets a tummy ache."

"Even more rare, I think."

"Well, he's a rescue dog. They found him in an alley behind a pizza parlor, or, anyway, that's what they said at the animal shelter. I think it has something to do with that pizza parlor. It is not in a very nice section of town."

"Let me understand," Wylie said. "Are you concerned about saving the tomatoes or are you worried that Roland, is it, will eat them and get sick?"

"Yes."

"Well, you can't apply noxious spray to your tomatoes. How about fencing them in?"

"He is an extremely athletic dog. He either knocks the fence down or jumps over it. He can clear six feet."

"How about using an invisible fence or even an electric fence to keep your tomatoes safe and avoid future stomach upsets for Roland?"

"That would be so intimidating. I was hoping you could recommend something not so extreme. He is a very sensitive dog – and talented too."

Wylie was sure that was so, but pointed out, "Look, what this seems to be getting down to is either Roland or the tomatoes."

"You are not being very helpful."

"I'm sorry. But, outside of fencing of some kind, or a cage, I am almost out of ideas. But, you know, uh, farmers sometimes plant a decoy crop to draw animals away from their primary crop. Does Roland like any other vegetables?"

"No. It is just tomatoes."

"Maybe a different variety of tomato? One he might not be fond of?"

"It's pretty much any kind of tomato, even the little bitty ones. He tried cucumbers once but didn't like them."

"So, definitely a tomato hound."

"I guess so… but he is quite the little entertainer."

Hoping this would open a different line of inquiry, Wylie asked, "Really?"

"Oh, yes. He wears a Hawaiian shirt and sings while I play the ukulele. He does the hula a little too. I made this little grass skirt for him. It's adorable."

"That's hard to believe."

"Believe it. You can see him any time you want. He's on YouTube. Thousands of hits!"

Wylie glanced at the other two Master Gardeners in the office who registered bewilderment and wonder. The woman glared at him, obviously not satisfied.

Weakly he suggested, "Perhaps a muzzle…"

She scooped up the oozing tomatoes and turned on her heel, out the door.

There was silence in the room. Wylie did not know about the others, but he had the vision of a chocolate lab with a tomato-rouged mouth wiggling his rump and warbling to the strings of a ukulele. Moments like this made the Master Gardener helpline so unpredictably rewarding.

At about eleven o'clock, a tall man in bib overalls carried in a branch of red maple and a large piece of its trunk. The gray bark of the trunk had the telltale drill holes of a yellow-bellied sapsucker and a quantity of sap seeped from those holes. Around them and on some parts of the branch a fuzzy cream-colored substance appeared.

"Damnedest thing I ever saw," said the newcomer, pointing to the fuzzy material that, on closer inspection, seemed to have little black bits writhing in it.

The Master Gardeners agreed that none had seen this before. Wylie decided to sniff the white blobs and discovered the material smelled like vinegar or, was it…beer?

"Yes," said the man who delivered the mysterious substance, "it smells funny like that and the yellow jackets go crazy when they drink the stuff."

Tawny carefully positioned some of the stuff under their microscope and adjusted the lens until it came into sharp focus. She saw the angry bubbling of what could have been a witch's cauldron – nasty opaque clouds tossing about bits of debris and reaching directly for her eyes.

"Holy shit," she said as she jerked away from the microscope, sending the offending material to the floor.

With her mild curse, Tawny rose in stature. She seemed stiff and somewhat distant before, but a healthy "Holy shit" confirmed her status as an everywoman. Wylie and Sue warmed to her.

Wylie retrieved the fallen material and returned it to the microscope. He saw what Tawny saw and remained mystified. When that happened, the Master Gardeners rose to the challenge. They carefully documented the event, wrote down the donor's personal information and promised to let him know when they were able to resolve the issue. Wylie looked at the reference books on hand and Tawny began searching the internet for clues about this strange material. Within the hour, they had their answer.

Wild yeast combined with maple sap during the current heat wave provided ideal conditions for powerful fermentation. Wylie was right. The stuff did smell like beer and clearly contained alcohol. That accounted for the tipsy yellow jackets. The little bits discovered in the maple beer were just fragments of bark and, on close inspection, insect parts. Tiny insects were overwhelmed by the expanding stuff and succumbed. They probably died happy, thought Wylie.

The results of their research were sent to the man who brought in the mystery substance and, as it was now lunchtime, the office was closed for the day. Wylie exchanged farewells with the two women and walked to his car in the parking lot. To his surprise, Anne Proctor was there, waiting for him. She wore a very worried expression.

"I saw from the schedule you would be here this morning. I really need your advice."

Wylie suggested they walk across the road to sit on a bench under shade trees on the town square. As Anne seated herself, Wylie noticed she was clutching an envelope that was slightly moist from being clenched in her hand. He saw the familiar logo of BIG AG in the corner, a large letter "B" surrounded by stylized leaves and vines.

"I knew no good would come of that damn interview with USA Today," muttered Anne.

"Just settle down and let me know what's going on here."

"You saw the article, right? The front page of the 'C' section with a picture of the corn plants and an inset picture of me that was less than flattering?"

"Of course."

"Apparently the article came to the attention of someone at Bemis, and they sent Dan Frimmel and me a nasty letter. Dan thinks they sent one to the University administrator too. They might sue me, for heavens sakes!"

Wylie reached for the letter and reviewed it carefully. He had seen the same letter or a variation of it many times. It contained all the appropriate buzz words: infringement, highly valued industrial property rights, Patent nos. attached as exhibits a, b, c, and d, and the demand that the infringer cease and desist.

Like an old warhorse responding to a trumpet call, Wylie became animated, unable to resist the possibility of engaging in legal action. It was like accepting a new case - an escape from the relaxed torpor of his retirement.

"Anne, it's a 'C and D' letter – for cease and desist. Patent and trademark lawyers send them out and hope they can scare whoever it is they think might be infringing their client's property rights. See, it's signed by some junior lawyer in Bemis' general counsel's office. This is a standard warning shot across the bow. Either that or it represents a misunderstanding or some overzealous junior lawyer pushing too hard. Also, their complaint seems to be based solely on a newspaper article. I don't see how they could have specific information about the plants themselves."

Wylie's words calmed Anne somewhat. As a conservative and law-abiding person, however, the threat of a legal proceeding was a very serious matter. She shifted in her seat to face Wylie directly.

"You and I know that there is something very unusual about those plants," she said." First, they germinated even though they had been sitting in the pocket of a suitcase for years. Now they are growing like crazy and yielding more produce than any three other plants. And they keep the soil moist and weed free. Undesirable insects give them a wide berth. On top of all that, they have received national publicity. I'm worried that someone will find out that I brought them into the country illegally. Now the second biggest chemical company in the country is threatening to sue me or something. This is not good."

Wylie understood her concern. He began to view her not only as a good friend, but as a client in need of his help. He had not involved himself in an actual case in years. Strangely exhilarated, he looked forward to beginning a process he knew well.

"Anne, my dear, if you will permit me, I'll review this with Dan Frimmel and see if the University plans to invest any legal effort in the matter. I'll take care of your involvement, if any. As I said, it is either a mistake or overreaching by Bemis. This will never amount to anything."

She calmed. Anne moved closer and gave him a grateful hug and kissed his cheek. Wylie took the letter from her and arranged to meet for lunch the next day. He planned to work in his own little condominium garden that afternoon. Rudbeckia needed thinning and his obedient plants demanded some weeding. In fact, there was much weeding to do.

The C and D letters to Anne and the officials at the University were neither a mistake nor an instance of overreaching. Etta Sporelli was asked to have her mole provide additional samples of the super plants at Van Poppen farm, and Randi Fochik assigned a special team to examine them in detail. These efforts were prompted by Dick Geier's observation that "these hunching plants could be a real pain in the ass if it gets into people's heads they should use them instead of our stuff."

However, the intensive study underway during the last two weeks of July and the first week of August added little new knowledge. They were, indeed, super plants almost identical to their North American peers with only slight and undecipherable variations in their genetic structure. Genetic engineering had not altered their makeup, and the subtle variations observed were within normal ranges. Somehow, though, the combination of all these minor differences resulted in their robust characteristics and the creation of mild toxins just powerful enough to thwart the growth of nearby invasives.

Newly discovered was the uncanny ability of the plants to transfer their noble characteristics to their more ordinary neighbors. They seemed to hybridize simply through proximity. And, of course, there was the completely mysterious glint of gold, visible both to the naked eye and electron microscope.

As their investigations progressed, it became clear that if seeds produced by the super plants carried the same characteristics as their parents, they could easily and quickly replace the use of Klobber and Bemis' genetically engineered seeds. That, according to Manfred Balducci, would be the inevitable kiss of death to twenty-five percent of the most profitable items in their entire product line.

"We are talking billions here," he announced.

Randi Fochik was gravely concerned the seeds would run true, identical to their parents. Dick Geier clearly understood.

"I don't know where these suckers came from, but we are going to stop them. There is no question in my mind that someone screwed with their genetic structure and probably stole things from us."

With his bright red face and apoplectic expression, the twin streams of smoke from his nose made him look like a kettle at full boil.

"That's our story and we will goddamn well stick with it. Simon, you need to get after this and grind those suckers into the dust. The dust! Right? Got it?"

Simon Targle got it. The General Counsel soon met with his senior patent team. Their strategy was to initiate a low-key attack, not to tip their hand as to the degree of seriousness they attached to the matter. They reviewed the information Etta Sporelli provided about Anne Proctor and the University officials involved and drafted the letter that Anne received.

Meanwhile, Targle met with the most prominent patent law firm New Anglia's major city, to secure their services should the need arise to move the case to Federal District Court. Considering the perceived weakness of the potential defendants, he did not believe that would be necessary. Nevertheless, he tasked Randi Fochik with contacting their most reliable paid outside scientific consultants to review their internal findings and prepare learned papers concluding that the super plants must have been created through genetic engineering which, in turn, violated numerous patents held by BIG AG. As sometimes happened within the scientific community, those who disagreed with such findings would be paid a handsome stipend to say nothing.

The three founding members of Magachem Limited S.A., the sole American subsidiary of a Bermuda company with a parent in the Cayman Islands, gathered in Dick Geier's office.

"Okay," said George Stirrup, "the papers that assign certain non-exclusive rights to the patented aspects of the chemical composition sold and distributed under the Klobber trade name have been transferred to 'MaLimSA." And, Malimsa is about to sign a contract with Home Warehouse as a second source supplier of the glyphosate-based herbicide they are calling Stomp®. That contract assures a minimum annual production rate of about two million pounds at a markup from the Klobber price."

The group quieted as Dick's executive assistant came into the room to answer his demand that she empty his overflowing ashtray. Stirrup continued, after she left, to detail the various other arrangements that were either in process or nearing completion.

"Labor Day – that's when she should be humming like a well-oiled machine."

Frank Edger added that warehousing and delivery were under control, and that Malimsa had rented an abandoned toy warehouse in the southern part of the state.

"It is too early to talk about hard numbers because we're still working on shipping costs to all of Home Warehouse's distribution points. But it looks very promising. We should be adding more than enough for after dinner drinks to our offshore accounts."

Even Dick Geier thought the line about after dinner drinks was worth a smile.

Uncharacteristically, Geier said, "Good job, guys. Good job."

Mary Smith sat waiting in the antechamber of Congresswoman Pewtree's district office in Middletown. She hoped for a brief meeting to introduce herself to the legislator while she was in her home district just before the Labor Day holiday. The receptionist, an earnest young college student, informed her that, sadly, the congresswoman was delayed and would not arrive until the following day. Would she like to meet with her chief assistant, Grover Merson? Not to waste the visit, she said she would be pleased to visit with Grover.

Hearing that a Mary Smith was waiting to meet him, Grover left his small office expecting to find a girl next door type with a request for some congressional favor. Instead, a petite Asian woman in a well-tailored navy-blue business suit rose to meet him. She wore a pale gray silk scarf fastened with a ruby studded clip. The scarf partially concealed a small port wine birthmark shaped like a new moon that descended below her left ear. From the right angle, it looked like an ebony earring. She was, by any standard, a beauty. Grover was not renowned for having a poker face, and his surprised look upon seeing an Asian beauty caused Mary to smile. The incongruity between name and physical appearance caused that to happen a lot.

"I'm Mary Smith, the new Assistant U.S. attorney for this district. I left word that I just wanted to drop by and introduce myself – especially since we are working in the same town."

She shook Grover's hand firmly, and he motioned her into the small conference room beside Representative Pewtree's office. In that moment, he recalled the newspaper article about the appointment of a new assistant Federal prosecutor. Without remembering the exact details, he recalled she had an impressive resume and an interesting background. He offered her one of the two easy chairs located near the room's large window.

"I'm very sorry the congresswoman isn't here to meet with you. There were some last-minute details involving legislation seeking to defund our national parks that delayed her. She asked me to meet with you in her stead."

"That's just fine," said Mary. "This is simply a courtesy call. Although we work for different branches of government, we all get our paycheck from the American taxpayer. And, there is certainly no harm in sharing information that could be of mutual interest."

"I agree. There is no question that the prosecutor has been very active in the southern part of the state. Three convictions for influence peddling and fraud by state legislators in the past year alone is quite a record. Is that going to be the emphasis of your office in Middletown?"

"I really can't say, but I can tell you that there's nothing like that on my plate right now. Financial institutions and shady business deals seem to be of interest. Of course, I can't identify anyone."

Their cautious banter continued for another twenty minutes and ended with Mary's departure. Each had taken inventory of the other and decided this was a person worthy of respect, even friendship. They added the other's telephone numbers to their ever-present smart phones.

Grover was correct in recalling that Mary Smith had an interesting background. As an infant, she was found abandoned in southern Thailand and sent to an orphanage near Bangkok. At that time, many boat people from Vietnam sought refuge in Thailand, and, in the confusion of the exodus, the population of Thai orphanages swelled. The government relaxed many regulations regarding adoption, especially since the origin of many orphans could not be determined, and childless couples, many from the United States, offered homes to the abandoned children.

Joseph and Barbara Smith were immediately attracted to the seven-month-old baby girl with button eyes, abundant black hair and a gurgling smile. Unlike some of the other infants, she was healthy and responsive. As Barbara leaned over her crib, the little one reached up with a tiny hand and touched Barbara's chin. The touch was an unmistakable sign. Within ten days, they completed the adoption, and the new family was airborne to the Smiths' home in western Pennsylvania, near Pittsburgh, where Joseph worked as an engineer for Alcoa.

As sometimes happens, the adoption of an infant triggers changes in emotional, hormonal and psychological dynamics. Eleven months after the arrival of Mary Smith, Barbara produced twins, a boy and a girl. Joseph joked they had prayed a little too hard for a family and had gone from two to five in a year. The three siblings were raised in a loving family atmosphere with strong middle-class values, including belief in the importance of a good education.

Mary grew up tiny and dynamic. She excelled in studies and sports. As a junior in high school, she won the state championship in acrobatics. In her senior year, she completed four advance placement courses and was the valedictorian of her high school class.

She chose Georgetown of the many college offers she received and, three years later, qualified for admission to Yale Law School. On graduation, she clerked for an appellate justice of the sixth circuit in Cincinnati, Ohio, and was recommended for a position as an assistant United States attorney. She elected to serve in New Anglia, not far from the new home her parents bought for their retirement.

Mary had numerous romantic liaisons but was too busy for a permanent relationship. She had one eye on a political career, which was an undisclosed reason for seeking out Pert Pewtree. Grover seemed nice, though. She needed to expand her social circle in Middletown.

She returned to her office just in time for an impromptu staff meeting, a recurring event under the administration of Francis P. Jones, prosecuting attorney. The other attorneys settled in chairs or stood along the walls of his office as he outlined various concerns and new matters of interest. Before adjourning the meeting, he brought up a final matter.

"I recently met with the Dean of Admissions at the University, who, as you know, is my brother. He and the university counsel are concerned about litigation threatened by Bemis International over some super plants. They take such things very seriously because of their close research association with that company. During their internal investigation, they interviewed university employees and some Master Gardener volunteers."

There was a low buzz in the room, signifying a lack of knowledge about Master Gardeners. The prosecuting attorney briefly explained their role and continued.

"It seems Bemis may have used improper means to gain proprietary information. Their actions might be construed as criminal behavior. We know the AG is especially sensitive to corporate shenanigans after Enron, WorldCom, payday lenders, and the financial institutions. I've been told to keep an eye on this."

He looked at the group of attorneys gathered in his room.

"Mary, would you mind being the point person on this? Make a few inquiries?"

"I would be honored," she said.

Winston Wu watched his young son consume chicken fingers, curly fries, and a strawberry milkshake at his favorite diner in Middletown. He enjoyed watching David devour his politically incorrect meal and leaned across the table to wipe off a milkshake moustache when he noticed Myron a few booths away in animated conversation with a blonde middle-aged woman. Winston thought it odd, since he had always seen Myron in public with his wife. What really interested him was that Myron pushed a bag of corn ears and beans across the tabletop to the woman, followed by a sheaf of papers resembling a computer printout. It occurred to him that he had seen Myron walking in the experimental patch carrying a similar bag that afternoon.

Winston was not a stickler for rules, but there was a policy at Van Poppen farm that volunteers were strictly prohibited from taking any produce for their own use unless offered by Dan Frimmel or Bruno Gladstetter. As an experimental program, careful records were maintained regarding all crops and uncontrolled removal by volunteers would play havoc with data and even affect programs under grant.

Of course, the leaders of the farm were very generous to volunteers at harvest time since none of their produce was sold. The food was offered to homeless shelters and soup kitchens around the state. As a scientist, Winston understood and approved of the "no picking" policy. He was bothered that Myron, the staunch supporter of his own milkweed project, seemed to be violating this policy by giving produce to an outsider.

Myron's activity nagged at Winston for a few days. His first impulse was simply to confront his friend and ask about what he had seen. However, he was worried Myron might think he was spying on him or be upset that he even brought up such a petty matter. Winston finally decided to mention his concern to Dan Frimmel.

On Saturday morning, as Myron arrived to put in a few volunteer hours selecting tomatoes for the annual great tomato-tasting event, Dan Frimmel engaged him in a little banter about working in the hot August sun. After Myron collected gloves and a sun hat from his locker, they wandered along the farm road together, and Dan changed the tenor of the conversation.

"Say, Myron, I just wanted to be sure that you recalled that stuff in your training about how we don't remove produce from the farm without authorization."

"Sure, yeah, I know that."

"Okay, that's good. See, someone thought they had seen you leave here last week with some of our corn and maybe other stuff. It's no big deal. I just wanted to be sure you remembered the policy."

Each participant to the conversation experienced it quite differently. Dan believed he was reinforcing a standing rule one of his volunteers might have inadvertently ignored. Myron, on the other hand, was in delicate emotional shape and believed the hand of doom was descending to smite him. The worm of guilt had been burrowing through his feelings for many weeks. As Etta demanded more information, more plant samples, more clandestine meetings, he became disgusted by his serial acts of betrayal. Moreover, his dislike of Etta Sporelli intensified with each meeting.

He had been physically sick before he saw her in the diner a week or so ago and felt he would not be able to stand seeing her again. When Dan brought up the subject of his liberating produce from the experimental farm, it was as though someone turned the petcock on a steam boiler. Myron was unable to control the words that poured forth.

"I'm sorry. I'm so sorry," he began.

In the next few minutes, as the two men stood on the dusty road beside a field of soybeans, Myron choked back little sobs and poured out his confession to the flabbergasted Dan. Myron spoke only of his role as a resource for BIG AG. He saw no reason to mention the milkweed project, of which he was quite proud.

As a matter of course, the details of Myron's story worked their way to the Provost's office and to the University's chief counsel. She contacted the Dean of Admissions as a conduit to the office of the prosecuting attorney who passed on the information to tenacious Mary Smith.

Doctor Harrison Oliver removed the lubricated glove from his hand and told Wylie to clean himself up with a tissue. Wylie was relieved that his prostate exam was over and waited nervously for further information.

Pleasantly, the doctor said, "Well, Mr. Cypher, it's not exactly normal. Human tissue is soft, and I felt hard spots on your prostate gland."

The tall black doctor motioned Wylie to the chair by the examining table. Wylie did not fully understand the meaning of the doctor's statement. Or, perhaps, he did not wish to.

"Not normal. I see. Might that account for the problems I've been having lately?"

"It could. However, we must consider those symptoms and the results of my exam a warning of something other than problems associated with an enlarged prostate."

Wylie remained silent for a moment.

"I get it. What comes next?"

"There are two ways to go," said Oliver. "Both require taking tissue samples, biopsies, of parts of the prostate. And they both are used to diagnose prostate cancer and grade its severity."

Having mentioned the "C" word, the doctor paused to gauge his patient's response. He was calm, listening.

"There is an office-based procedure done under local anesthesia that takes about fifteen minutes. I will take samples from the mass I detected, as well as surrounding areas. I could set up that test here for later this afternoon."

"And the other?" Wylie asked.

"You would need to go to New York City for the closest clinic that uses very sophisticated imaging and computer-guided biopsy technology. The technique is more precise than what I can perform in my office and is very promising. The literature says it can detect cancer sooner than the standard approach."

Like many his age, Wylie was not enthralled with the latest technology.

"I'd like to get it over with and have the test here this afternoon," he said. "How long before I know the results?"

"The biopsied tissue is viewed under high magnification by a pathologist to see whether it differs from normal prostate tissue. The review takes a few days. I will certainly let you know as soon as possible."

"Thank you, Doctor Oliver. I'll be back this afternoon."

The procedure was uneventful, and Wylie did his best to appear untroubled at dinner that evening. It was a special occasion. Portia had invited Grover for the first time to join them for dinner, and Linda and Portia prepared a meal featuring Turducken breasts, a delicacy for the family. Grover arrived with a berry pie and ice cream for dessert. The meal was a great success.

Wylie was happy to talk politics with someone with similar views. He quickly warmed to Grover, which pleased Portia. The young couple went for a drive as Linda and Wylie cleaned up in the kitchen. Linda seemed tired and asked Wylie when he was coming to bed. He thought he would read for a while, but the book lay open on his lap as he looked blankly out the dark window. With clear knowledge that something was amiss, Emma trotted from her bed in the kitchen, sat and placed her chin on Wylie's knee. She searched his face with warm brown eyes, and he patted her head. She moved only when he was ready to climb the stairs.

Chapter 7

SEPTEMBER

Middletown Courier-Times

Mastering your Garden

By Elizabeth Pendleton Crangle

Odd as it may seem after the hot days of August, September is the time to think about winter. Segregate any plants you plan to bring indoors and examine them carefully. Any pests that come in on them can infect all your other houseplants. You can also pot up bright summer plants to add color to your home. Use 6-10-inch pots to collect coleus, begonias or impatiens and let them rest outside for a couple of weeks before placing them in a sunny indoor spot. Bring the plants in before night temperatures drop below 55 F.

Now is the time to plant ornamental cabbages and kale, as well as chrysanthemums and early blooming perennials such as peony roots. I like to plant the ornamental kale in pots near the front door. They are amazingly hardy and can withstand temperatures well below freezing. Seeing their bright colors under a frost brightens many a November day for me.

If you have been "summering over" amaryllis, remember they need to rest in a cool dark spot for two months before beginning a new growth cycle. Bring them in by the end of this month to ensure (close to) Christmas bloom.

If you are old fashioned enough to can fruits, make jam or preserves, this is the time to check your supplies. I am assured that some hardware stores still carry canning supplies! Anyway, there are wonderful harvests of fruits this month – from Anjou pears to baby Watermelons (couldn't find a fruit that begins with "Z"). Don't forget you can freeze peach and apple slices now to use in pies later, and those not so perfect apples make great applesauce. Try adding a few pears to your applesauce!

It is especially important this month to clean up debris containing fungus spores. To avoid black spot next year, prune infected areas of roses and rake up debris and dropped leaves. Many perennials will show powdery mildew infections, and you might want to cut down heavily infected plants. Resist the temptation to toss them in the compost pile. It is unlikely to generate enough heat to kill the spores. Dispose of the debris in plastic bags.

But, remember this is just for debris containing fungus spores. Many valuable insects overwinter in dead plant stalks or leaf litter. These materials may be used as mulch. For example, maple leaves can protect perennials in your garden, and leaf litter provides hiding places and food for your beneficial insects including ground beetles, centipedes, millipedes, pill bugs and spiders. To encourage their return in the spring, leave dried plant materials standing over the winter. Good bugs can't help your garden if they overwinter in a plastic bag buried in a landfill!

This is a good month to plant shrubs and trees and to complete any lawn renovation or seeding plans. Just be sure new plantings are well watered and mulched. But not too much mulch around trees and especially not the "volcano" approach. Little critters burrow into the mulch and feast on tender tree bark during the winter.

You will notice leaves beginning to turn by the end of the month. Resist the impulse to bring in those gorgeous red three-leaved branches; they are probably poison ivy! But enjoy the brilliant sugar maples, dogwoods and blueberries. We are blessed to have such beautiful fall colors in our part of the country.

Blissful gardening - Bitsy

Portia

Although she carried a full course load for her third and last year of law school, Portia planned to continue participating in the law school's legal aid program a few hours a week. She enjoyed interacting with and solving the legal problems of real people. She saw it as a respite from belaboring the minutiae of legal cases and dueling with professors who always seemed to find ways to expand all facets of an issue while dancing away from its resolution. Although her class standing was such that she could have worked on the law journal, she chose to help manage the school's moot court program and became vice president of the Dames, the law school's feminist group dedicated to thwarting challenges to Roe v. Wade.

This afternoon she met with other women of the Dames to consider recalling New Anglia state legislator Phineas Allgud, author of Bill No. 13-047. Allgud was the long-time assembly member for the district where Middletown was located. Rumor had it that he found Attila the Hun too moderate for his tastes. Younger legislators suggested that he had been the Hun's tutor. Others believed his political beliefs prohibited him from making a left turn when he drove.

What incensed the Dames was the content of Bill No. 13-047, subtitled Best Medical Practices for the Care and Good Health of Women, which had narrowly avoided passage the previous June. The bill required all women seeking an abortion in New Anglia to undergo a non-invasive sonogram prior to the procedure and that the embryo's purported male parent be present and obliged to view the image of the sonogram. There were exceptions in cases of rape and incest, so long as two witnesses were available to confirm the existence of the exceptions.

In addition to the outcry from numerous feminist organizations when the bill was proposed, various fraternal lodges, men's clubs and the Boy Scouts hired lobbyists to protest the potential inconvenience and embarrassment to putative donors of the Y chromosome. This lobbying effort ultimately persuaded a majority of New Anglia legislators to table the legislation. As reported in the Courier-Times, it was a close vote. Since the proposed legislation could be revived, the Dames were determined to remove its author and, they hoped, put the issue to rest.

Allgud himself was of slight, but fit, stature. He recently stopped using a comb-over to conceal the ever-broadening bald spot on his head. His hairdresser now artfully arranged carefully pomaded curly hair about his ears to resemble a laurel wreath. He was always impeccably tailored in a style reminiscent of the 1920s -- dark suits with lapels on his vests and white shirts with rounded collars and ties retained by collar pins. Razor creases in his trousers threatened to cut his knees, and his highly polished shoes rose to mid-ankle. He was perhaps the most stylish legislator in Capitol City. The most dangerous place in town was between him and a television news camera.

His voice was sonorous and helpful in debates, so long as one concentrated on the voice and not the words it formed. He had one unfortunate linguistic habit. Between utterances, perhaps to avoid having to listen to other voices, he made little humming noises, like the opening note of a mourning dove's song. "Whooo" he would intone, followed by a slightly higher pitched "Humm." Sometimes he would absentmindedly warble an elongated "U" sound, like the word "you" spoken in a shower stall. He drove those sitting near him in the legislative chamber crazy.

Portia's fellow law student, Forsythia Bandage, was charged with researching the most effective means of removing Legislator Allgud from office. She rose to address the eleven women assembled in the room.

"There are two ways of getting rid of that supercilious idiot: impeachment or recall. Impeachment is a legal process that must be initiated by the legislators themselves, while recall is a political process where an individual voter can petition for a special election to remove and replace an elected state official. Given that Allgud has been in the legislature for more than thirty years and runs the central valley political machine, there is little chance we could pressure the legislators to impeach him."

There were knowing looks and sour faces among the young women.

"So, let's consider recall. That is an attractive alternative. Just recently state Senators in Wisconsin and Arizona were successfully recalled, as was Representative Paul Scott of Michigan. Fortunately, New Anglia has very broad grounds for recall. Our statute says: 'The sufficiency of any statement of reasons or grounds ... shall be a political rather than a judicial question.' That has been interpreted to include lack of fitness, incompetence, and neglect of duties or corruption. And, last year our high court stated that – and she pressed a few times on her tablet to bring up the exact words – 'No recall submitted to voters shall be held void because of the insufficiency of the grounds by which the submission was procured.'"

"Well," said Portia, reflecting the sense of relief among the group, "that's excellent, Sythy. Great job of research!"

"How complicated is the recall process?" asked another participant.

"Not complicated. One of us files an application with the county clerk to circulate a recall petition, and we gather signatures from within Allgud's district.

We need signatures from twenty percent of the registered voters in his district within sixty days after we begin, and a recall election is held."

"And how many voters would that be?"

"I figure about eight thousand, but nine to be sure," she answered.

That number seemed daunting. There was a pained silence around the table.

Portia spoke. "Come on. We can get a lot of help with this. Planned Parenthood, NOW and many other women's groups will support us. The fraternal lodges might be with us. They spent a lot of money to help defeat the bill. It won't cost them anything to sign a petition."

The discussion resumed. The bright young women began planning a campaign to dislodge what one of them called "that geriatric popinjay."

As the meeting was about to adjourn, one of them asked,

"I guess we need to propose an alternative candidate for the recall election. Any idea who that might be?"

No one had a candidate in mind. That could wait until a later meeting. Portia, flushed with enthusiasm, rushed to her Industrial Property Rights class.

"That young woman is tenacious as a 'gator with a piglet," mused Senator Pete Rowe, causing the two assistants near his desk to lean toward their boss in hopes of further explanation.

"Those tea bags or whatever they call themselves over in the House came up with the horseshit idea that we could save the taxpayers a bundle if we defunded the national parks and turned them over to private businesses. Raise the price of admission a bit and manage the parks as well as American businesses always do. Casually forgettin' that a million and a half American businesses go bust each year and that the profit motive surely adds significantly to the cost of doin' business. How much did we pay the CEO of Fannie May before he was canned – can't remember his name…"

"Michael Williams," offered the assistant more familiar with financial matters.

"Yeah, Mike Williams. Canned his sorry ass in '08. What'd they pay him for the two years before he ran that business into the ground? 'Bout ten million, I recall. Good businessman, right?"

The senator listened for murmured agreement among his aides.

"Anyway, Miz. P. explained in a very ladylike way that the house would have their respective heads up their asses if they handed our national patrimony over to the businesses represented by all the K street types. You could hear them over here salivatin' to get a chunk of, say, Jean Lafitte National Historical Park in the great state of Louisiana, or Big Bend in Texas or Yellowstone in Wyoming. Well, she did a good piece of work there, throttling that notion back and shaming them into adding a little something extra for the park service in the next three years. I think I'd like to have a little meetin' with her."

The assistant more familiar with matters in the house saw the light.

"Representative Pewtree, you mean?"

"Yeah. That's the one. They call her 'Pert.' Cute name."

Within the hour, Grover Merson received a call from Senator Rowe's office, inviting his employer for tea with the Senior Senator. Would Thursday be convenient?

In her almost four years in the nation's capital, Representative Pewtree had visited the Hart Senate Office building only three times, and that was as a member of a group there for ceremonial purposes. As she entered the building, she noted that Senator Rowe's office suite was on the first floor, a preferred location based on his seniority. The massive atrium with the Calder sculptures was designed to impress, and it did. She walked through the lobby toward the senator's office looking forward to her meeting with, what pundits referred to as, the "Cajun legend."

She admired the senator for his direct, unvarnished approach to economic and political issues. Unquestionably canny, he always found simple ways of expressing complicated issues, frequently with a "down home" voice or expression. Although the recent fracas in the house about defunding the national parks died there without reaching the senate, he had supported her position, publicly stating that "my hound dog, Blue, would a been smart enough to scamper away from that mess - would a known it smelled worse than a polecat."

She was curious about the summons to Senator Rowe's office, and wondered what might be on his mind as she pushed open the door to his anteroom. Zelda

Barnickle, the senator's executive assistant, rose from her desk and greeted the congresswoman warmly.

"It is so nice you have taken the trouble to visit with the senator. I know he is eager to speak with you. The senator takes tea this time of the afternoon – not like in older days when he scoffed at anything less than eighty proof. But as we get older…" She trailed off.

"Tea would be just fine. Do you perhaps have Earl Grey?"

"Of course. Let me show you into his office."

Senator Rowe said his knee still smarted, but he had graduated from the detested four-footed contraption to an aluminum cane. He supported himself with it as he rose to meet congresswoman Pert Pewtree.

"Miz. Pewtree, so good to see you, my dear."

He shifted the cane so he could shake her hand. She returned his grip firmly.

Small talk began. Yes, their families were fine, there was a morning chill in the air, mutual respect was expressed for the fine and underappreciated work done by their staffs, and it was a terrible shame how divisive the atmosphere in the capitol had become.

Zelda Barnickle pushed open the door to his office and deposited a tray with tea and scones, honey, and butter. Pert had not expected such treatment in the office of a grizzled Louisiana oilman turned politician.

"Yes, I know," Pete sighed. "Between my wife and my doctor, they've gradually eliminated almost everything I like to drink and eat. Up till a couple years ago sweet bourbon was my teatime drink. Now it's really tea, but I'm getting used of it."

Zelda poured a cup of Earl Grey for the congresswoman and the senator larded his cup with four teaspoons of honey. She gave a slight, disapproving shake of her head and left the two legislators. Pert relaxed in her chair and sipped as Pete leaned toward her.

"I was admirin' the way you handled those people on the other side who wanted to take away money from our parks. You managed to sound like the only sensible one in the room and got the press to feel that way too. That was a nice piece of work. And I say that with respect, even though some on the other side are so dull they think 'asphalt' is a rectal problem."

Pert laughed loudly at his last observation and thanked him for the kind words.

"I was just wonderin' if you followed that bill about requiring legislators and executives employed by Uncle Sam not to profit from information that comes their way. Sort of a new take on insider trading. Kind of makes unlawful what most of us thought was that way all along."

"Of course. It seemed to be one of the few things that had bipartisan approval."

"Yes – and that's a shameful thing," Pete said. "Anyway, I been reviewing other things that seem as though everyone believes they are wrong and subject to the law. I began looking at all the rules established to curtail outrageous lobbying. You know, how gifts have to be worth less than twenty-five dollars, and meals and tickets to sports events and such are outlawed."

"Sure. We are being very careful about that in my office."

"As is good and proper," Pete agreed. "What me thinking was that scandal last year where that lobbyist for the National Mortuary Association, Liz Todthill, was discovered in, what do they call it? Flagrante delicto? On her knees. In Congressman Adverse's office. By his wife."

Sentence by sentence his grin grew broader as the honeyed words painted the picture for the congresswoman. Certainly, she knew of the incident. It made front-page news throughout the country and the international blogosphere. And, within the week, another senator, Maxwell Hardesty, was discovered being massaged with scented oils by Randy Folk, lobbyist for the Amalgamated Weightlifters Union.

Both stories fed on each other for at least a day. Pundits expressed various forms of indignation until two fresh scandals from Hollywood and the N.F.L. eclipsed commonplace sexual antics in Washington. That story drifted away.

"What surprised me was that there is nothing in all our rules regardin' working with lobbyists or the findings of our ethics committee that prohibits activities like that. Sure, some voters might hold peckerdillos like that against their chosen political leaders come election time, but I believe this is not a matter that should be left to politics. My intention is to offer legislation to make such activity unlawful, and I would be honored if you would sponsor the same proposed act in the House."

"I agree that would be worthwhile legislation if, as you say, it fills a legislative void," she said. "However, neither of us has a reputation for hasty decisions, and I need to think this over a bit, discuss it with my staff. Might I get back to you in a day or two?"

The senator thought that would be just fine. Their conversation shifted toward the recent poll conducted by Fox News and MSNBC that concluded not only that Congress as a whole had an approval rating of less than eight percent, but contained the startling revelation that thirteen percent of voters would like to hit their legislators in the mouth with a bat if they came across them in a supermarket. Prudent legislators were avoiding supermarkets.

The senator then enumerated recent bipartisan agreement on a few bills that required no use of federal funds. The Defense of Marriage Act, for example, purported to support high moral American principles and cost nothing. Except, of course, that it was probably unconstitutional and huge sums would be spent on lawyers' fees as the constitutional challenge worked its way to the Supreme Court. But, said the senator, the number of legislators willing to climb to high moral ground was impressive.

"Well," said Pert, "that being so, it is very likely that bipartisan approval of your proposed bill would be forthcoming."

"I'd like to think so. By the way," said the senator as he lifted some papers from a desk drawer, "here's a draft of the act. Since I hope you are inclined to be with me on this, you're entitled to see what my staff has come up with."

Pert thanked him and glanced at the papers. They were headed The Probity Act (Ethical Considerations regarding the Relationship between Members of Congress, Officials of the Executive Branch of Government and Registered Lobbyists and their Ilk). Tightly spaced "Whereases," "Wherefores," and "Therefores" marched across the pages. A glance refused to reveal its gist.

Pete Rowe interjected.

"When you cut out the dog poop and bull hockey, it says it is unlawful for any member of congress or people who work in the White House to have sexual relations with any lobbyist or his or her proxy. And, the 'sexual relations' definition section is pretty complete. It's covered by these two pages here."

Pert followed the words the senator pointed out and blushed slightly.

"It certainly seems so," she said.

The congresswoman placed the papers into her attaché case and offered a fond goodbye to the senior senator from Louisiana.

Wylie kneeled in his tiny vegetable garden behind the condominium harvesting a few plum tomatoes warm from the afternoon sun. Portia had not yet returned from law school and Linda was in the kitchen talking on her cell phone with her daughter. In these restful moments, he evaluated the morning's discussion with Dan Frimmel and the University's General Counsel about the repercussions from Bemis' C and D letter.

Being friendly with Dan Frimmel, director of the Van Poppen farm, Wylie sought information from him first. Dan said he couldn't discuss the matter unless he had clearance from the University's top lawyer, General Counsel Andrea Popov. Wylie knew Andrea well enough to request a meeting, which was held that morning.

General Popov, knowing of Wylie's reputation for discretion, described the meeting between Myron Ng and Dan Frimmel which led to the discovery that Bemis had extracted potentially confidential information through its "moles," and that discussions with chief lawyers in other state agricultural colleges and universities were underway.

Meanwhile, Andrea responded to the C and D letter with a letter of her own, saying she appreciated the guidance contained in Bemis' letter, that she was looking into the matter and would advise them accordingly. She was sure they would understand that the gravity of the matter demanded a thorough investigation

"Wylie," she said, "I think that will hold them while we firm up fact finding and research similar cases."

"Yes," he agreed. "Patent law was not in my wheelhouse, and I wonder if you could say more about the allegation that Anne Proctor's super plants somehow infringed Bemis' industrial property rights."

"Of course," she said. "With Ms. Proctor's agreement, we tested her plants in our own laboratories to see whether there is any merit to that claim. They are super plants, indeed, what with that peculiar golden sheen and robust growth patterns. But their genetic makeup is almost identical to our own heirloom plant varieties, with no deviation beyond the standard. We can't rebut Bemis's claim, but we do not believe they can prove infringement either."

"Mexican standoff?" asked Wylie.

"Looks like."

"So, unless our side can sandbag Bemis with sustainable claims of illegal, unethical or anti-competitive dealings, we are looking at a long, drawn-out and expensive legal proceeding."

Andrea made a sour face and shrugged her shoulder to signal her agreement, and Dan Frimmel looked discouraged by Wylie's assessment.

Under normal circumstances, and assuming a client with deep pockets, the prospect of extensive litigation and numerous billable hours would be an attorney's dream. However, Anne Proctor was, by now, a dear friend with limited resources – and Bemis, with seemingly unlimited funding, might prevail in a legal proceeding by the application of money. Bemis could exhaust them financially and emotionally with pleadings, delays and demands. Wylie thought of Dickens' Bleak House and the generations-long Chancery case of Jarndyce and Jarndyce. At times Dickens' unfavorable view of the legal process was deadly accurate.

Andrea offered her thoughts.

"Well, it's early days. I'm collaborating with the Prosecuting Attorney's office, and they are considering whether any of the information might lead to claims of unlawful behavior, criminal liability. I think that Bemis interfered with our business opportunity, which exposes them to civil liability too. I plan to play for time and convince Bemis we are terribly concerned about their infringement claim and need time to investigate."

Good strategy thought Wylie. Now he had to figure out how best to protect Anne Proctor. He had advised her not to respond to the C and D letter while he assessed her situation. Now he proposed to Andrea that he draft a letter for Anne that told Bemis she was working with the University to clarify the status of her plants and certainly had no intention of infringing Bemis' property rights."

"Fine," said Andrea. "They'll probably want some sort of timetable, and we can haggle over that while continuing our preparation."

"Don't be so glum," she said to Dan. "You know the cliché about 'walks like a duck?' I think we are going to find a large, fat duck on our hands. And it might be ready for the oven."

Dan perked up. He hoped that Andrea was right.

As Wylie worked in his garden, he edited in his mind Anne's letter to BIG AG. It would show her concern and vulnerability and beg for time to resolve the matter. There would be no legal jargon. He would need to…

Linda, backlit by the afternoon sun, cast her shadow across the tomato plants.

"I'm going to do some grocery shopping. Anything you need?"

A completely ordinary question, yet Wylie felt a chill despite the warm September air. In the close relationship that develops between loving couples, unarticulated discontent, emotional pain, or physical unease felt by one may be transmitted to the other.

Wylie felt guilty and upset, without knowing why, other than there was something wrong.

"No. I'm fine," he said, unable to see her face silhouetted against the afternoon sun.

"So, do you know how to describe what happens when you get a sneezing fit and end up coughing, sneezing and farting at the same time," asked Billy as they examined their cards after a fresh deal.

His partners tried to ignore this bizarre question, coming out of nowhere, yet quintessentially Billy. A studious silence hovered over the card table, broken, finally, by Arnie.

"I just know I'll regret this, but…how?" said Arnie. "Snoughart," said Billy Clarke. "I learned it from one of my managers in Pennsylvania. It perfectly suits that unfortunate situation."

"Snofart?" asked Arnie, debating with himself whether to pursue the issue, about to speak when Sy interrupted.

"Well now, that drives what passes for conversation here to a new low," he said.

"Maybe not," said Wylie. "I think that's a legitimate new word--a clever combination of three words that sounds something like what it means. The Oxford English Dictionary of new words will probably cite it next year, like 'screenager' and 'threequel.'"

"Wylie, where do you come up with that stuff? 'Threequel' and 'screenager?'"

"Well," he said, "you know when I wrote legal briefs and contracts for a living I was paid by the word, with a bonus for multisyllabic words that required a reference look-up. So, I do give an occasional glance at a dictionary."

"Enough," said Arnie. "How about giving an occasional glance at your cards? We don't move this game along, I'll be sleeping on Sy's couch."

By ten in the evening, comments about wives and girlfriends rounded out the evening's agenda. Sex was a touchy subject among septuagenarians, so the talk was mainly G-13 rated. The unspoken assumption among three of the card players, however, was that Wylie was getting some – which was more than he was entitled to or deserved. However, speaking fondly of feminine foibles was permitted, even encouraged. It was Wylie's turn.

"Happily, I haven't heard from Mavis for a few weeks. I think she's been busy redecorating her living room or something. Porrie is a pleasure to have around. I see something of myself in her, Arnie. Remembrance of the great times we had in law school. She is really involved in local politics with the Allgud recall."

That generated comments about the legislator's character, past service and prospects. Consensus was that it would be character building for the Law School feminists, but that they were tilting at windmills.

Wylie did not mention Anne Proctor because of his involvement in an ongoing legal proceeding, but he hoped his friends might provide meaningful guidance about the situation with Linda.

"I don't know what's going on with Linda. There is this coolness between us that I can't put my finger on. I suspect she wants me to propose, but I can't commit to that. It's complicated. I feel like I'm being pushed in a direction I just don't want to go."

His companions looked thoughtfully at their dour companion.

"Jewelry," said Billy. "Works for me every time. Just go for platinum and diamonds – necklace, bracelet, whatever. I go to this guy over on Broad Street."

Sy considered a medical aspect.

"Could still be change of life? Hormones, hot flashes, little extra weight, all that. Cry occasionally? If it becomes a problem, there's an excellent woman GYN specialist in my building. I hear she works wonders. Uses Prozac, the husband's best friend. Here, I'll jot down her name," he said, reaching for his ever-present prescription pad.

Judge Brackett placed his cards on the table and gazed at Wylie for a moment

"Band-Aids on a cancer, Band-Aids on a cancer," he said. "Those ideas might work for a little while, but the focus there is on Linda. Wylie, you've got to figure out why you are unable to commit. I know you had a bitter divorce with Mavis, but that was Mavis, not Linda. You've been with Linda for what, now? Almost three years? Man up, Wylie. Consider for a moment that the problem might be you."

That observation ceased further conversation on the subject. It was time to settle and go home.

Wylie thought over the advice received from his friends as he walked to his car. He was disappointed that his old friend, Arnie Brackett, failed to understand that Linda, herself, was at issue and that he, Wylie, was concerned with her well-being. To suggest that he should engage in introspection as a potential solution was not relevant. It was subversive. Anyway, that advice was unsolicited.

He glanced at the paper where he had written down the name of Billy's jeweler and made a mental note to discover the identity of Linda's current lady parts doctor. Perhaps the one suggested by Sy Wiser could be more helpful.

When he worked for Chevron, Dick Geier sought to improve his management skills by reading the latest articles in popular business magazines. One that caught his eye was "managing by walking around." Improving his visibility by wandering around plant sites and chatting with workers was appealing, principally because it gave him an opportunity to smoke away from the smoke-free office building. He didn't know whether walking around enhanced the quality or style of his management abilities but, since he enjoyed the process, he kept doing it through his various career changes.

Bemis headquarters was built years earlier next to one of its the larger manufacturing operations. Time went by, and modernization programs enhanced and expanded both the corporate offices and manufacturing facilities. Although the large city near headquarters also expanded during that time, their office setting remained bucolic. As other companies spent large sums relocating their operations to suburbia or even rural areas, Bemis management felt smug about the money they saved because they were already there.

In earlier days, only poor accommodations for customers, potential employees, and other visitors to headquarters were locally available. The company built some comfortable guest cottages in a secluded area near both the main offices and the fertilizer mill. These little houses still served their original function, except that they were reserved for VIP guests invited by the company's executives. Use of a guest cottage by top managers was unquestioned.

After four failed marriages and the heavy costs of moving from wife to wife, Geier concluded the sanctity of marriage was outweighed by the convenience and lower maintenance costs of having a mistress. In doing so, he blended his ambulatory management style, the availability of a guest cottage, and the need for carnal knowledge of the pneumatic Priscilla Sudby. She had been in his horizontal employment for five months.

The most direct route from his office to Priscilla's guest cottage was out the side door of the Headquarters building, into the plant nearby. There he navigated a catwalk over the main blending area in the huge fertilizer production building, out a side door, across the manicured lawn surrounding the guest cottages, and into the "Rendezvous" cottage.

The route's minor inconvenience was not being able to smoke. Although all environmental controls Bemis could not avoid were in place in the blending area, a spark or flame could ignite the almost invisible dust particles. Smoking and open flames were strictly prohibited.

That Tuesday afternoon he advised his executive assistant he was going to be walking around the plant for a while, see how things were going, keep an eye out. He didn't want to be bothered so he handed her his pager. He planned to be gone an hour or so.

The cottage door opened to his secret knock. Priscilla greeted him in what she called her "trikini," a Victorian flowered hat, eyeglasses with red heart-shaped rims and red patent leather stilettos. She offered Geier a long kiss and turned toward the bed, revealing a tasteful star-shaped tattoo on her right buttock, with the name "Dick" flowing from it like the tail of a comet. Enthralled, he moved to the bed. This girl was full of surprises.

Later that afternoon, Geier held a brief meeting with the other founding members of Malimsa. It ended in self-congratulatory high fives on the report that all distribution problems had been resolved and the second source company was already so profitable it seemed as though gold coins were raining from the sky. As Edger and Stirrup left Geier's office in a giddy mood, Simon Targle entered to report on the status of two acquisition proposals and various items of litigation. Geier enjoyed hearing of the many ways in which Bemis was "sticking it to" competitors, infringers, and any who might threaten the continued welfare of his company.

"So, that brings us up to date on the Rosen and Stern acquisitions and active litigation," he said. "I have had no additional feedback from Randi about those 'super plants,' and Etta says that local intelligence has dried up. We received a standard 'we're looking into the matter further' letter from the University and a rather poignant letter from Anne Proctor, saying how sorry she is to be causing us any trouble, and that she is cooperating as fully as possible with the University's investigation."

"What's your take on it, Simon?"

"They're not about to stand up to the threat of a lawsuit from Bemis. There will be some bluster and delay, and then they will sign a non-compete agreement and promise never to do it again. Whole thing should be settled in a couple of months."

Wylie had not been asked to remove any of his clothes as the nurse ushered him into the small examining room that connected to the doctor's office. The office door was open, and he could read the "Harrison Oliver, M.D., F.A.C.S" on the mahogany nameplate on the desk. The desk itself was stacked high with papers that spilled onto shelves and a pile in the corner of the office. There was no sign of the doctor and Wylie, quite nervous, chose not to sit on the small chair in the examining room.

He wandered into Dr. Oliver's office and looked at the various framed diplomas, honors and awards on the wall. He learned that "F.A.C.S." stood for: Fellow of the American College of Surgeons. That was reassuring, he supposed.

The doctor bustled into his office and discovered Wylie looking at the framed documents. He held a suspiciously thick manila file with "Cypher" displayed in large block letters.

"Fine. You're here," he said. Why don't you just sit here on the couch and I'll join you as soon as I shift some of these papers.

Which he did, and moved to sit next to Wylie, offering his large brown hand in the process. Wylie took the hand and managed a weak "How are you?" which he immediately deemed completely inappropriate in the circumstances.

"Fine. Well, Mr. Cypher we have the complete biopsy results. They took a bit longer than expected...."

"And?"

"And it appears you have a very slow growing form of prostate cancer. It is classified as grade one. May well have been there for some time."

Doctor Oliver extracted some black and white electron microphotographs and showed them to Wylie. For all Wylie knew, they could have been pictures of a plate of spaghetti with tomato bits and Marinara sauce. The doctor pointed to several spots on the pictures and Wylie tried to focus on the words he spoke.

"Non-aggressive; early stage; lucky we found it now; there's another little spot over here; medical option..."

It all seemed to blur together, like the sound of raindrops hitting a copper roof. He experienced a slight sense of relief. The results did not seem as bad as they might have been.

"I see. So, what's next?"

"We needn't take aggressive action now. Certainly, it is too early to consider surgery, radiation or chemotherapy. In cases like this, I recommend a strategy of active surveillance. That means we monitor the cancer non-invasively with a view toward further treatment when and if it becomes necessary."

Wylie experienced the sensation of invisible fingers clutching at a spot just below his scrotum. His prostate gland seemed to awaken and say "hello." He did not like it.

"Those symptoms I have, the burning…"

"I can give you medicine for frequent urination but, may I ask, do you still have an active sex life?"

"Well, I'm not sure how active it is. Until recently, it was once or twice a month. Does that count?"

Wylie hesitated.

"Um, going forward, will I still have that sex life?"

"Of course. In my experience, you should consider yourself lucky. Look at it this way. You are quite a healthy seventy-five-year-old man with a little touch of cancer. Life goes on."

That, thought Wylie, is a peculiar way of putting it.

"Come back to me again in three months. We'll see how things look then."

Even before leaving the doctor's building, Wylie began evaluating his situation. Not as gloomy as it might have been. Certainly not the best news but, as his father said in his eighties, "Every day past seventy-five is a gift. Use it well."

This is going to change a lot of things, he thought. A lot of things.

Wylie pulled his car into the parking lot of the Middletown arboretum for the monthly Master Gardeners' meeting and nodded to others who were moving toward the building's entrance. Three days had passed since he received his diagnosis of prostate cancer. He had now arrived at the fifth stage of grief – acceptance. Denial flitted through his mind briefly as he watched Dr. Oliver's fingers poke at areas of the photograph of the plate of spaghetti that depicted cells in his prostate. Anger arose upon his return home and the discovery that neither Linda nor Portia was there that evening. As he began sipping his third tumbler of Glen Morangie, however, anger gave way to bargaining.

He was an excellent bargainer, honed over years of countless negotiations with other attorneys and businesspeople around the globe. However, he was unable to identify the party with whom to bargain. Or, for that matter, what he might have to bargain with. He was not sure there was a God, but he was certain that if He had blessed him with prostate cancer, there was little Wylie could offer in exchange for an immediate cure. Consequently, depression set in.

Since Linda was spending a few nights at her daughter's home, and he did not care to discuss his medical situation with Portia or the card players, he had no choice but to review his condition with Emma. She responded by licking his hand and sighing as she burrowed her nose in his lap, not far from the offending gland. So, by the third morning after Doctor Oliver's diagnosis, acceptance set in. Only Doctor Oliver, Emma, and he knew of his condition.

The monthly meeting consisted of announcements, reports on various programs underway, and a lecture by a seasoned horticulturist on a subject of general interest. The meeting also featured refreshments provided by designated Master Gardeners who vied to increase the girth and cholesterol levels of their peers with lavish and delicious breakfast treats. Wylie always hurried to see whether Bitsy Crangle had provided her miniature cinnamon rolls that suffused his mouth with ambrosia of sugar, cinnamon, butter and more sugar. Unfortunately, she was not on the list of providers that day, and Wylie made do with little salmon quiches.

He found a seat near Anne Proctor, who signaled she wanted to speak with him later. The morning's lecturer, Anonia Scott (known in gardening circles as the "Great Scott" in reference to her expansive mid-section), prepared the computer and projector for her lecture on Replacing Invasives with Native Plants.

Most in the audience understood the dangers of allowing undesirable invasives and non-native plants to proliferate in the landscape. In simplest terms, that destroyed the balance in nature created over the ages. The ornamental tree from Australia would not support the caterpillars that fed the birds that spread the seeds that replanted the native forest. The exotic flowers from Africa did not feed butterflies that laid the eggs that fed the birds, etc. Thickets of multiflora rose, an invader from the Far East, aggressively covered fields and forests, choking out desirable understory. Deer preferred native plants, opening new areas for the invasive rose plant.

Wylie kept careful notes as Anonia spoke. It was unlikely he would be using her information in the little garden surrounding his condominium, but he wanted to be able to tell helpline clients with larger properties about the dangers of non-native invasive species. A list of alternative choices would be helpful.

As he reviewed his notes, he realized, signaled by a brief shocked expression, that Anonia's subject also referred to happenings in his own body. Invasive species indeed! He imagined minute multiflora roses attacking his prostate. He felt their tiny thorny branches there. For a moment, he regressed to an earlier stage in grieving process – anger.

Then Anne Proctor caught his eye, and they met outside for a quick conference.

"Anne, I haven't heard anything more since our last meeting," he said. "Andrea Popov sent her letter about the University's stance in the possible infringement to Bemis and has not received a reply from Bemis. That is how this legal game is choreographed. The steps are predictable, except in this case there is the strong odor of wrongdoing on Bemis' part. University agents and the prosecutor's office are looking at that aspect of the situation carefully."

Anne thanked him for the update and complimented him on the artful letter he drafted for her to write to Bemis.

"I haven't heard anything from them either," she said. "Do you really think this will go away? I can't tell you how much this is bothering me. Nobody ever threatened me with a law suit before. I am worried about what might happen to my savings."

"Anne, this situation is becoming much more complicated than a simple argument over patent infringement. It may take a while for it to go away, but. I'll be looking out for your best interests all the way."

A disembodied hand motioned through the rear door that the meeting was about to resume.

Anne seemed to need the consolation of a friendly gesture. Wylie wrapped an arm around her shoulders and provided an affectionate squeeze.

Relaxed and muzzy, they touched lightly as they lay together. Grover rested his hand on the curve of her waist, and Portia spread her palm across the center of his chest. Passion abated, they shared current events in their lives.

"We're moving into high gear with Pert's campaign," he said. "Since she has served two terms, the odds are greatly in her favor that she will be reelected. But the opposition is seizing on the issue of her challenging the privatization of our national parks. Sammy Trencher, the used car dealer they are running against her, is saying the business of managing our national parks is too important to be left to the government. He's characterizing her as a 'tree-hugger' and a socialist."

"That's ridiculous!"

"Of course. But that's modern politics. Orwellian. Say it often enough and someone might begin to believe it. The polls say he's not gaining any traction, but we still have six weeks before the election and strange things can happen. We are not dropping our guard."

She moved to achieve closer contact.

"Just so you know, your political savvy has been most helpful in the Allgud recall. We have almost all the required signatures already. Your idea of getting signatures in front of Planned Parenthood offices was great, and we were helped a great deal by Boy Scouts soliciting signatures at supermarkets."

"How about an opposition candidate?" he asked. "Any decision there?"

"Not yet, but the Dames are interviewing. The good people don't seem to want to be bothered with political office."

Something stirred.

"I think that's enough political talk for one night."

The Dames booked Andrea Popov for one of their evening meetings of informal talks by successful women, and Andrea talked about her position as General Counsel of the University. She enjoyed her evenings with the young women students at the law school she had attended. To them, she epitomized a modern working mother who managed an important job, two children, a husband who was a noted author, and a gracious home located near the University campus. Despite her important position, she remained a free spirit, athletic and with an antic sense of humor. She was the University Frisbee champion, and students challenged her at their peril. The Dames looked forward to learning about difficult decisions taken in managing the University's legal affairs.

Before the meeting, Forsythia Bandage and Heather Perriconi, fellow third year students, huddled with Portia to assess chances of persuading Andrea to challenge Phineas Allgud.

"I don't know," said Heather. "She has so much on her plate, and I've never heard her express any interest in a political career. Of course, he'd be a fabulous candidate."

"Maybe you're right," said Forsythia, "But, you know what they say – you want the job done, give it to a busy person."

"All she can do is say 'no.'" added Portia.

Portia agreed to ask Andrea to begin a political career as an alternative to Phineas Allgud.

After her talk, the three gathered near her lectern and thanked Andrea for her excellent talk, she would soon return for another chat with the Dames.

Portia then raised a new subject, explaining that they had enough signatures on their petition to recall Legislator Allgud, and that they were looking for a candidate to challenge him. Then Portia hesitated, searching for the right words to ask the crucial question.

Andrea noted the pause.

"Should I suppose you want me as challenger?"

"Oh, yes." managed the three women, "We think you would be a wonderful candidate!"

Seeing the eager faces of the three students, Andrea looked thoughtful for a long moment.

"That Allgud is a nasty piece of work. He is both mean-spirited and ignorant. He has singlehandedly obstructed needed funding for our University. He has sought to install his unqualified political cronies in high paying positions at the University and has blocked tenure for well-regarded professors because he considers them immigrants. It would be a very valuable public service to end his career."

Andrea gathered her notes and appeared to be ready to leave. There was consternation among the young women. Was that her answer? Had they missed something?

"I will discuss it with my family," said Andrea. But, now, I am inclined to accept your offer. You had better think about some fund-raising."

The law students hugged. It was going to be an exciting October.

Chapter 8

OCTOBER

Middletown Courier-Times

Mastering your Garden

By Elizabeth Pendleton Crangle

Picky, picky, picky! Many of you argued that Zucchini is a fruit and it should have been my "Z" for last month. I think that is still open to argument, but one reader explained that the Zinfandel grape is a fruit, so I sit (I don't stand while writing) corrected. I used to teach school, and it's nice to know you are paying attention.

We can expect the first touch of frost this month, and you might want to extend the color and life of your annuals by covering them with a sheet or tarp on evenings when frost is expected. This is also the time to gather completely dried seedpods, collect the seeds, put them in a sealed container and refrigerate. Why pay the big seed companies their ever-increasing prices when your seeds are free? I especially encourage you to harvest Asclepias (milkweed family) seeds to plant next year. The monarch butterflies love and need those plants.

This is also the month to give new plantings and container plants plenty of water. With cooler weather, we don't notice how dry it gets, but the plants do. The good news is that you probably will not have to water again until spring. Along those lines, you may still plant trees and shrubs now. Once watered in and dormancy sets in, they will begin to establish themselves over the winter and get a good start next spring.

Apples! They are so good and so many varieties of them are available at farm stands and markets now. Last year I bought a little apple-peeling machine that saved me hours of work. Look for the ones that core and peel apples by turning a crank. If you know how to use the www web, you can learn how to make applejack from the peelings. Strictly for medicinal purposes, of course.

Chances are fall rains will saturate the soil around your home, making weed control a bit easier. Perennial weeds will only become more of a nuisance next year so remove them (such as thistle, dandelion, dock, Japanese knotweed and plantain) with an appropriate tool and try to get all the roots. Mulch your garden heavily with an organic mulch (I've had success with well-rotted horse manure) to thwart winter weeds and protect perennials from freezing and thawing.

I have a friend who can't wait for the first frost to harvest rose hips for tea and jelly. He breaks off the stems and spreads them out on newspapers (he says the Courier-Times works best) to dry. When they begin to shrivel, he removes the seeds and lets them dry completely. He stores them in sealed plastic containers and crushes a teaspoon full to make one cup of tea. With honey, it's summer all over again.

In my garden, I have many berry plants to help feed birds over the winter, and I also put out suet and seeds, especially in early spring when food for them is scarce. I've discovered some of them love peanut butter, which I now buy in bulk from a wholesale warehouse. What we tend to forget is that birds need water over the winter too. There are heaters for birdbaths that keep them from freezing. Also, place a pile or two of brush around the yard so the little birds can find shelter from predators.

As you can see, there is plenty to do in the garden in October. Resist the idea of putting it off until November. As you will see next month, a garden and a gardener never really rest!

Blissful gardening – Bitsy

Mary

Myron could see early touches of color gilding the sugar maples surrounding the Middletown square from the glass-walled conference room on the fourth floor of the federal building. He checked his cell phone to discover that he had been sitting alone in the office for more than thirty minutes. He assumed the wait was a strategy to enhance his apprehension of the coming meeting. It was working.

He had spent many hours in unpleasant meetings during the past few weeks. Since he disclosed his involvement with Etta Sporelli to Dan Frimmel, he had been interviewed by University Security, by two attorneys in the University's office of General Counsel, and a team of scientists from the University's agricultural research department.

His wife suggested that he visit a psychiatrist who questioned him about childhood experiences escaping from Vietnam and nearly starving in Thailand. Those repressed memories brought forth tears and increased his sense of worthlessness. Fortunately, no one had suggested he did anything unlawful. That is, until he was summoned to the assistant Prosecutors' office for this morning's interview. On Bitsy Crangle's recommendation, he hired Attorney Clem Gatz to intercede for him. Clem told him an appropriate arrangement had been reached. Nevertheless, it was a fragile and worried Myron Ng who waited for his meeting with the prosecutor.

Mary Smith entered the conference room. Petite, well-groomed and all business, she placed a large file on the table and sat across from Myron. He involuntarily glanced toward the door, expecting the actual Mary Smith to arrive. This young Asian woman, barely five feet tall, with pulled back glossy black hair and an ingratiating smile, could hardly be the prosecuting attorney Clem Gatz described as "tough as they come." But there was something about her, something familiar yet threatening, that caused him to be wary. He involuntarily shifted in his seat.

Mary extended her hand to Myron who grasped it weakly. He mumbled "hello."

She responded, "Thank you for meeting with me today, Myron. May I call you Myron?"

"Sure."

"As I believe your attorney has explained, you have waived the need for counsel at this meeting, in exchange for our granting you immunity from prosecution. Is this your signature?"

She removed a paper from her file and passed it across the table for his review. He confirmed that he had signed it.

"Now, Myron, our agreement is that you will be completely truthful and answer my questions honestly and to the best of your ability. I'm sure you understand that."

Mary asked similar questions that demanded a positive answer. She wanted to get Myron into the habit of saying "yes." It was a standard interrogation technique.

Her next series of questions dealt with Myron's personal history: education, marital status, employment, hobbies and similar items that purposely stayed away from his involvement with Etta Sporelli and Bemis. Mary wanted him to talk as comfortably as possible about himself, to focus on familiar and uncontroversial matters. As she spoke, she ticked off confirming information in the personal history file in front of her. His date of arrival in the United States interested her. It was almost exactly six months before she joined the Smith family in Pennsylvania.

"Myron let's talk a little about how you first met Etta Sporelli. How long ago was that?"

"It's been about three years now."

"And were you aware that she was a Bemis employee then?"

"Yes, but I thought she was one of the technical people who visited Van Poppen farm to go over the plant testing programs. She was very friendly and took me to lunch a couple of times."

Mary paused and said, casually, "Friendly in an intimate manner?"

"God, no! The idea of getting close to her physically is frightening. You see her yet? She is scary."

"Did she ask you for information about the programs at the farm then?"

"Well, it was just shoptalk at first. I don't really remember exactly when she wanted information about stuff that I wasn't comfortable with. But, as time went on, she offered nice vacations as a 'reward for our friendship' and because I was being so helpful to Bemis."

Myron began looking at the floor, and his face reddened.

Mary continued in her matter of fact way, gleaning details about information that Myron passed on, and cataloging places and dates of meetings with Bemis' agent. Keeping the bargain he made with himself, he mentioned nothing about Winston Wu's milkweed project. He now understood that he could have important information about BIG AG's challenge to the "super plants" grown at the farm, but he wanted to assure the success of his little group of improbable warriors. Once he was certain that the seeds were distributed, he would consider revealing his role in the project – if it did no harm to the participants.

Mary's earlier discussions with Dan Frimmel and an attorney in the University's General Counsel Office revealed that University employees at Van Poppen farm had not notified the volunteer master gardeners that their activities were confidential or proprietary, except for ongoing projects that already involved Bemis. If anything, Myron provided early notice of what would later be revealed.

Passing on plant materials was another matter, since that was clearly a violation of University policy and could be construed as a theft. Were that so, Ella Sporelli and Bemis could be recipients of stolen goods. That was a felony in the state of New Anglia. Until additional evidence highlighted other possible crimes or misdemeanors, the prosecutor's office was hinging its preliminary investigation on the theory that Bemis was a "fence."

As the interview continued, Mary focused on the times Myron had handed samples of the super plants to Etta Sporelli. He disclosed five different meetings at which this occurred, and Mary made careful note of them: date, time of day, place, and duration of the meeting. Apparently, Bemis wanted specimens of the plants during their entire growth cycle. The University, on the other hand, tested samples received at the end of summer. Mary was assured, however, that there were no seasonal variations in the genetic makeup of the material. Yet, there was no proof that the plants had not been genetically altered.

In concluding the interview, Mary asked whether Etta had shared with Myron any information about results of Bemis' tests of the purloined plants. As Myron searched his memory for the answer, she noticed that he seemed distracted.

"I can't remember anything like that. I just handed over the plants and left as soon as I could," he said.

"Well, Myron," she said, "I have no further questions."

Reaching over to shake his hand, she saw him wipe his eyes with his knuckles and look searching at her.

"Was there something you wanted to ask?"

"Would it be all right to ask a personal question?"

Curious, she agreed.

"It's about that little mark under your left ear. I couldn't help noticing it."

Mary adjusted the silk scarf that usually covered the birthmark with a flick of her hand.

"That? It's a birthmark.".

"My baby sister had one like that. I remember it from when I was a kid."

Mary was confused. There was no mention in his file about a sister.

"Something happened to her before we came over here. Nobody talks about it," he added.

"I see. I'm sure it's just a coincidence," she said self-consciously, touching the discoloration with a fingertip. "If need be, Myron, I'll be in touch with you as our investigation progresses. Please, enjoy the day."

"Sure."

The Cessna returned from its foray over frost-silvered fields as the sun crested the horizon. Jerome decided the culmination of their long effort should occur in the stillness of early morning, when no strong wind could divert the milkweed seeds from their designated landing areas. He and Bitsy rose at three and met at the Cessna's parking spot at the aerodrome a half hour later. All the seeds had been placed in the airplane the afternoon before, carefully arranged in storage areas of Jerome's design.

Once airborne, they released the little brown seeds following the pattern designed by Freddy C. Within two hours, the pattern had been covered. Half a peck of seeds remained. On a whim, Jerome flew over meadows near his apartment north of Middletown Center, and Bitsy released the last of them where Jerome would be able to monitor the effects of their program next spring. She reached across the instrument panel and gave Jerome a hug and a kiss – the first time she had been so forward with him.

Chill air struck them as they crossed the tarmac to the aerodrome office, but Bitsy ignored it and excitedly called Winston Wu on her cell phone to report the success of their mission.

"It was too dark to see most of the time, but those little brown seeds shot from the back of the plane and are in their places right now. I'm so happy! I'm going to miss all our meetings and planning, though."

Winston said there might still be some mischief their little group could get involved in. He thanked Bitsy for the call and suggested she get some rest after their early morning excursion.

Jerome signed the flight log and suggested they find a cup of coffee and a cruller. Bitsy thought that a fine idea.

"Okay," he said. "Tell you what. Why don't we go to my place? I have lots of stuff for breakfast."

She followed him to his "apartment," located in a gated community north of town. The guard motioned her car through after Jerome spoke with him, and they pulled up in front of a four-story brick federal building. His apartment included six thousand square feet comprising the first three floors. The top floor was an office for the assistants who managed his business interests. The basement, Bitsy later learned, consisted of a shop equipped with the latest CNC machines, computer-assisted design capabilities and every digital and electronic whizz-bang known to man – and some, courtesy of Jerome Hastings, yet to become known.

Compared to her modest cape, Jerome's place seemed enormous. The man she had known to wear worn, possibly cast off, clothes and a leather jacket from a Hell's Angels refuse bin did not seem to fit with this tastefully decorated mansion. Jerome, who seemed to have grease permanently embedded in his fingertips, stood by an elaborate copper cappuccino machine and asking how she liked her coffee.

Bitsy removed her jacket and joined Jerome at the granite breakfast counter. She thought she would have a latté with her cruller – which turned out to be fresh croissants with a choice of honey, imported marmalade, and pumpkin jam.

As she finished her breakfast, she tried to suppress a yawn. The excitement of her early morning adventure was beginning to wear off and drowsiness set in. She welcomed Jerome's suggestion that they take a little rest. The two sexagenarians moved to the bedroom, and Bitsy marveled at the huge bed at its center.

They sat next to each other on the bed, and Jerome leaned toward her and delivered a proper kiss, not airborne or quick, but earthbound and naughty. Involuntarily she drew back, thought better of it and responded by clutching his shoulders, accepting the powerful emotions that his closeness inspired. Bitsy, who in her wildest imaginings would never have believed the arrival of a sexual partner in her seventh decade, accepted her good fortune, not once, but twice. A while later, she wondered: what was that marvelous thing he did? Never in their married life together had Fred ever done that! Soon after, Bitsy Crangle found herself in the throes of goofy senior love, very similar to hormone-fueled goofy teenage love, but with wrinkles.

Aldo Rechnitz flashed his Air Marshall's badge at the young man behind the desk in the aerodrome office and for the first time announced his name. the young man placed the latest flight log on the counter, and Marshall Rechnitz again made notes in his leather-covered pad. He loosened his bolo tie as he left the office and turned toward the black van in the parking lot.

Rechnitz had diligently completed his background investigation of the two in the Cessna, and got a headache reviewing the file of scientific information From the Desk of Randi Fochik about the allegedly purloined genetic material contained in the allegedly genetically engineered milkweed seeds.

This was a far cry from investigating terrorist activities in metropolitan areas, and he was somewhat annoyed of this assignment. In any case, he still awaited notification from state headquarters in Capitol City about which section of the Patriot Act his prey had violated. It would be fine with him if the notice never came. He had difficulty imagining how sowing seeds from an airplane could threaten the nation's interests and, anyway, he was beginning to develop a certain fondness for the miscreants in question. They seemed like a nice older couple.

Less than three weeks before the election, Pert Pewtree's campaign was in full swing, and the polls predicted a very close race. To her benefit, an investigative reporter for the Courier-Times responded to several customer complaints about recent car sales at Sammy Trencher's used car Honest Deal Dealership. While no one believed that the cream puff they were considering had been driven only on Sundays to church by a little old lady, other claims about the cars' provenance were supposed to be accurate. So, when certain late model vehicles, which were represented as loaner cars and recent trade-ins, developed mold on the carpets and floor panels, the reporter obtained the VIN numbers and checked the cars' histories. He learned that they all had been parked too close to the Monongahela River during last spring's flooding. They were submarine models that dried out on their way east to Sammy Trencher's lot.

Sammy claimed no personal involvement and took advantage of the incident by firing his sales manager, during this long-awaited opportunity to rid himself of his wife's baby brother. He chewed out the service manager for not having dried the cars thoroughly before sale and made a public show of taking the cars back and refunding payments. The cars were then sold to a salvage company that exported used vehicles to South America. However, Pert Pewtree's campaign gained but a small advantage from this incident. Most voters expectations were low in any case. After all he was a used car salesman.

Although robocalls, e-mail blasts and local television advertisements were routinely employed in congressional races, both Pert and her challenger also relied on large postcards to communicate with voters. Each side selected unflattering photos of the other candidate and plastered well-chosen negative phrases on the glossy paper. Since Sammy was a political newcomer, he had no record to challenge, so shady business dealings, his DWI arrest, questions about whether he lived within the congressional district, and his substantial political contributions to Phineas Allgud and his cronies were highlighted.

Sammy's team produced a post card with Pert's head superimposed over that of a bear hugging a tree. The copy complained that her flagrant effort to keep the nation's national parks from being privatized cost taxpayers billions of dollars in lost revenue. In the post-truth political environment of the day the card pronounced that Pert's defense of the parks was shortsighted, un-American and smelled of socialism. The bright red post card arrived in voters' mailboxes on the last day of October.

Grover and Portia, both in bathrobes, were enjoying a bottle of red wine. For some weeks now, they had slipped into the habit of having a dinner together at his apartment every Friday evening. Neither had other obligations then and they enjoyed the time to wind down from the week's exertions.

Grover was explaining how the levers of political power were manipulated to obtain needed endorsements, in this case the teachers union headquartered in Middletown. Government money, certain promises, and the congresswoman's agreement to reconsider a "pay for performance" scheme offered by a state commissioner were involved. What was political reality for Grover was disappointingly banal for Portia, whose legal training still focused on founders' bright ideals and solid ethical considerations.

"So, that's what's going on this week. Sorry to do a data dump on you, but I really appreciate having someone I can trust to discuss this with," said Grover.

He divided the remaining wine between their glasses.

"But, with all this stupid, vicious politics as usual going on, there was a very bright spot this week. You know Senator Pete Rowe, the one they call the cagy Cajun? Well, he and Pert are working on legislation together, and he arranged to have a very nice sum of money provided to the campaign from the national coffers. Among other things, we will now be able to hire that local actor who plays the president on the Casa Blanca television series to pretend to endorse her."

"O.K. Look, enough. Let's talk about something else," Portia said wearily.

"Well, like the saying goes: that's enough about me. What do you think about me?"

She punched him in the bicep, and he retaliated by reaching for one of her soft parts under the bathrobe. She withdrew and settled in the corner of the couch.

"So, he risked, "how is it going with the Allgud recall?"

That was a political situation Portia was eager to talk about. She was excited that more than enough signatures on the petition to recall had been collected. The election was scheduled to concur with the general election in November, two years before the expiration of Allgud's current term. Allgud loudly rejected this challenge to all the wonderful things he had accomplished for the community and rebelled at the impertinence of the "girls" besmirching his lofty persona. Unfortunately, during the heated speech in which he rejected the uninformed, malicious and unjustified attacks by his enemies, the microphone picked up his peculiar warbling that made part of his locution resemble the sounds of mating red-footed boobies. It was not his finest hour.

Andrea Popov, on the other hand, behaved like a seasoned campaigner, making the most of the time she allotted to the race. With the blessing of the

University administration, she addressed numerous women's organizations about the mean-spirited and aggressive abuse of women during Allgud's reign. She was very persuasive and comical at the same time. She frequently opened her talks with a recording of a segment of Allgud's speech in defense of his political contributions, which included his little whistles, chirps and humming sounds. The audience was asked what those sounded most like, and the responses were uniformly hilarious. Fornicating penguins was among the milder analogies.

After the raucous opening, Andrea provided a rundown of the ways Allgud challenged women's rights over the years, focusing on his defeated plan to require sonograms in order to receive an abortion. At this point, she usually introduced a member of the local chapter of "Raging Grannies." The older woman wore a judge's robe and carried a spatula. She disclosed that she was among the group of self-appointed "judges" who held court to determine whether politicians should be allowed to obtain prescriptions of Viagra or other drugs that corrected erectile dysfunction under their federal and state health programs. The "judge" offered her comments with deadpan delivery. The audience, including the men who were more frequently attending her talks, loved this satirical approach. Andrea's light touch and careful enumeration of Allgud's past misdeeds were very effective. The Dames were thrilled. Their first foray into the political arena had a chance to succeed.

"Just don't get too overconfident," cautioned Grover. "There are still three weeks until November fifth. Allgud probably has something up his sleeve."

"You think he will be endorsed by Sarah Palin?" snorted Portia.

"Not that, but he is a canny little bugger. You don't stay in office that long without being an astute politician. Even at the state level."

"Point well taken. Eternal vigilance and all that."

The corner of the couch seemed lonely. Portia returned to Grover's side.

Two weeks later, Mary's sense of unfinished business, of irresolution, continued. It bothered her as she tried to sleep, and last night she dosed herself with three fingers of whiskey before finding fitful slumber. Several little things nagged her: the odd feeling that came over her when she first met Myron Ng; the sense that she had known him before; and his comment about the scimitar birthmark that he recognized as like his baby sister's.

She recognized that there was a simple way to resolve her concerns. However, such a personal matter was completely inappropriate given her role as Myron's interrogator and potential prosecutor should he fail to live up to the terms of his immunity arrangement.

Yet, Mary's heart leaped at the minute possibility that she was related to Myron Ng, and with that an opportunity to learn about her true family. She loved deeply the family that raised her and did not feel conflicted about the long-suppressed desire to know her true origins, to learn who her real parents were, to understand how it was possible that she had been abandoned. My God, she thought, is it possible my parents are still alive?

She decided to consult with her, boss, her friend and mentor, the prosecuting attorney.

Frank Jones was a crusader and a reformer with a warm heart. He listened carefully as Mary described her dilemma. Was there any appropriate way, she wanted to know, for her to contact Myron Ng with a view toward determining if he was related?

"Mary, I have no doubt that you would be able to discharge your duties, regardless of the outcome of such inquiry, " said Jones. "But there is always concern about perceptions of impropriety. That, however, would be avoided if I simply transfer the Ng investigation to another assistant AG now, before that inquiry is even broached. Would you be willing to hand your files to, say, Francine?"

Mary was not pleased with the idea of passing her work on to anyone else. That might be considered a setback, a diminution of her authority. It might even block her carefully orchestrated career path. The decision was not easy.

"Yes, that would be all right. I deeply appreciate the offer."

Myron volubly and eagerly agreed to her suggestion that they compare DNA profiles. He, too, was experiencing unexplained feelings and fantasies about the inappropriately named Mary Smith. Yes, he would be there, in her office, tomorrow, just to be swabbed. He understood there was nothing else. She might not even be there. That was fine. She would arrange for the tests through the lab her office used. Sure, forget about what is on the TV shows. Even if the lab isn't backed up, it takes two weeks to get the results. Sure.

The founders and investors in Malimsa discovered a slight setback that afternoon. While revenue continued to flow like spring floods into their offshore accounts, there was this little problem with one of the young women in the headquarters accounting office. She had the temerity to ask George Stirrup if he was aware that Malimsa seemed not to have filed state certificates of tax exemption for the current year. Apparently, his simply checking the box on the corporate form that profiled Bemis customers was not enough. She was terribly sorry, but, in the absence of proper documentation, someone would have to tell Malimsa it would be required to pay state taxes on the significant purchases made to date.

"So, what's the problem?" asked Geier. "Give her the frigging paper and let's move on."

"Well, Dick, it's a little complicated," said Stirrup. "We originally thought we would have a single distribution point, which is what we asked the consultant to set up. They got papers on that. Then, when we added warehouse space to be closer to Home Warehouse's locations, the whole tax thing slipped through the cracks."

"Slipped through the cracks! What kind of horseshit is that?"

Stirrup was getting red in the face.

"So, when we set up the other locations, that meant we were doing business in those other states, but we just didn't bother to let our consultant know about that."

"This is beginning to sound like a classic cluster fuck!" said Geier

Frank Edger spoke up.

"Listen, George and I are doing the operations part of Malimsa, and you've got to admit the process and materials flow are excellent. And the corporate structure is beautiful. We got that so confusing no tin horn government bookkeeper will ever trace ownership. So, we screwed up a little on this detail. Shouldn't even have bothered you with it."

"Not so sure about that." Geier whipped the space in front of him with a glowing cigarette. "You trip on a path and you break a hip. You a-holes get this thing fixed – and fast."

"Sure. We just need to redo some paperwork and adjust some filing dates. I have a good man working on it."

"And that young woman over in accounting? You going to deal with that?"

"Yeah. I don't think she's going to be around much longer."

Geier dismissed his business partners. His experience suggested that he keep close watch on what they perceived as a "minor glitch." People never stumbled over mountains. It was the pebbles that brought you down.

As though prescient, the young woman in question, Rayseen Jackson, was at that moment occupied in transferring certain information about Malimsa to the thumb drive she always carried in her purse.

It was Thursday afternoon, and Geier appeared at his assistant's desk to announce he was going to walk around the plant for a bit. He headed out the side door of the headquarters building toward the fertilizer operation. He scolded himself for absentmindedly lighting a cigarette just before entering the building and crushed it out beneath the warning sign. He was concerned about the accounting issue raised by George Stirrup and almost failed to wave at the workers managing the controls for the blending operation on the floor below.

The huge silos at the far end of the building contained the basic chemicals conveyed to the tanker truck-sized vats below the catwalk where paddles like ship's propellers slowly blended the granules to a uniform consistency. The heavy air above the walkway had a strong chemical smell resembling a loaded cat litter box. Geier rushed along the catwalk, exhaling to avoid that smell.

Priscilla opened the door to the cottage slowly, dramatically revealing the outfit she selected for that afternoon's entertainments. She wore a gossamer negligee so transparent it could have been made of dragonfly wings. Her nipples were rouged, and she wore a leather choker studded with brass cones. She held a riding crop in her right hand and placed its leather tassel under Geier's chin as she drew him into the room.

"Have you been a good boy today?"

"I think so."

"We'll see."

Wylie believed himself to be a decisive person. Yet, more than two weeks since his diagnosis of prostate cancer, he was unable to make up his mind whether and to whom to tell about it. He had come to terms with his condition, concluding that some other currently unknown ailment would dispatch him before the cancer. An early life experiences provided him with a form of fatalism that, in this case, offered optimism.

He recalled with great clarity the time, now almost fifty years past, when he peered over the sandbags of a command post in Korea and saw masses of Chinese infantrymen surging toward him across the narrow valley below. The stinging white light of flares etched their movements as they climbed the steep abutment directly toward his position. Their grease guns spat deadly fire, and mortars thudded relentlessly as they marched up the hill to his front. For the next three hours Wylie and two of the men who would become his closest friends routed the enemy.

During that time, he experienced simultaneously the crushing fear of imminent death in battle and the exhilaration of the victorious warrior. Those moments provided two life lessons. First, as he told his army buddies, if he could get through a shit storm like that, he could handle just about anything. Second, someone up there must like him.

Finally, he decided to announce the fact of his illness to his loved ones in a letter. He would send identical letters to his children and let the ripples from that message course toward the larger circle of his acquaintances. He felt it unnecessary to inform any Master Gardener friends of his condition except, perhaps, Anne Proctor. He remained uncertain about telling his Pinochle group: perhaps he would await the right moment during one of their games.

Linda and Portia required special treatment. He would tell them individually and directly about the cancer. Linda had been so cool toward him lately, however, that he was concerned his illness would tip the scales of her affection against him. Nevertheless, he felt his housemates were entitled to know.

Portia had a long lunch break between classes and hurried home to pick up running shoes she had forgotten that morning. She and Grover had scheduled a run around the Big Bum Reservoir later that day to enjoy the brilliant fall colors. Wylie was standing in the kitchen when she arrived.

"So, Porrie how is your new career in politics going?" He asked. "You about ready to take over Grover's job after you graduate?"

"Hardly that," she laughed. "But we think that the recall campaign is doing well. Your friend, Andrea, is an awesome campaigner. She's total energy and really connects with the voters. We're optimistic about the coming vote, but that Allgud is no dope and we expect shenanigans from him."

"And school is OK? Any feelers about future employment or clerkships?"

"Nothing noteworthy. It's a bit early, of course."

"Sure."

Wylie finished drinking a glass of water, settled into the wooden chair next to Portia, and placed his hand on the arm of her chair.

"I need to bring you up to date on a little health matter."

She stiffened.

"It turns out that I have grade one prostate cancer, which is about as benign as that kind of cancer can be. It's not life threatening, and the doctor simply plans to keep an eye on it. I just…"

Portia, eyes moist, took Wylie's hand in both of hers and observed him intently, as though she might discover a change in his eyes, his mouth, and his age lines.

"The doctor who diagnosed it, he's a good doctor?"

"Sy Wiser recommends him most highly."

"Did you get a second opinion?"

"Yes, in the sense that my biopsy was reviewed by two of the best doctors at Columbia Presbyterian. But, listen, it's O.K. I'm fine. I'm just getting a little older."

His granddaughter moved from her chair to crouch next to him and threw her arms around his neck. She sobbed and wet tears rolled to the hollow of his throat.

"Oh, Wylie, I love you," she murmured, quite a few times.

He was deeply moved and embarrassed in equal parts.

He and Linda shared tea that afternoon when she returned from the part-time nursing position she had temporarily accepted at the hospital. The work seemed to agree with her, and she was more animated and cheerful than she had been for a while. He regretted breaking the mood with news about his condition.

"Grade one?" she asked, confirming she had properly heard the diagnosis.

"Right."

With her years of medical experience, no additional information was required. She understood clearly the degree of involvement, seriousness and prognosis of Wylie's cancer. She was concerned, of course, but understood her Wylie would be around for many years.

What she did not understand was the great sense of relief and powerful attraction she suddenly felt for him. The words were hardly out of his mouth when she rushed to where he sat and nearly smothered him as she clutched his head to her chest. Her strongest desire was to comfort him. He did not understand this reaction to his bad news. Whatever the reason, he ceased to care as she ministered to him.

As she wakened from a languid post-coital nap, with Wylie snoring softly at her side, she tried to comprehend the sudden change in her attitude toward the man next to her. Was it that she had become irritated by his lack of vulnerability, his always wanting to be in control? When they first met, she was attracted to his assuredness, kindness, and generosity, but for some time now, that was not enough… or, perhaps, it was too much. It was confusing.

Now Wylie was no longer invulnerable. He had a serious imperfection, and she decided she liked him much better, very much better that way. She reached around and impulsively patted him on his left buttock. Wylie snorted mildly in acknowledgment and tried to recapture the tattered wisp of the dream he was dreaming.

His carefully worded letter to his children elicited concerned telephone calls from all three. He provided reassurance, insisted that he was feeling just fine, and stressed there was no need for immediate concern. Yes, he promised to let them know if there was any change. Of course, he wanted to see them as soon as their busy schedules permitted. Within a few days Portia's mother, Mercy, arrived for a visit. Because of their adventures together in Peru, Mercy was closer to her father than her siblings. She was relieved that Wylie looked much as always and hugged him repeatedly before she left. She reported that he looked well, was positive and funny to her siblings and mother soon after her visit.

It did not occur to Mavis to contact her ex-husband and offer sympathy when she learned his condition. Mavis suspected that Wylie contracted cancer so he could diminish what she considered to be his sizable fortune in an attempted cure, thereby reducing his estate and, as she put it, "screw our kids." Fortunately, that supposition was not shared by the kids, and they rejected that notion immediately. Rebuffed, Mavis googled Wylie's disease. She was pleased to discover actuarial tables that indicated Wylie probably would not make it to his ninetieth birthday. She was three years younger and now had a tangible goal – outlive the bastard.

She unsealed the manila envelope and held the letter it contained in both hands, carefully reviewing the rows of comparable numbers and the bold bottom paragraph that announced the conclusion. The proper Yale Law School graduate, who never swore, whose strongest oath was "goodness," stared at the letter and muttered "son of a bitch!"

The Bemis mole, the betrayer of possible confidential data, the source of information about charges against BIG AG, Myron Ng, was her brother.

SON OF A BITCH!

Chapter 9

November

Middletown Courier-Times

Mastering your Garden

By Elizabeth Pendleton Crangle

Inexperienced gardeners believe November is a quiet month where everything is getting ready to rest for the winter. While that might be so for most of your plants, many chores remain for the gardener.

Before it becomes uncomfortably cold, attend to final stages of cleaning up, raking leaves and disposing of potentially diseased debris. It is especially important to bag and discard leaves under roses that had black spot during their growing season, and plants such as bee balm and lilacs affected with powdery mildew. While spring is the time for careful pruning of roses, this month cut back tall canes and reduce the overall size of the bushes to three feet or so. Winter winds, freezes and thaws are less hurtful to lightly pruned rose plants.

Pine needles make excellent winter mulch. Rake them on your perennial beds and under new plantings. Two or three inches around favored shrubs will protect them from frost heaves. This is also a good time to order organic materials for your garden. Spread well-aged horse manure and your own compost on the vegetable garden to weather over the winter. Proper organic material will help suppress weeds next spring and should be lightly turned in so as not to revive weed seeds lurking below the surface.

Of course, this is the month for continuing to work with the fall harvest – apples, pumpkins, squash and, for the truly old fashioned, parsnips, which taste wonderful after a good frost. Don't forget to collect seeds from these late veggies and save them for next season. Or, roast and salt them for "pioneer" treats. Your children and grandchildren will be impressed!

I'm not exactly computer literate (my grandkids suspect I still live in the Middle Ages) but I can find my way onto the internet – where I search for local gardening lectures. This Google thing is amazing. I can type in a question dozens of words long and get good answers. The Agriculture Department of State U sponsors numerous meetings and lectures during the winter months. I find it is always pleasant and informative to visit with other gardeners.

While your plants might be declining as they prepare for winter, there is no reason to abandon them entirely. This is the perfect month to bring color indoors and overwinter your annuals to start in the garden next spring. The process is straightforward, and our local Master Gardener group has brochures that explain it. Tricks of the trade are to water plants thoroughly before taking cuttings, don't add too much rooting hormone (the stems might rot), be sure to supply bottom heat and use plastic bags to control humidity around the cutting. Sterilize your cutting tool with alcohol or a dilute chlorine solution after each cut. Also, if the plants will be getting light from a window, be sure it is clean. That makes a big difference.

Finally, since you won't be watering for a few months, drain your hoses and put them away out of the sun. Clean and oil garden tools and sharpen spades. Look at your garden and decide what to dig up or move in spring. A note in next March's calendar and a picture on your cell phone will be helpful reminders. Enjoy the produce of your garden at Thanksgiving and be thankful for another year of blissful gardening.

Blissful gardening – Bitsy

Linda

Linda added hot coffee to his cup and sat across the breakfast table from him. The morning light illuminated Wylie's face was not flattering, but her rekindled appreciation for him affected her vision. Linda saw a kindly older man, secure in his wrinkles and spots of age, smiling at her, reaching for her hand, offering affection, even love. She squeezed his hand. He squeezed back.

'I was just thinking," he said, pulling his hand away.

"Now, that's dangerous," she said.

"No, I mean, the trips I like to take always involve flying somewhere. It's habitual. Unless it is to go someplace around here, I always look for a plane schedule. I just got used to working with clients and travelling abroad. That could be interpreted as excluding you on purpose because you won't fly."

"I must admit, the thought crossed my mind."

"I'm sorry. So, why don't we consider taking a road trip somewhere? Maybe visit a national park or two. Hang out at a nice resort for a few days. Something like that?"

Linda was not surprised at Wylie's suggestion. Two days before, she had finally explained to Wylie how hurt she was that he had asked Anne Proctor to accompany him to Spain. Wylie protested that he had asked her first, that she had agreed he could take Anne and swore that the trip was completely platonic. Linda granted all that.

"The thing is, after you came back the hurt set in. I thought it would be okay., that I could handle it, but it turns out I was wrong," she had said.

Wylie did not challenge her. Facts and arguments never conquered feelings. When the idea of a road trip came to him, he was surprised that he had not thought of it before. This sort of thing, the errant realization of simple solutions to life's little problems, seemed to be happening more often lately. Reluctantly, he decided it was a matter of aging.

Wylie decided to bolster his restored alliance with Linda by offering a vacation together, a road trip to places of her choosing. The more he thought about it, the more appealing it became. Fortunately, Linda agreed. It would be an adventure with Wylie. She would not have to share him with anyone, not even Portia.

Linda paused long enough to worry him, then gladly agreed

"So, what do you think. When should we go?" he asked.

"I don't have serious plans for the end of the month. How about then?"

"Well, that would be fine, but weather could be problem at the end of November."

"So, we would just go south. About thirteen hours of driving would get to a place like Miami," he suggested.

"Oh, that would be nice! I've never been. Is that near the Everglades?"

"I think so."

Linda became more animated as the conversation continued. She was more "computer literate" than Wylie and eager to research a trip to Florida on the internet. Wylie encouraged that exploration, particularly since it had been some time since he had seen his housemate so happy.

Tersh Brandon was in his element. It was the first time he had invited his current girlfriend to his workspace at Plankton Communications LLC, and he busily explained the art and science of creating robocalls, discussing mass communication techniques and testing whether she would accept his hand creeping inward from her knee. He prided himself on his ability to multitask.

Imelda Stratton was mildly interested in the array of glowing video screens surrounding Tersh's desk space and not interested at all in the movement of his hand across the faded denim of her skirt. She removed the now tasteless wad of chewing gum from her mouth and pressed it firmly into the palm of the hand moving on her thigh. Tersh continued his monologue while trying to remove the mess that now stuck to the fingers of his other hand. Multitasking.

"Okay. So this screen shows the list of e-mails and telephone numbers that we have generated over the past four years from numerous sources, broken down by zip code, political affiliation, age, social demographics and stuff like that. We use several "bots" to mine information from search engines and social media on the internet, and sometimes we can hack e-mails for internal addresses. And Facebook, how great is that? Billions of dummies broadcasting all that personal information!"

"Bots?" asked Imelda.

"Yeah, they're bits of software that we send onto the internet like little robots that gather of personal information and deliver it to our servers. We get millions of hits, like every day."

Imelda pointed to another screen that showed zip codes and ten-digit numbers streaming across the lime green background.

"That unit assigns phone numbers for robocalls. We use it for initiating conference calls and broadcasting identical messages to thousands of telephone numbers at the same time. With this computer, we can dial a huge number of telephone numbers at once, and then play a single message. We are using that a lot now, with the election so close."

"Umm. So when I get a call from, like, that congress lady, Pert whatever, it comes from here?"

"Very likely."

"Cool."

"Yeah."

Tersh looked at the clipboard on the desk with that evening's schedule and asked Imelda if she would like to see how the robocalls system worked. Sure, that would be amazing.

He pressed keys on the board and the screen changed to show a sliding scale with a "start" button, a graph resembling a heart monitor and the bold letters "Allgud Announcement."

He moved the cursor to the "start" button and a very official sounding bass voice was heard over the speaker.

"This is an important public announcement," the voice said. "Due to recent problems in the delivery of voting machines, the location of your normal polling place has changed."

The voice continued to identify polling locations in various districts and directed voters to other places. The announcement ran for almost two minutes. Imelda had difficulty following those directions.

The announcement was a ruse designed by Phineas Allgud's chief of staff, a long-time devotee of Lee Atwater, the political consultant who demonized Governor Dukakis during the George H.W. Bush campaign. Recognizing that his employment was at risk because of the recall campaign initiated by the Dames, the chief of staff decided to take advantage of the latest computer technology to discombobulate the competition.

He hired a plummy voiced announcer to record the bogus declaration about changes in the voting places and contracted with Plankton Communications LLC to call all voters likely to favor the recall the day before the election. He hoped the voters would be either confused or angry – and not vote. His research indicated this had worked before in upstate New York.

"See, this is what I'm going to be sending out in just a few minutes. I have three telephone databases available: all the voters in his district, voters likely to vote against Allgud and for the recall, and voters likely to vote for Allgud and against the recall. Somebody else assigned the voters to the various classes."

Imelda inserted a fresh stick of spearmint to help her take it all in. She pointed a well-manicured finger at the screen.

"So that's why you got them labeled 'all, against and for.' You just need to click one little button and all those calls go out?"

"Yeah."

"Bitchin'."

Finally, with the aid of a tissue, the gum was off his hands and fingers. Thoughts of future conquest arose.

"Want to send it out? Click the button?"

"Oh, yeah. Be amazing."

She stood, leaned forward over the console, and poised her forefinger, the sparking, shiny design on the nail catching the overhead light, over the array of buttons.

"So, he's a politician, right? And we need to call the people who are for him, right?"

Tersh, distracted and focused on Imelda's nearby bottom, said "Right."

The sparkling digit touched the key, and the announcer crooned over thousands of telephone lines and into the homes of tomorrow's voters.

The evening's work was done and Tersh and Imelda turned their thoughts to the night's remaining prospects.

As they began to leave the office, a bright yellow square surrounded by a red line announced the completion of the robocalls, with statistics about calls completed, messages left and dropped calls. Tersh casually reviewed the information.

"Wait! What? You clicked on the for Allgud button, the ones likely to vote against recall. Oh baby, am I in deep doodoo!" wailed Tersh

It was clear that the recall vote had succeeded before the polls closed. Allgud made a bitter announcement in the early evening conceding defeat. He refused to refer to Andrea Popov in any way. He planned to comment at length about the underhanded use of dirty tricks by the Popov campaign until he was reminded that his name was on the Plankton contract. In frustration, he fired his chief of staff who he considered fully responsible for this debacle. It bothered the chief of staff, but not too much. He was almost immediately unemployed anyway.

Tersh Brandon eloquently told his supervisor that the computer must have had a "brain fart" which issued the wrong set of instructions. He was fired anyway.

Given that used car dealers received voters' approval ratings much higher than members of congress, many voters decided that Sammy Trencher should retain his exalted status in the used car industry. That, coupled with confused Allgud supporters searching for nonexistent voting places, granted Pert Pewtree a comfortable margin of victory.

On Tuesday night Portia and Grover attended two victory parties. Pert and her family held forth at the Grange Hall south of Middletown. She offered thanks to her supporters and buckets of shrimp etouffee provided through the generosity of the senior senator from Louisiana, a fervent Pert supporter. Wine and beer flowed generously, but Portia and Grover imbibed little and left early for the law school auditorium.

Andrea Popov was there, surrounded by the entire membership of the Dames and her other supporters to celebrate the departure of Phineas Allgud and the ascension of their new Assembly Person.

It was a splendid night for the two young people who worked so hard in support of their principles and candidates. They were high on victory. Well after midnight, they found themselves in Grover's apartment where they mutually declared an honorary Friday night and rushed to the bedroom to continue their celebrations.

Myron, having heard nothing for two weeks about the DNA test, was frustrated and more nervous than usual as he walked toward Winston Wu's office. He had remained silent to the authorities about his involvement in the milkweed project, but all the recent confidential interviews and examinations about his association with Bemis' agents worried him greatly. Eventually, he thought, his entire sordid involvement with BIG AG would come out and his friends on the milkweed project would reject him. He had difficulty sleeping and thought his hair was beginning to fall out. With effort, he put a smile on his face as he greeted Winston, Bitsy, and Jerome. Freddy C. arrived moments after he did.

Jerome retold the story of the successful delivery of milkweed seeds to neighboring states, and there were mutual congratulations.

Myron noted that Bitsy not only hung on Jerome's words, she hung on him as well. Her hands constantly rested on his arm, wrist or shoulder. Myron found it disconcerting to see old people carrying on like that. Here I am, he thought, full of self-loathing and ageist too.

He pulled a metal chair away from the table and sat a few feet from the others as Winston opened a notebook and addressed the little group.

"I know we all feel good about the completion of our project – and we have every right to be! Bitsy joked last time about what we need to do next and I said I would try to figure that out. Well, it doesn't seem to be a joke anymore. I've been called in to consult about herbicide 'drift' by a farm consortium in Missouri. We might have more work to do."

None in the group knew what "drift" was.

"I'm sorry," said Winston. "That's when herbicide sprayed on one field drifts a mile or two to another location and affects another crop. Drift is especially prevalent with the herbicide 2,4-D, which can vaporize days after being sprayed and travel in the air for miles."

Jerome looked confused.

"Hang on. What's this talk about 2,4-D? Isn't that the stuff they used in Agent Orange to defoliate Vietnam?"

"Yes, that was part of the formula, but it remains considered safe to use here."

A sense of discouragement pervaded the room.

Winston continued, "So, remember how surprised we were with how quickly our treated milkweed seeds began to resist glyphosate? Well, seems many weeds have developed resistance to glyphosate over the past few years, and spraying doesn't work to keep them down any more. There's a plant called pigweed that has overrun cotton fields down south and is driving farmers crazy."

"I'm not sure what that all means," offered Bitsy.

"It means" Winston said, "that the process of engineering crops to resist 2,4-D is now beginning. The Agricultural Department seems ready to approve 2,4-D resistant corn, soybeans and cotton."

Winston shuffled through papers in his notebook.

"And, to make matters worse, a troublesome weed called waterhemp in Nebraska is already resistant to 2,4-D."

Myron understood, perhaps before the others.

"When does this crap ever end? Are we just going to have to keep developing plants that resist herbicides until we run out of herbicides? This is nuts! If we keep this up the weeds will overrun us all. I really believe you can't screw with Mother Nature!"

Winston shook his head.

"You're right. Modern agriculture may well be genetically engineering itself out of business."

"To say nothing of possibly poisoning our soil forever," muttered Freddy C.

No one spoke for a while.

"Let's calm down," suggested Winston. "I guess we have to figure out whether we need to rework milkweed to resist these other herbicides as well. Anybody up for another two years of work to help the Monarch?"

Silence.

"Let's think about it for a week or so and get together again."

There were nods of ascent.

"Damn, Winston, you surely are a buzz kill," offered Freddy C.

"It's what I do'" he admitted.

Simon Targle rose to address the members of the staff meeting about the latest developments in the legal arena. He explained that the Antitrust Division of the Justice Department was challenging their acquisition of Marble Chemical because the surviving monopoly in ground calcium carbonate would tend to limit competition and increase consumer prices.

"Of course, it will! Why the hell else would we be shelling out twice what it's worth to acquire them?"

Targle winced at Geier's outburst. He managed a slight scowl in his superior's direction.

"Oh, come on. I'm just pulling your chain, Simon," said Geier. "Not often I get a rise out of you. I get the anti-trust thing. If it's pro profit, it's anti-trust. Let's move on to the situation with the 'super plants?' Have the university and what's her name come to terms?"

"I have to say – not yet. They are taking their time investigating the case. They have promised to get back to us right after Thanksgiving."

"But you have that fancy patent law firm in Middletown ready to go on this, just in case?"

"Certainly. Of course."

They moved on to other matters.

Frank Edger and George Stirrup were glum and edgy. Earlier in the day, they had reported to Geier that the state tax issue was almost resolved and that the young accountant who pestered George about the situation was completing her last week of employment. Since resolution was not at hand, Geier waved his cigarette madly and promised to tear them new assholes. They were unusually eager for the current staff meeting to end.

When it did, Geier asked Lavitra Gascoigne if she would stay for a moment to discuss sections of the draft of the new human resources handbook. She returned to the chair beside him.

"The handbook looks as though it's ready to go. I have no questions about it. It just pisses me off that we have to conform to all those intrusive government regulations. Why should we worry about people with disabilities, provide extra leave for girls who get knocked up, no discrimination about sexual orientation. I wonder what socialist figured that one out!"

He continued in that vein for a few more minutes, venting about social issues that affected his bottom line. The attractive black executive had heard it all before and bit her lip. The hardest part of her job, it seemed, was to foster compliance with relevant government regulations and laws with which she agreed. He was winding down.

"But, Levitra, I'm looking at you and you seem tense. Is everything OK with your family? Those nice kids of yours?"

"Everything at home is just fine. Thanks for asking, Dick."

He rose and moved behind her chair. Both hands reached for her shoulders.

"Yeah. Look at that. Tight as a drum. Let me give you a little massage."

She turned in the chair and put her hand against his.

"No, that's not appropriate. You should know that is a form of harassment."

"What? A friendly little neck massage?"

"It is inappropriate."

He grinned and again placed his hands on her shoulders. Before she could move away, he slid both hands down past her shoulders and cupped her breasts.

With his mouth close to her right ear, he asked

"So how inappropriate is this?"

She recoiled immediately, disengaged from Geier and quickly left the room.

That miserable bastard, she fumed. Now I've got to figure out what to do about this situation. Damn him. This is another "he said, she said." That prick. That disgusting honky.

She stormed down the corridor to her office, kicked off her shoes and curled up on the couch near the large window. Deep breaths, she thought. In through the nose, out through the mouth. Slowly she calmed and raging disgust changed gradually to thoughts of cool reprisal. He will regret this, she vowed. Time wounds all heels.

Mary sorted through conflicting emotions about her newfound relationship to Myron. Principally, she felt disappointed in the actions of her brother. That he betrayed cherished principles of honesty and loyalty in spying for BIG AG bothered her. Yet, he showed sincere remorse that, as an attorney involved in various criminal matters, did mean something. He also was forthright in passing on all his recollections. With his help, their office was piecing together a case against Bemis, beginning with the offense of receiving stolen property and developing a pattern of heavy-handed intimidation of smaller competitors. It was slow going. They needed more information.

Mary feared that she might share some of Myron's less than admirable qualities. She didn't believe that was possible, but you never know. Putting those thoughts aside, she recognized that he represented a pathway to other family members. She did not know, for example, if either of their parents was alive. How could she ask this difficult question?

She stood as tall as possible, drew her shoulders back and pushed open the door to the small conference room where Myron was waiting.

"I didn't think it was appropriate to discuss this with you on the telephone... and I wanted to be with you when you read the results."

That was all he needed. He immediately guessed the outcome of their DNA test.

As she passed a paper to Myron, she blurted out, "It shows that I'm your sister."

For days, he anticipated the outcome of this meeting, even rehearsed his response to either alternative. Remain cool.

Instead, he stood and stared at his sister, tears welling in his eyes.

"Oh. Oh. That is so amazing. So unbelievable. You are my sister? That's amazing!"

The file she held slipped away and fell to the desk as she stood and looked at her brother. Myron moved toward her and offered a clumsy embrace, a cross between a handshake and a hug. It did not last long. He returned to his chair and stared at her, emphasizing the shock of this discovery by continuing to mutter "amazing," "can't believe it," and similar exclamations under his breath.

"Oh my God, Mom is not going to believe this." Myron repeated several times.

Mary was thrilled. Her mother lived. It was beyond imagining. Her mother. Lived.

Myron regained coherence and began to describe the relatives she had to meet. Their father died some years before, but their mother, in her sixties, lived in a modest fifty plus condominium development less than fifteen miles from Mary's office. A sister, an uncle and two aunts, all lived near the mini-Saigon area of Middletown, created when the city offered its hospitality to Vietnamese boat people. Myron would call them all. There would be a great celebration. He would call them right away.

"I don't think that would be a good idea. It's going to be a surprise for everyone, especially me. I'd like to meet my mother first, alone with you. She's not fragile or anything? She won't be too shocked with this news?"

"Fragile? She coaches women's basketball at the high school. Her American name is Irma, and they call her the 'Irminator.' No, I don't think we have to worry about that."

They discussed how and when to meet Irma, their mother.

Of the two, only Wylie had been in Florida before, and that was for a hurried business meeting in Tallahassee twenty years earlier. In her thorough way, Linda researched points of interest on the internet, talked with friends at the hospital and decided that the focus of their vacation trip would be Miami Beach and the Everglades, and then a run across Alligator Alley to Sanibel Island and a leisurely drive back to Middletown. The trip was scheduled to last for about two weeks. Wiley Wylie was happy that Linda took full control of the vacation planning. On the two occasions she asked about his preferences, he told her he trusted her fully. Whatever she thought was best was fine with him. His instincts were good. Linda felt newly empowered as a travel guide. Her role as caregiver to her imperfect mate was validated. Harmony reigned.

On Wylie's past trips away, Linda, Portia or both were available to care for Emma. Their trip would include the Thanksgiving holiday, when Portia had agreed to meet Grover's family in the Merson compound on Lake Pisquatch in the northeastern part of the state. She would be gone almost four days, so there would be no one to care for the dog during that time. Wylie was reluctant to board Emma since the only time he had done it before she developed kennel cough. He did not care to spend another three weeks dosing her with cough suppressant.

"Simple enough," said Linda. "I'll check to see if the motels and the Miami Beach hotel accept dogs."

Linda checked, and Emma was included in their vacation plans.

"Well, young lady," she said to the hound lying on her bed in the kitchen, "it looks like you're going to hit the road with us."

Linda gave her a proper massage behind the ears. Emma understood that "young lady" referred to her. The other verbiage was white sound, but the tone... the tone was lovely. Whatever it was, she was ready – ready right now!

Early on the third Monday of the month, Linda and Wylie packed his car and installed Emma in the back seat – recently covered with a custom-fitted blanket guaranteed to be impervious to dogs. Of the three, perhaps Emma was most eager to go, although Linda also looked forward to a great adventure. Wylie had the legal issue between Anne Proctor and Bemis on his mind but spending more than a week with his renewed Linda pleased him. Portia, in a bathrobe and holding a mug of coffee, waved to them from the back porch. There was a chill in the air, and she pulled her robe tight as they rolled down the driveway.

Their route took them through Pigeon Forge, Tennessee so Linda could visit Dollywood, but that was disappointing. It was late in the season; many rides were closed, and few people were on hand. The ride through the Smokies, however, was impressive. Oaks retained their leaves that glistened in the afternoon light, and the views of endlessly rolling blue mountain peaks from high points were spectacular. Emma enjoyed a rest stop every few hours and reveled in the generous assortment of new scents encountered. Black bear, gray fox and bobcat were unknown but deliciously familiar, carryovers from her ancestral past. She savored them until Wylie gruffly pulled on her leash.

They arrived late the next day at the Delano Hotel in Miami Beach where they stayed for two days. The weather was perfect, and the balcony of their room offered spectacular ocean views. Linda applied numerous coats of sun protection and absorbed vitamin D while Wylie, thin skinned and bereft of most of his hair, kept to the shade and read the latest thriller on the Times best seller list. Emma was not allowed on the beach, but they walked her along the palm-fringed streets, where she assessed the size and breed of dogs that had gone before.

The languid days roused amorous feelings for the couple, and Emma spent half that night penned in the bathroom while her two favorite people made noisy love. As a reward upon her release, she could sleep at the foot of the king size bed. Life had never been so good.

The tires of the Cadillac crunched across white gravel as Wylie maneuvered the car to a parking place under dusty palm trees by the Anhinga Trail section of the Everglades National Park. There was a place for Emma to obtain relief near the trail, but she was required to wait in the car as Linda and Wylie explored the park.

As they waited for a lecture about the animals and birds in the park, Linda wandered to a low stone abutment separating visitors from a large watery area dotted with hummocks of grass and low shrubs. She concentrated on a group of anhingas drying their wings in a low tree, white speckled cruciforms against the brilliant azure sky. Wylie approached.

"Listen. Don't lean too far over the wall. I'm not sure it has had breakfast yet."

A large motionless alligator, perhaps twelve feet long, smiled at Linda from the other side of the wall, not five feet from her. She looked down and involuntarily stepped back from the wall. The alligator made a distant rumbling sound and Linda saw its nostrils ripple as air escaped. Feeling less exposed, she observed the huge reptile more closely. It lay partially submerged in the water, its tail obscured by grass and reeds. Massive teeth were clearly visible, eight ivory daggers protruding on each side of its snout. Shiny gray scales reflected sky and water, giving the beast an indigo hue. She gazed at it for some moments as Wylie joined her, held her hand and looked at the alligator.

She noticed fluid oozing from the animal's eye. An orange butterfly with black markings balanced itself just below the eye and sucked the liquid through its slender proboscis. The insect nourishing itself from such an unexpected location fascinated Linda and Wylie.

"It's a monarch," said Wylie. "Probably tanking up before it makes its way down to Mexico."

The butterfly repositioned itself on dainty feet and shifted its feeding tube. Coincidentally, the alligator, which had been motionless for hours, swiftly pushed itself forward on stubby feet and with a mighty flick of its tail slid into the water. For a moment, it seemed the butterfly would be stuck to the beast as it submerged, but it flew above the water and made a lazy arc toward yellow flowers along the bank. A hapless turtle became the alligator's breakfast.

The couple continued along the trail, observing the hundreds of anhingas, ibis, herons, other waterfowl, turtles, fish and dozens of alligators smiling peacefully among red mangroves and royal palms. Fluffy anhinga fledglings festooned low trees like shaggy tennis balls while young alligators waited below for one or two to lose their balance and tumble into a white toothed, pink grave.

"This is very nice," said Linda, "what with the little museum, the shop and facilities. And this paved trail with all these wonderful creatures. I am so glad we came."

Wylie also enjoyed the visit. However, he was thinking about the balance of nature and the way this microcosm reflected an idealized view of an environment's essential elements. Human management of the wetlands, he knew, threatened many native species. He did not share those negative thoughts with Linda.

"Yes, it is a beautiful and interesting place. I'm glad we came, too. But we better let Emma have another walk now. She has been cooped up in the car quite a while."

They continued along the Everglades Parkway, also known as Alligator Alley, at a steady sixty miles per hour. The road ran straight as a bowling alley through the Big Cyprus National Preserve, and many alligators were visible along the alley's broad shoulders. As the car sped along, Emma dashed from side to side on the seat behind Wylie, smudging the back windows with nose prints. Linda took in the passing scenery. She rested her left hand on Wylie's thigh.

"Hun, you having a good time?"

"Absolutely. I haven't felt this well rested in months."

"I wish we had thought of this sooner."

He recognized the "we" really meant "you." He admitted to himself that she was right. Without nagging daily chores, pesky e-mails and unanticipated interruptions, the past few days exploring with Linda reinforced their physical and emotional bonds. There was no question that she was a happier person. By the alchemy of adult relationships, that made him happy too. He had almost forgotten his cancer. Happiness might not be a cure, but it was an effective treatment.

"You're right, Sweetie. Sooner would have been better, but this isn't so bad."

Until this week, he had never called anyone "Sweetie." It just came out one day, unbidden, and Linda seemed to appreciate it. He began to sprinkle the word over his daily comments.

"We've been driving for a while now. How about we stretch our legs and let Emma do her business?"

That was fine with Linda, and Emma got her first solid whiff of alligator. What a wonderful place she was in.

That afternoon they stayed at an attractive motel in Naples and enjoyed a seafood dinner with a bottle of good Sancerre. Emma joined them for a walk as the sun set across the ocean and Linda cried out with delight when she thought she saw the legendary "green flash" just as the sun sank below the horizon. Wylie missed it but was happy for Linda.

As they prepared for bed, Emma took her customary position near the foot of the large bed, hoping that she would be permitted to hop up and stretch out just before they extinguished the light. Wylie and Linda were barefooted and in pajamas. Suddenly Emma left her post, moved to the corner of the room by the desk, and showed great interest in the black plastic paper basket there. She growled and clawed at the confined space behind the basket.

Wylie came to her just as she nosed aside the basket and began to sniff the baseboard. As he reached to pull her away, she recoiled as though shocked by electricity and cried in pain. Linda comforted the dog as Wylie turned on the desk lamp and searched the area where she was injured. He saw a black spider almost three quarters of an inch long moving away from the light toward a small fuzzy ball that Wylie assumed was its nest.

The receptionist responded immediately to Wylie's call. Spiders were serious business in Florida, which was home to four species of widow spiders. A maintenance woman arrived within minutes carrying a hand vacuum and a flashlight. She located the spider and its nest and prodded it with her gloved hand.

"Yeah, it's a southern black. Got the full red hourglass. Don't know how we missed this bugger. Lucky you didn't step on it. They pack a wallop."

She adjusted the nozzle on the vacuum and sucked the spider into a transparent container.

Linda held Emma around the neck, trying to calm her. The pain and shock were a new and unpleasant experience, and she was shivering, looking from Linda to Wylie for help.

"Better get that dog to a vet," said the woman. "I'll get you some ice in a bag to put on her nose. That will help with the swelling. Nice dog, too."

The motel manager located a veterinarian for Emma, and Linda held her on her lap in the back seat of the Cadillac, pressing the ice bag to her nose, as Wylie drove.

Apparently, it was not rare for dogs in the area to get spider bites on the nose or feet. The veterinarian sedated Emma and gave her the appropriate anti-venin. The doctor supposed she would have swelling and some pain for a few days, along with itching. However, she was not in danger and would make a full recovery.

Returning to the motel, Linda pointed out that Emma had saved them from potential danger. She hugged the groggy dog.

"You good girl! God knows how you located that black widow, but your daddy or I could have stepped on it instead. You are such a good girl. You are our heroine."

Emma accepted the accolade graciously and yawned a mighty dog yawn. Her nose was sore and swollen but that was all right. Her humans were okay.

The return trip to Middletown was uneventful, and the trio arrived in excellent spirits. The motel with the black widow spider did not charge them for that night's stay.

Some days later, when Wylie returned from a walk with Emma, Portia waited for him in the kitchen, sipping a glass of wine. As Wylie joined her, she described her visit to the Merson compound with Grover and how pleasant his parents were – even with all that money.

"Sounds like things might be getting serious with Grover," he suggested.

"I think he wants that, but I'm not sure how I feel about a stronger commitment. After all, I have always been taken care of by my dad, and you, and now Grover wants to step into that role. I want to try being on my own and see if I can make it without some man's support."

"I understand how you feel," he said. "but there is no doubt you will be successful at whatever you do. You are gifted."

"Thanks for that. But I detect a bit of bias."

"Gee, you noticed."

They talked more about events at the law school and Andrea Popov's ascension to the New Anglia assembly. Portia reported that Grover had been rewarded for his hard work during Pert Pewtree's campaign by a promotion to chief of staff, the youngest in the state.

"Bright future for that boy, right?"

"Yes. I think so."

Wylie made a mental note to arrange a lunch or dinner with young Grover. His interest in him was fortified by a recent conversation with Senator Pete Rowe who referred to him favorably in connection with a project involving Congresswoman Pewtree. It wouldn't hurt to get to know a potential grand-son-in-law better.

Porrie changed the subject.

"You know, I'm really enjoying the industrial property rights class with Professor Forster. We're studying 35 USC 161 right now, dealing with what is patentable, and I was thinking about your case with Anne Proctor. Could something have been overlooked, what with all the scientific discussion about genetic engineering, stealing genes and such?"

"You know that isn't my field. What's your argument?"

"It's simply that naturally occurring plants, in the absence of any breeding or genetic engineering, aren't patentable," she said. "If those seeds Anne brought back from Peru are from plants that grow in the jungle there, they can't be challenged by anyone."

"It's just a thought," she added.

Damn, thought Wylie, there it is. The simple concept overlooked because everyone was focused on arcane minutiae. Portia provided the best argument he had heard in months. Of course, this was the way to proceed.

He stood and kissed his granddaughter on the forehead.

"Brilliant, my love. Brilliant."

The lawyers dealing with the Patriot Act were located on the sixth floor of the same building where Mary Smith had her office. The attorney most familiar with Title II of the Act dealing with surveillance procedures was Cameron Crasskey, a dedicated public servant of middle age who partook perhaps too much of his daily bread. Crasskey required a special office chair to support his more than three-hundred-pound girth and, contrary to popular belief, he was neither merry nor jolly. In fact, his longtime association with criminals and miscreants of all stripes gave him a somewhat sour outlook. He grumbled a lot.

He was the only lawyer in their section who could recite the actual words the ten-letter backronym, USA PATRIOT, stood for. Uniting [and] Strengthening America [by] Providing Appropriate Tools Required [to] Intercept [and] Obstruct Terrorism Act of 2001. He wished he were creative enough to fashion such an astute acronym.

Marshall Aldo Rechnitz worked with Cameron, who retained the growing file on what he called the Middletown eco-terror group ("METG" for short). That file contained the information about the group obtained by Etta Sporelli from Myron Ng and summarized by Randi Fochik. There were also two ominous memoranda prepared by scientists on Fochik's team that predicted dire results from the introduction of glyphosate-resistant milkweed.

The file also contained chronologically arranged reports from Aldo Rechnitz regarding the activities of Elizabeth Pendleton Crangle and Jerome Hastings. Further, as Title II of the act permitted the suspension of numerous civil liberties and second amendment constitutional rights, copies of e-mails and telephone calls to and from the METG filled folders on Cameron's desk.

While Cameron had a perfect understanding of what was allowed under the Act's surveillance procedures, his knowledge of what constituted unlawful actions under the Act was somewhat fuzzy. Terrorist conspiracies to blow up a bridge or building were one thing, but a group of citizens working on a horticultural project designed to support butterflies was quite another.

He could argue that their actions constituted a conspiracy, which was thwarted by the apparently benign purpose of that conspiracy. However, Rechnitz' last report contained circumstantial, hearsay information that the Crangle woman and Hastings had actually released the seeds into air space. If so, this was definitive action and demanded a response, if only he could properly categorize it under the Act. Surely there must be a fingernail hold of an idea that could serve his purpose.

He reviewed the Act carefully. Clearly, it disapproved of the dissemination of terrorist information and materials, and it permitted heavy penalties. Recently an American cleric in Yemen had been blown up by the American government for inciting terrorist activities and disseminating such information on the internet. So, Dissemination might be the theory on which to base a case, if only he could liken the seeds to, say, pamphlets extolling the virtues of self-immolation by airplane or suicide vest. That was a tenuous argument, however.

He reread the papers prepared by the Bemis scientists. They referred to millions of acres of glyphosate-resistant milkweed hindering the nation's agricultural industries at unimaginable cost. In his reading, Camron overlooked Footnote No. 36 that noted in small print the existence of numerous glyphosate-resistant weeds and Bemis' work to introduce other herbicides. He began to devise the flawed theory that the imminent destruction of segments of the country's agricultural industry was tantamount to a terrorist act. In his experience, cases had been argued successfully on less.

He shifted his bulk toward the computer by his desk, highlighted the Warrant form on the drop-down list and began filling in the names of the METG members. The arrests would be made because of their conspiracy to disseminate materials designed to impede and disrupt the agricultural industry of the United States of America. That had a solid ring to it, he thought. Tomorrow he would assign two of his marshals to make the arrests. In the meantime, he extracted a handful of chocolate peanut butter cups from a desk drawer to consume while he reviewed his handiwork.

Bitsy Crangle was close to the deadline for completing her monthly gardening column. For a while now she was much more interested in being with Jerome Hastings than in passing on her horticultural knowledge. But she always honored her commitments and, now, just after Thanksgiving, she was in a cubicle on the second floor of the Courier-Times building drafting her column on a legal pad before typing it into the computer. Most of the column was completed, and she was laboriously typing the words from the legal pad to the newspaper's database. As she finished typing her unfavorable comments about the Colorado blue spruce's culture in New Anglia, a burly man wearing a string tie and leather jacket appeared beside her desk. He showed her a bright golden badge.

"Is your name Elizabeth Pendleton Crangle?"

"Yes," she admitted.

"Ma'am, I have to ask you to come with me. We need to ask you some questions about milkweed seeds."

Chapter 10

DECEMBER

Middletown Courier-Times

Mastering your Garden

By Elizabeth Pendleton Crangle

This is the joyous month in which we celebrate our redeemer's birth, even though there seems to be evidence that he was born in July. It is also the time of gift giving, so consider gardening-themed items to delight friends and family. Consider a miniature bamboo rake to attack the debris under shrubs, or permanent identification tags. A lovely bud vase will always be appreciated, as would cut-and-hold pruners for the rose garden next summer. Garden gloves and a kneeling pad could be fine stocking stuffers.

Looking out at the two dustings of snow we had reminds me that almost all physical work in the garden has ended for the year. However, if you plan to purchase a live Christmas tree, this is the time to find the spot and dig the hole to place the ball after the holiday. And, please, try not to succumb to the non-native live evergreens. Take the Colorado blue spruce, for example. In our area, it is highly subject to Rhisosphaera needle cast, a very common fungal disease that causes needles to turn brown and fall off. The disease spreads from the inside out and from the bottom of the tree up, and there is no known cure. Eventually the tree dies. Why would anyone sell a Colorado tree in New Anglia?

Editor's Note: Unfortunately, Ms. Crangle was unable to complete this month's column. As reported elsewhere in this issue, she was arrested at her desk in our offices on suspicion of dissemination under the Patriot

Act. We trust this matter will be cleared up before next month and our dear friend will create another wonderful gardening column.

Anne

Wylie spent almost two hours that morning with Andrea Popov and the outside patent counsel she contacted after Wylie passed on Portia's insight about the unencumbered use of things found growing in nature. According to counsel the law was clear. The difficulty was in establishing and documenting that the plants grew in the wild and confirming that they were the same as Anne Proctor's super plants. And that they had never been subject to genetic engineering.

"That's a very tall order," noted Andrea.

"Unfortunately, that is the kind of proof necessary to thwart Bemis' accusations," said the patent attorney. "Otherwise, the matter will hinge on the conflicting claims of scientific experts hired by both sides. In my experience, that will be costly, time consuming and probably unsatisfying to both litigants. Also, it will be difficult to find a trier of the facts whose eyes won't glaze over the first time someone explains how plants are engineered genetically".

Having provided the benefit of his counsel, the patent attorney prepared to leave, reminding Wylie and Andrea that he was always ready to proceed as they wished. Goodbyes were exchanged.

"Well, at six fifty an hour I'm sure he will be glad to proceed," said Andrea. "Wylie, I hate to say it, but perhaps we should give in to Bemis for the time being and see what the Justice Department can find to bludgeon them with later. I don't see a clear conclusion to the super plant problem in the absence of better information about the plants' origin. And that may be impossible to develop. I am inclined to accede to their requests for the time being."

Two of Wylie's personality traits combined to make him challenge Andrea's proposal. He was an optimistic person, made more so by the reestablishment of a harmonious bond with Linda. Consequently, he saw most obstacles as interesting challenges to be surmounted – and he was usually right. Second, he found it virtually impossible to accept defeat in the pursuit of a client's interests. Dammit, Anne Proctor may have been a little off base in importing her magic seeds, but there was no way the draconian demands by Bemis were either right or fair.

Further, it appeared that the super plants could be of great benefit to agriculture generally, and Bemis should not be allowed to deprive the larger community of them. He felt a kick of adrenalin. He was ready for fight, not flight!

"Before we take a final decision," said Wylie, "let me quiz Anne Proctor about the time and place she found the seeds in question. Surprising as it might seem, I have experience and contacts in Peru, where she obtained the seeds."

"Really?"

"It's a long story."

"Some other time, then. Talk with Anne and get back to me."

That afternoon he found Anne at Van Poppen farm scrubbing out plastic pots and sterilizing them with a chlorine solution so they could be recycled in the spring. He suggested they talk in a quiet corner of the building. Glad to be relieved of the scrubbing duty for a while, Anne removed her long rubber gloves and followed Wylie to a makeshift kitchen where they both prepared a cup of tea and retired to a table by a window where snowflakes dusted the corners of the panes.

"If I understand it correctly, the big question about the seeds is their 'provenance?'"

"Yes, that's pretty much it, "he said. "If we can show that the plants your seeds came from occur naturally, Bemis' claims fall by the wayside. Their case evaporates. But, you know, this whole thing has focused a lot of attention on their own shady practices. They might well regret opening this can or worms!"

"But, Wylie, how on earth do we prove the seeds are all natural?"

"Go to the source."

"You mean go to Peru?" she asked. "Go to that crazy little town on the Amazon?"

"Exactly."

"Boy, that's really a long shot. It was such a long while ago."

Wylie had heard similar objections from his cronies at the weekly pinochle game, Portia, Linda and, he suspected, Emma as well. She seemed to cover her eyes each time she heard the word "Peru." However, thirty years before, he had a great adventure in Peru. In one of the defining moments of his life, he and his daughter, Mercy, Portia's mother, had to flee from angered communist guerillas and government thugs across the high Andes.

Wylie sensed the possibility of another Peruvian adventure – hunting for super plants in the dense jungles of the upper Amazon. True, he was thirty years older and not as spry, well balanced or strong as in his forties. But, except for his "touch" of cancer, he was fit, and he certainly had the spirit to undertake a new mission.

"You are probably right," he admitted. "It may be so, in my case that there is no fool like an old fool. But, if those seeds showed up in the Iquitos market all those years ago, they must have come from the local area. In my view, it is worth the slim chance of finding where they came from to avoid a long drawn out and certainly costly legal argument with the Bemis people. Anyway, I've never been along that part of the Amazon before. I think it would be a great way to avoid the New Anglia winter."

"What can I do to help?" she asked.

"Well, to begin with, I would like you to come along. You have precise knowledge of the plants and could certainly help identify them."

"That's so, but it would still be looking for a needle in a haystack. And the expense..."

"Not a big issue. Ms. Popov has given me a stipend to act as her counsel on a fact-finding visit to the jungle."

Lost in their own thoughts, Anne and Wylie gazed at the snow falling on the stubble of the cornfields out the window. Anne decided the only part of what Wylie said made sense was a return to the warm and steamy pleasure of the tropical forest during a cold January.

Wylie's ancient rolodex files had migrated to the "contacts" folder on his computer where, later that afternoon, he searched for Rodrigo Weschler, the son of his old friend from Lima. Weschler Senior had been the leader of a business conglomerate in Peru that formed a joint venture for mineral and petroleum development there with Wylie's American client. During the negotiations leading to the completion of that venture, he and Wylie became friends. Weschler supported Wylie while he and Mercy were in danger. He had probably kept them from being killed.

Wylie maintained contact with the Weschler family over the years and flew to Lima for Wechsler's funeral, which occurred a few months after his divorce from Mavis. Rodrigo, known to his American friends as "Rod," had succeeded his father as head of the family businesses and had employed Wylie from time to time for help with stateside business dealings. His friendship with the younger Weschler continued.

By the time Wylie located Rod's telephone number and written out the questions he intended to ask, it was evening – too late to call. He would wait until tomorrow.

Their arraignment was uneventful. Winston, Freddy C., Bitsy, and Jerome stood before Judge Marsh Thurgood. He considered them unlikely flight risks and asked for a five-thousand-dollar bond from each of them. Attorney Gatz was pleased, but Cameron was miffed. He argued that, given the serious nature of their offenses, such a low bond was insufficient. As a possible harbinger of the case's outcome, Thurgood stared down at the porcine lawyer.

"These people are charged with dropping seeds from an airplane, Mr. Crasskey. I applaud your creativity in shoehorning this into a Patriot Act violation. You will have an opportunity to justify that during the preliminary hearing next Tuesday when we consider Mr. Gatz' motion for dismissal for want of jurisdiction. Meanwhile, they will be home with their families."

Cameron thanked the judge, closed his oversized briefcase and clumsily made his way out of the courtroom. The defendants followed and surrounded Clem Gatz. Jerome was the first to speak.

"How come Myron didn't get arrested? Did he manage to skip town or something?"

"No, he is not listed as a defendant," said Gatz. "The prosecutor told me he had been granted immunity from prosecution, but he wouldn't say any more."

"Immunity? If you believe all those crime shows on TV that could mean he is working with the prosecutor."

"I wouldn't jump to conclusions," cautioned Gatz.

"Yes," added Bitsy, "that's not fair to Myron."

Because Myron was a cooperating witness in the Bemis matter, he received a broadly defined immunity from prosecution regarding all activities relating to, among other things, his work at Van Poppen farm. Although Myron's name came up as Cameron reviewed Etta Sporelli's information about the eco-terrorist group, his grant of immunity precluded him from being charged as a member. Although relieved of avoiding another legal entanglement, Myron now worried about how he would explain his "good luck" to his notorious eco-terrorist friends.

Clem Gatz had a cool head for business. Over the years, he fostered a relationship with the University Law School under which he employed senior law students, at a favorable hourly rate, to assist in legal research. The arrangement avoided the expense of hiring full time associates. Now that he had secured the release of his four "eco-terrorists," he required prompt help in dissecting the jurisprudence about the Patriot Act developed during the past decade. To that end, he contacted two talented students on the law journal and decided to offer temporary employment to Portia Venezia, who had impressed him during a job interview the previous spring.

Intrigued by the nature of the case, all three accepted this part-time employment. When they appeared at his office the next afternoon, each received a copy of Cameron Crasskey's criminal indictment and his offers of proof, including the memoranda from Bemis' scientists.

They retired to Clem's conference room and began to read the materials. One by one, they began to chuckle, and then laugh.

"Talk about bootstrapping! He put his argument together with spit and bailing wire!"

"Dissemination? What next? Indict dandelions for losing their seeds."

"That's not bad. We could probably use that in Clem's brief."

The gleeful band deconstructed the indictment and assigned research. Portia agreed to parse the Patriot Act and depose Bitsy Crangle and Jerome Hastings. The other two would contact Winston and Freddy C., research the footnotes buried in Bemis' scientific papers, and create the first draft of the brief.

Jerome spoke with Gatz' assistant on the telephone to confirm their meeting. The young woman who knocked on their door did not fit his preconception of a female Perry Mason. Slim and attractive, she explained that she worked with Clem and needed to understand their involvement in the milkweed project, learning exactly what happened on the morning when the seeds were dispersed.

She was thorough and charming as she questioned Bitsy and Jerome who warmed to her. During a break in the questioning, as they enjoyed a hot drink, Portia noted that her grandfather was a Master Gardener like Bitsy and wondered if she knew him. Of course, she did! They shared many days on the help line. He was such a nice man. So, she was his granddaughter. How nice for her!

As Portia began to outline the legal tack they planned to take, Jerome interrupted.

"I'm no legal eagle, but it seems to me this whole thing is a crock. Big chemical companies are genetically engineering their seeds to a fair thee well, and then they charge farmers who plant the seeds through the nose. Their objective is to make big profits. We are "guilty" of engineering the seeds too. Just cut out the middleman and sowed the seeds directly. And our objective was to save the monarch butterfly. Like I said, it's a crock."

"What he said!" offered Bitsy.

Portia added a few more notes to her tablet.

"Certainly, that will be a part of our argument next week," she said. "The more we dig into it, the flimsier their case appears. Clem is considering charging the government attorney with prosecutorial misconduct. There are strong indications that he is in BIG AG's pocket and is pursuing this on their behalf. That is not the way the system should work."

Bitsy and Jerome were temporarily relieved by her comment, but after Portia left, and they returned to the kitchen for coffee Portia's comments caused them both to relive the moments that they were arrested.

"Nothing like that ever happened to me before," said Bitsy. "I was really scared. Those two big men bundling me in their car and taking me to be arraigned…" She put down her coffee and shook away the chill growing between her shoulders.

Jerome reached across and took her hand, offering words of comfort, telling her he was unconcerned.

But it was a lie. He tried not to show it, but each time he entered the courtroom he battled a feeling of impending doom. This thing could be really serious.

Rayseen Jackson carefully considered how to respond to the e-mail notice that she would be terminated at the end of the month. During her six years of employment with Bemis, she received exemplary annual reviews that resulted in generous pay increases. The statement, in the e-mail, that her position had become "redundant" was nonsense. She was a team leader with heavy responsibilities that could not easily be transferred to someone else. Moreover, she noted that a position strikingly like hers was listed as available on the company employee openings list. Not "redundant" then, she thought

Her thoughts lingered on George Stirrup's discomfort and angry words when she followed up on the need for documentation in the Malimsa tax issue. Is it possible that she was being punished for that? Had she inadvertently become a whistle blower?

She needed to look deeper before her time was up.

As a diligent General Counsel, Simon Targle frequently informed members of management not to put anything into an e-mail that they wouldn't want to see on the front page of the Washington Examiner, or its web site. George Stirrup ignored this advice as he created the network of ownerships intended to confuse anyone trying to understand who was a Malimsa investor. There were exchanges of e-mails with a banker in the British Virgin Islands and a solicitor on the Channel Island of Guernsey.

No fool he, he carefully deleted all those damning messages from his desktop computer. The corporate main frame and the two arrays of backup systems buried in remote locations acknowledged the request for the deletion and saved those messages all the same. Rayseen was familiar with the backup system and knew how to access it. She spent an hour or so the previous afternoon looking at Stirrup's e-mail. Then she added more information to the thumb drive in her purse.

With more than a thousand employees at Bemis' headquarters complex, it was understandable why Lavitra Gascoigne could not exactly place Rayseen Jackson. She consulted the employee database, discovered the young woman's employment history, and noted that she was being terminated at the end of the month. Apparently, there was nothing wrong with her performance. She simply had the bad luck of finding herself in a redundant job classification. Lavitra was not looking forward to the scheduled meeting, which would probably be emotional. Unlike the cowardly termination procedures in other corporations, where employees were fired coldly by e-mail or during "conference calls," Lavitra believed that exit interviews, no matter how difficult, were her responsibility. She reviewed the folder containing Rayseen's termination package - weeks of pay after termination, accounting for 401(k) contributions, instructions for retaining medical benefits under COBRA, and outplacement assistance. It was a generous package for a midlevel employee.

The interview initially followed the expected path.

"Thank you for seeing me," said Rayseen. "As I told your assistant, I need to tell you about some aspects of my 'termination' that really bother me."

"It is natural that any termination might come as a shock," said Lavitra. "And I am always glad to have your input during our exit interview. But, dear, the main reason for our meeting is for me to go over various benefits you will retain even after your employment ends. Because of your excellent service, we have put together a generous..."

"Before we talk about that," Rayseen interrupted, "may I go over with you some other benefits that I've been thinking about? As head of human resources, you are probably familiar with them."

"Of course."

This was a novel experience for Lavitra. This cool young woman was trying to dominate the conversation.

"In my position as a team leader in the audit department I sometimes notice simple improprieties that I draw to the attention of various department heads. A few weeks ago, I discovered a sales tax problem that I discussed with Mr. Stirrup. He seemed very irritated. That surprised me, because I was just looking for a piece of paper to justify the legal avoidance of withholding state taxes. He cursed me and mumbled something about nosy bean counters."

"I see. Yes, Mr. Stirrup does occasionally come on strong."

"Anyway, I tried to follow up with Mr. Stirrup a week or so later. His assistant, who is a friend of mine, told me he ordered her not to let me see him. I thought that was unusual, so I began to look more carefully at the little issue that bothered him so."

"And you found something of interest?"

"Definitely. And that brings me to the other benefits I mentioned before."

"Not the company benefits I have in this folder?"

"No. These are bigger benefits."

Now, thought Lavitra, this conversation breaks new ground. She leaned across her desk toward Rayseen, closing the gap between them.

"I've learned that employees who expose tax fraud are entitled to thirty percent of the dollar amount involved" said Rayseen, "and that there is a whistle blower protection program administered by the Department of Labor that imposes heavy penalties for retaliation, like firing."

Lavitra closed the file on her desk and stared at the composed young woman sitting opposite. She rose and shut her office door.

"Say more about this. Are you telling me that you think you should have whistleblower status?"

Rayseen removed three folded sheets of paper from her purse and handed them to Lavitra.

"These represent the cash flow status of a little company called 'Malimsa' that purchases Klobber from our company. You will note that it is an extremely profitable company, having accrued profits of over two million dollars on sales of eleven million in just the past three months."

"Yes, I can see that. But, what does this have to do with anything?"

For the next forty-five minutes Rayseen Jackson described in minute detail her findings about Malimsa's tax avoidance scheme, the self-dealing of three top executives, including Geiger, (at that point, Lavitra almost pumped her fist into the air) and the diversion of profits rightfully belonging to Bemis. She explained to Lavitra that she had documentation to support those findings and passed on a flash drive with copies of the pertinent materials, including Stirrup's e-mail correspondence.

If the subject of their conversation had surprised Levitra, Rayseen was taken aback by the HR executive's response when she finished her report.

"You know, there is much more to this than your profiting from a share of recovered taxes. If this disclosure is handled the wrong way, it will not only be devastating to top management, but would also affect the lives of thousands of employees, the stock value of our 401(k)s, and the reputation of the entire company. This could be devastating!"

"I get that."

"Would you be interested in working together for our mutual benefit? See if we can't use your information to make needed changes and shake up management? A significant financial reward and a secure position could certainly be arranged."

"What exactly do you have in mind?"

"I'm not sure yet. There are so many possibilities. And, for you, they are all good".

Rayseen settled back in her chair, pausing to consider this unexpected turn in their conversation. Leaning forward, she said, "Just so long as I keep control of all the information I've gathered so far. I have it all in a safe place."

Both women realized there would be some time before trust was established between them, but each sensed the powerful benefits of working together.

"As a first step, how about I cancel your termination and assign you as an HR Director, reporting to me? And, to keep you out from underfoot, we'll put you on indeterminate medical leave, with pay. And Rayseen, a Director gets a bunch more money than you are making now."

"You'll confirm this in writing?"

"This afternoon."

"You've got yourself a deal, girl!"

As Cameron Crasskey rose to stand before Judge Thurgood, he wished that he had been able to enhance the charges contained in his initial complaint against METG. As he and an assistant prepared the brief supporting those charges, they came across the footnote in the scientific papers that diminished the argument that the miscreants in Winston Wu's group were preparing to singlehandedly take down the nation's agricultural industry. Clearly, their intent was to benefit the monarch butterfly, a desire difficult to paint in a criminal light. Further, as the brief offered by Clem Gatz and his team of researchers noted, there was nothing inherently unlawful about sowing seeds in nature, even genetically engineered ones. Portia had even come across a case from Missouri where a neighbor's inadvertent dumping of genetically engineered soybean seeds on adjoining property did not give rise to a cause of action.

Judge Thurgood was looking at section headings of Clem's brief, which rested next to Cameron's slender argument on his desk. Both attorneys stood as he prepared to comment on the briefs and Clem's motion to censure Crasskey for prosecutorial misconduct. The judge signaled the four defendants to take their seats and turned his gaze toward Cameron who stood beside his assistant at a table in front of the courtroom. Never a natty dresser, his bulk was encased in a rumpled navy-blue suit, a white shirt of questionable cleanliness and a red tie that curled upward at the bottom. The knot of his tie was obscured, from the judge's perspective, by the drooping flesh under his chin. Cameron looked warily in the judge's direction.

"Mr. Crasskey, I'm going to deal first with Mr. Gatz' argument that this case should be dismissed for lack of jurisdiction. That is denied. Parties are all resident and the seriousness of the matter places it within the jurisdictional limit. I fully accept that this court has jurisdiction."

The judge looked at Gatz.

"I now turn to the defense's claim that your office has engaged in prosecutorial misconduct. Bluntly stated, Mr. Gatz contends that, since your evidentiary materials are principally documents provided by various agents of Bemis International Group, you are acting on their behalf, and not as a completely independent prosecutor representing the government."

"Your honor..."

"Are you interrupting me?"

"I beg your honor's pardon."

"You don't have it."

"Yes, Judge."

Cameron experienced palm-wetting anxiety and wished courtroom etiquette permitted him to take his seat. Cool as the weather was, a puddle of perspiration collected around the waistband of his undershorts and threatened to trickle rearward and downward. He shifted his weight uneasily. Clem Gatz stood comfortably at attention as the judge continued.

"The term of art for Mr. Gatz' suggestion is 'hogwash.' Flimsy as your argument is, Mr. Crasskey, I believe it is offered in good faith and clearly within the purview of your charge as a public servant. While it is troubling that much of your information comes from a potentially tainted source, I nevertheless reject the suggestion that you have engaged in prosecutorial misconduct. You have dodged that bullet, Mr. Crasskey."

Cameron felt obliged to acknowledge that determination with thanks of some sort, but Clem Gatz interrupted.

"But..."

The judge directed a dyspeptic gaze at Gatz.

"Your 'but' is overruled. I shall continue."

Judge Thurgood looked at each potential defendant for a moment or two. They were an innocent looking bunch, he thought. From their worried expressions, it seemed obvious that they understood the potential gravity of the charges concocted by the prosecutor. It was time to put them out of their misery. He adopted a more benign expression.

"Mr. Gatz, your brief is detailed and persuasive. The research is well documented and your analysis of the act under which the charges are brought is thorough. It was interesting to discover that a magistrate in Missouri failed to find a cause of action for the dissemination of genetically engineered seeds in neighboring property. Mr. Crasskey alleges similar seeds were disseminated from an aircraft but offers only circumstantial evidence of such activity. In any case, that is a distinction without a difference."

The judge continued in that vein for another ten minutes, carefully delineating the ways in which the government's case refused to stand up to judicial scrutiny. One by one, the faces of the eco-terrorists began to show relief. Cameron Crasskey seemed to grow shorter and more spherical, like a blue serge toadstool. Judge Thurgood completed his analysis.

"So, this matter is dismissed, with prejudice. Defendants are free to go, and I wish you all very happy holidays."

The elated group bustled from the courtroom as the judge retired to chambers and the two attorneys bundled up their papers and prepared to leave. In a demonstration of legal fraternity, Clem shook Cameron's hand and Cameron mumbled something about "good win." Almost as an afterthought, Clem asked,

"Have you been in the judge's chambers recently?"

"No, not for a while. Why do you ask?"

"No particular reason. Have a good holiday."

Clem's question, of course, was designed to nag at his corpulent adversary. However, Cameron had no occasion to visit Judge Thurgood's office until well into the New Year. When he did, he noted new decorations on one of the walls. There were two handsome raised-glass frames exhibiting large, colorful butterflies resident in Merida, Mexico and the highlands of Costa Rica. The lovely azure blue morpho appeared in both frames. He couldn't be certain, but Cameron thought he spotted the black and bright orange wings of the monarch as well.

"Is that knee about healed up now?" asked Wylie.

"A twinge or two, but it's coming along fine," said the Senator.

As confirmation, Senator Rowe stood and walked from behind his desk to sit on the upholstered chair next to Wylie. Guilty that he had postponed a visit to his old friend for too long, Wylie had accepted the Senator's invitation to visit, stay overnight with him and Sunhee, and enjoy a Christmas performance at the Kennedy Center. A shower of fluffy snowflakes fell on his cheeks as he made his way to Pete's office, and he welcomed the offered tumbler of Glen Morangie as the two friends began a chat that lasted for almost two hours.

During that time, Wylie outlined the story of Anne's super plants and explained his plans to visit Peru again in January. Pete wrinkled his nose at that news.

"Last time you were there, as I recall, you were a real troubleshooter – trouble and shootin' all the way, and you and Mercy damn near got yourselves dropped off the side of a mountain. Wylie, you are just a glutton for punishment!"

"Not at all," he said defensively. "This will be just a little exploration in the Amazon jungle looking for vegetables. It's just a vacation from the Middletown winter, and we will have local guides to lead us through the waterways down there."

The Senator remained skeptical.

Wylie explained further.

"You remember Don Weschler from Lima? He came up to visit about fifteen years ago, and you arranged a visit to the Capitol?"

"Yeah. Nice man. Lovely wife."

"Well, he's passed on now, but his son, Rod, recommended a guy in Iquitos to help with logistics for the visit. Rod called him a trustworthy gringo named Paul Beaver who runs jungle lodges with his wife, Dolly. She's from Iquitos and well connected. Rod says they are tight with many of the local communities along the Amazon and are highly regarded. Beaver works out of Florida, and I talked with him last week. He sounds okay and has set everything up for our arrival in Iquitos in two weeks. I'm excited!"

"I understand," said Pete. "You're just as audacious now as you were fifty years ago. But, Wylie, you were saying something about documentation and evidence?"

"Yes, well, on the off chance that we do find the source of Anne's super plants we need clear evidence of the discovery and their existence in nature. We will need that for any legal proceeding and to convince the patent examiner to confirm that Anne's plants in no way infringe on genetically engineered plants. As I said when we talked last week, I was thinking some astute politician sitting nearby might have some idea about how we could do that."

The Senator laughed and slapped Wylie's knee.

"Wylie, did you know that a wild goose chase was originally a kind of horse race? That was before it meant a dumb fool thing to do. You know that?"

"Pete, subtlety was always your strong point."

"Glad you remember that."

At that point, Zelda Barnickle arrived with more refreshments. Having consumed his quota of scotch, Wylie pointed to the tea tray, and. Zelda poured tea for both.

"Well, there's a real sharp girl working with me. Graduate of LSU. I talked to her about your problem and she figured a senior member on the staff of the Associate Commissioner for Patent Examination Policy would be a reliable observer. There is a feller there about ready to retire who, it seems, would love a jungle boondoggle. So, if you can afford another seat on the bus, he's willing to go. Name is Fritz Gumbach. Here's his stuff."

Pete handed Wylie Fritz' curriculum vitae. Wylie nodded appreciatively to his friend. As usual, he never failed Wylie when needed.

The following day, after spending a pleasant evening with Pete and Sunhee, Wylie returned to Middletown on the Acela Express. As the train sped north through snow-dappled towns and countryside, he reviewed the particulars of his planned visit to the Amazon jungle. Linda, still leery of flying, understood the necessity for Anne Proctor's presence on the planned expedition. After all, Anne's visit to Iquitos years ago set in motion the need for a return. In any case, Linda's newly rekindled feelings of warmth and affection for Wylie, along with the fact that others would be along, melted her concern. Yes, it was all right. No, it really would not be a problem. Really. Not a problem. Anne should go.

However, Anne did not agree to join the expedition until Linda, herself, called and urged her to go. Assured, Anne Proctor began to organize clothes for the trip. She knew that the weather would be hot and humid.

Andrea Popov offered a few thousand dollars in "fees" to help subsidize the trip. Wylie, knowing Anne had limited means, refused her offer of a financial contribution and prepared to invade his retirement savings to cover trip expenses. That was, until Portia proposed she and Grover join the expedition.

She pointed out that it was her suggestion to locate the plants in the wild, and the timing of the trip coincided with her winter break from law school. Grover, always keen on adventure, also wanted to come. He offered to document any findings with his high definition recorder and fund the rest of the trip with part of his quarterly check from Merson Holdings LLC. Wylie readily agreed. Aside from the financial support, he looked forward to spending some time with a likely grandson-in-law.

There would be six people involved in the search. Rod Weschler insisted that his son, Domingo ("Sunny"), accompany Wylie's group. Rod well remembered the difficulties Wylie experienced on his last extended visit to his country and knew that Wylie's Spanish was weak at best. Sunny had graduated with a degree in petroleum engineering from the University of Colorado in Denver four years earlier and was familiar with the Iquitos region. He was more than willing to help his father's good friend and, being a free spirit, thought bushwhacking through the jungle would be a pleasant change from calculating collapse strength of casing streams and downhole static pressure in Lima.

Paul Beaver explained that he would make available not only the hospitality of their two lodges in the Tamshiyacu-Tahuayo Reserve but would assign one of his most experienced guides along with two helpers to support Wylie's group. In fact, Paul and his wife, Dolly, expected to be in Iquitos when they arrived to give personal attention to their needs.

So, thought, Wylie, there will be at least six of us on what Pete Rowe thinks is a wild goose chase. Was this whole thing getting out of hand? Was he inviting failure?

What the hell, he thought, at my age I am entitled to a bit of folly. And failure no longer had the sting of earlier years. Sometimes, he recalled, failure was a stepping-stone to self-awareness and later success. Should he, now in the last quarter of his first century, still look for stepping-stones? Not so much, he thought. Winning remained paramount. Let's plan on finding those damn plants!

The members of the milkweed group were elated and in a generous and forgiving mood. Bitsy suggested they invite Myron to a small party of celebration to commemorate their escape from the clammy clutches of Cameron Crasskey and the Prosecutor's Office. Her suggestion was sincere, but she also was very curious about the reasons behind Myron's avoidance of prosecution. Jerome offered to host a brunch at his apartment and call Myron.

When Jerome called, Myron had just returned from the meeting with Mary and their mother. Irma, for all her ferocious coaching capabilities, was almost as diminutive as Mary and could not restrain herself from hugging her daughter for what seemed to be half an hour. She rocked her back and forth, as though to compensate for the times she could not do so in the past and, within moments, both women were in tears, wordless. Myron also wept "for happy," as his mother finally said, and the reunion continued for hours.

The amazing coincidence that brought Mary and Myron together was discussed and considered to be divine intervention, a mystical blessing designed to bring comfort and contentment to Irma's remaining years. Mary provided details of her upbringing in the Smith family and spoke lightly of her higher education and current job. Irma detailed the story of the family's arrival in the United States and identified all the relatives Mary had yet to meet. They began to outline a program of visits. For a while, they were caught up in the details of planning when, as though a curtain had dropped, discussion ceased.

Light in the sunny room seemed to dim and the two women looked again at each other. Irma beckoned, and Mary went to her, was held and rocked again. Irma whispered French and Vietnamese words in her ear and tears again rolled down Mary's cheeks. A long disused bond was reformed, and Mary, orphaned no more, felt a bursting in her chest. She was with her real mother.

Myron was describing the emotional visit to his wife when the telephone buzzed.

"That you, Myron? This is Jerome. What you been doing, man?"

"Oh, Jerome. I'm fine. Been kinda busy."

"Listen. Bitsy, Winston, Freddy and I want you to join us for brunch tomorrow. At my place. We're celebrating getting the long arm of the law off our necks. Come on over, okay?"

"Well..."

"Yeah, come on."

"When is it?"

"Tomorrow. Eleven in the morning."

"Jerome..."

"Good. You know how to get to my place?"

"Well..."

"Okay. So, what you do is..."

And Jerome offered directions to his apartment. Myron scrambled for pen and paper and scribbled down the directions. Since he asked Jerome to repeat part, Jerome believed Myron would come.

Mercy and her husband celebrated Christmas with Wylie, Portia and Linda. Wylie helped Linda decorate the condominium with electric candles in the windows, a smallish Christmas tree and a large lighted wreath on the front door. A fine dinner was arranged and "fun" presents exchanged. This year Wylie did not receive the usual gifts poking fun at his advancing years. No glass to hold his teeth at night or Depends for bladder control. The pall of his cancer discouraged those, and he received an alpaca scarf and woolly earmuffs for brisk morning walks with Emma. There was no mention of his condition.

He, in new scarf and earmuffs, and Mercy took Emma for a walk Christmas morning.

"Dad, Portia says she is going to Peru with you."

"Right."

"I can't forget what happened last time, and how dangerous that was. I mean, they were going to cut you into little pieces! Promise me you will take care – don't do anything foolish."

"Sweetie, this is a totally different thing. There are no bad guys involved. Not high Andes – Amazon jungle. Not just the two of us, but a whole expedition. And we will have an experienced guide. I am looking forward to having a little fun while we are there."

"Yes," she said. "Portia filled me in on the details. But, listen. You're not a youngster anymore. You need to take it easy."

Wylie bridled at that. Walking every day, watching his diet, doing all things in moderation, he felt as well as he had twenty years ago. And he resented being lectured to by a woman he had and diapered and powdered as an infant. They walked a while in silence, except for Emma's excited yips at the scent of a squirrel or deer.

"I doubt that this will be my last hurrah. Let's consider the trip to Peru my penultimate hurrah. I'm pretty sure I have at least one other hurrah left in me."

"Okay, dad."

Mercy took her father's hand and held his arm tightly to her side. You'd think by now, she mused, I would know better than to challenge him.

By old habit, they matched their steps, one to the other, and continued their walk in the crisp Christmas morning air.

Myron was surprised that he had to give his name to the gatekeeper at the entrance to Jerome's compound. He was surprised there were a gate and a keeper. They did not fit with his image of scruffy Jerome on his shiny Indian motorcycle, the only vehicle he had ever seen Jerome drive. As he followed the broad roadway winding toward Jerome's home, he resisted the impulse to turn around, to avoid this meeting with the group he had supported for almost three years. Freddy C., perhaps the member of the group he was closest to, had called two weeks ago to offer a ride to the arraignment of the eco-terrorist group. Myron demurred, saying he was involved with "other things" and didn't have to go at that time. Certainly, the members of the milkweed group were eager to hear from him. Myron was afraid that today's celebration could result in his ostracism from the group.

Jerome decided he would have "help" for the occasion, and two of his assistants were pressed into service through the application of a very generous tip on top of their Christmas bonus. A young woman took Myron's coat, and another offered him the choice of a bloody mary or a kir royale. He almost took both to steady his nerves but settled for the kir royale to find out what it was.

Bitsy was settled next to Jerome on a large couch near a fireplace flaring resin from fir logs. Winston and Freddy stood nearby, in animated conversation. The two young women waited to offer drinks and tidbits before serving Jerome's idea of brunch.

Bitsy rose as Myron entered and walked quickly to him, gave a little hug and said how glad she was that he came. The others offered their greetings, and the conversation turned to the wintry weather, how they celebrated the holiday and anything but their recent legal entanglements. The elephant in the room sidled to a position next to the fireplace and waited, patiently. Jerome finally prodded the beast.

"So, Myron, what magic did you use to avoid having to go to court with us? Our attorney told us you managed to get immunity from prosecution. Nice going."

"Yeah," said Freddy C., "you missed all the fun."

Myron was grateful that Mary had provided advice, in another context, that helped him answer Jerome's question.

"Well, I don't want to be mysterious about it, but I am going to be a witness for the United States attorney. It involves some things going on at Van Poppen farm. To protect me down the line, they offered me immunity and that somehow applied to our milkweed project as well. But I can't say anything about this thing that I am being a witness for. If I did, I would be in real trouble."

"Oh."

"But, really, I didn't have anything to do with your case. Never spoke with the prosecutor or anything. It certainly was a relief that the whole thing was dropped."

"Tell me about it!"

The others were now standing around Myron. Their curiosity had been only mildly satisfied, but they understood that Myron probably could not add more to his explanation. In any case, their legal issues were behind them, and the milkweed project was successfully concluded. There was little interest in pursuing a new venture to thwart 2,4-D. Certainly, the monarch butterfly would be well supplied with sustenance for at least a few more years. None felt a sense of urgency. Even Winston Wu was content, at least for the moment.

He moved closer to Myron and placed a friendly arm across his shoulders.

"So, we are all glad that you are with us, and I hope whatever legal stuff you are involved with is soon resolved."

He clinked Myron's almost empty glass with his.

"Here's to a great holiday, to good friends and a job well done!"

"Yeah, what the hell. It's Christmas, okay?"

Glasses were refilled and one of the assistants informed Jerome that brunch was getting cold. They moved into the adjoining dining room to sample the cornucopia of delights Jerome called his "little brunch." From smoked salmon to beef wellington to crepes almandine to truffled quiche, they moved around the table and settled on chairs. There was something about joining together in a holiday feast that rekindled the atmosphere of purposeful friendship they enjoyed while pursuing the milkweed project. Myron lost his nervous concern and laughed with the others when Jerome recalled the time when the cabin of his little aircraft filled with granules of perlite and Bitsy instantly aged ten years with the white stuff covering hair and eyebrows.

By early afternoon, there were signs that the marathon brunch was ending. Freddy C. tried to conceal yawns behind his napkin and Bitsy became tipsy, nodding and giggling as she clutched Jerome's arm. To Jerome it seemed the right time to deliver his announcement.

Taking Bitsy's hand, he said, "I want you three friends to know that this young lady and I are engaged to be married this spring. Ms. Crangle has agreed to make me the happiest old man in the county."

The party rejuvenated immediately. Toasts were exchanged and compliments provided. A spring wedding! How wonderful!

Bitsy glowed.

At Christmas Dick Geier was alone.

Of his four former wives, only one remained in contact, and that was through infrequent discussions about his only son's progress, or lack thereof, in pursuit of employment. He detested nepotism but, in the end, he probably could find work for his son at Bemis – far away from his location.

Priscilla announced that she would be taking her five-year-old daughter to visit her grandparents in South Dakota for the holidays. He had received holiday dinner invitations from George Stirrup and Frank Edger but turned them both down. He was in a solitary mood.

So this is how it is, he thought. A Jewish Christmas. Eat Chinese food and go to a movie. He scoffed at the thought and lit another cigarette as he looked through the expanse of glass surrounding his penthouse apartment at the glowing yellow lights of the city below and the deep blues of the hills beyond, receding into the late afternoon dusk.

He must have dozed. The acrid smell of scorched wool filled the air, and he saw the glowing fibers where his cigarette had fallen on the sleeve of his robe. There was momentary panic until he saw the partially full bottle of beer beside the chair. That extinguished the smoldering fabric. The unpleasant odors of charred wool and stale beer coupled with the sticky wetness along his left side caused him to feel unclean. He disposed of the ruined robe and took a shower, managing a cigarette as he dried himself.

He dined on cereal and bourbon. The television channels burst with cheery or maudlin Christmas dramas, and he clicked through them until he found the replay of a college basketball game. He settled deeply into the overstuffed leather couch and toasted the players with his glass.

"Merry Christmas, motherfuckers.".

Soon after Wylie and Mercy finished their walk with Emma, Mavis appeared to deliver little presents for her daughter and granddaughter. She arrived as Wylie and Linda were discussing Emma's care while Wylie was in Peru on what Linda called his "expedition to the lost pole." Linda had agreed to extend her hours at the hospital during Wylie's absence to help train a contingent of Philippine nurses recruited for their skills and knowledge of English. Portia, of course, would be with Wylie. Feeding their dog would not be a problem, but it would be virtually impossible to take her for a walk during daylight hours.

Although Mavis concentrated on ignoring Wylie and chatting with her female descendants, her peripheral hearing picked up the conversation in the kitchen. Since the Emma matter did not seem to be resolved as she prepared to leave, she turned to Linda.

"I overheard you talking about finding someone to take Emma for walks. I have free time and I could use the exercise. If you'd like I could come over and walk her in the morning. Unless there's a blizzard or something. You know."

Linda disguised her surprise with a broad smile.

"Oh, that would be so helpful. You sure you don't mind?"

"No. I'd be glad to do it."

Mavis patted the dog's head as she left the kitchen.

When informed of the proposal, Wylie wondered. Doesn't sound like Mavis, he thought. Maybe she's changing. That would be nice.

Chapter 11

January

Middletown Courier-Times

Mastering your Garden

By Elizabeth Pendleton Crangle

I'm certainly pleased to be able to write the column again this month. You might have noted in last month's paper that government agents arrested me and charged me with dissemination under the Patriot Act. Fortunately, Judge Thurgood refused to believe that dispensing seeds from an antique Cessna violated the Act. He also told the overweight prosecutor that "dissemination" was not a recognized crime under any statute and dismissed the charges with prejudice. Fortunately, I was represented by fine young student lawyers, especially Portia Venezia, at the University Legal Aid Society. They helped my lawyer, Clem Gatz, with my "case." He says the ruling means that they must leave me alone from now on.

Here we are in January, looking at snow-covered fields and piles of seed and garden catalogs on the chair by the fireplace. Many of the seed catalogs are promoting "Heirloom" vegetable seeds of many types. Before you give in to nostalgia and look for peas like grandma used to grow, remember that plant scientists have been isolating the best qualities of many veggies, and hybridizing plants for many generations since grandma planted her peas. Corn, tomatoes, peas, beans and other favorites have improved greatly in flavor, texture, size, etc., and organic seeds are readily available to the home gardener. Order some of them for your garden this year.

About marking catalogs: I never seem able to find pages where I have turned down the corners. A stack of sticky notes marks pages where I've found seeds of plants I can't do without this spring. While it is too early to plant any seeds, now is the time to make sure you have all needed materials for starting seeds – flats, potting soils, grow lights, markers, heat mats and fertilizer. Once you have decided what you need, order early to be sure that desired varieties are available. If you didn't find time to clean, oil or wax your garden tools last season, do it now. Also, be sure pruning tools are ready for early spring, when fruit trees and vines are trimmed.

When I look at my side yard covered with snow, I get colorful relief from the yellow and red-twigged dogwoods boldly showing their branches above the snow cover. I also enjoy the orange berries on our hawthorns and the bumpy maroon fruits still hanging from our Kousa dogwoods. There are still bright spots of red on our winterberry hollies and pyracantha. And the scruffy, peeling bark on the hawthorns and Kousa dogwoods is a pleasing change from the smooth maples and ashes along the tree line. The point, of course, is that we should not ignore garden features that enliven the drab winter months. All the plants I mentioned are extremely easy to grow in our region.

We are only about eight weeks away from the first crocus bloom, and I suspect the hellebores hiding under the snow in front are now ready to send their flowers toward the sun. Another remarkable spring plant is skunk cabbage, which you will see coming up near streams and in swampy areas in early March. This plant produces its own heat to help push through snow and ice. Its internal temperature can rise to 36 degrees Fahrenheit higher than the surrounding air temperature. When you learn things like that, it is understandable why gardening is such a popular and fascinating hobby!

God willing, I will be back next month – Bitsy

Edson

The people of the Amazon in Peru have a unique relationship with time. In the equatorial expanse of the jungle there is little change in weather, seasons, sunrise and sunset. Time seems to glide by slowly, accommodating itself to the languid ways of the region. Or, perhaps, the languid ways of the region reflect the almost imperceptible way that change occurs. The Amazon cares little about that. The river rises and falls twenty or more meters throughout the year, but the water level along its banks and on the hardwood stilts supporting homes by the river seems to move hardly at all from day to day. Dugout canoes glide almost effortlessly along, so low in the brown water that only surface tension keeps water from rushing in. The lush foliage challenges the observer to count its shades of green and obscures the way into the jungle, only hinting at the dark, impenetrable wall of intertwined vegetation just a few meters from the river's edge. Huge trees, buttressed by wall-like roots, gradually rise above the jungle to offer support to the thousand species of birds in the region. The strangler fig takes its time as it slowly reaches upward to surround a tall tree. It dies in its grasp and crumbles away, leaving the delicate latticework of the fig to host the birds that don't notice that the big tree is gone.

The people of the river live with slow time. If fish do not bite today, they probably will tomorrow. If the river transport boat is a few hours or days late, that becomes an opportunity to chat with the neighbors, maybe make new friends. If it rains too hard today to gather building materials from the jungle, it is fine to wait a day. Perhaps a cousin, uncle or sister will be here to help then. It is, of course, important to have a job, to make a living, to be able to buy rubber boots, cell phones, headlamps and machetes. However, the jungle offers much for the taking -- food, shelter, charcoal to sell, exotic barks to cure many illnesses. It is, of course, important to have a job. But even without a job, one can survive. There is no need to rush.

Outsiders who come to the jungle must learn about the different time along the Amazon. Of those who arrive in search of consolation, adventure, redemption or riches, the earlier they learn the better. Not all do, nor do they achieve their ambitions. Paul Beaver was one who did, though it took a while before he understood about the time.

He had a hardscrabble childhood in Nova Scotia before his family moved to Massachusetts. He realized that education offered opportunities for advancement and matriculated at the University of Chicago where he earned a Ph.D. in animal behavior. In 1977, he took a teaching position at the University of Washington in Seattle, looking forward to a secure and uncomplicated life.

Then his life came apart. He failed to gain tenure and lost his job, his wife, two children and home, almost simultaneously. His dog didn't die, nor was his car wrecked or his house burned down at the same time, but what happened was miserable enough to immerse him in abundant self-pity. An old friend offered him an escape route: a two-month sinecure studying the behavior of tropical birds and consulting on the construction of zoological exhibits in the green paradise of the Amazon. He arrived in Iquitos in the early eighties.

Not too long afterwards, Paul conceived of creating an adventure camping company – something for rugged individuals like him who sneered at the comfortable lodges and posh riverboats plying the Amazon. His idea was to offer the ultimate jungle experience, living off the land, sleeping on the soft and mucky bed of jungle floor, hunting and fishing. It was an obstinate rejection of the secure and comfortable life in Seattle that he was forced to abandon.

Realities of the tourist trade gradually asserted themselves, and the adventure camping company added primitive accommodations styled after the native homes along the river, and included meals, housekeeping and guides. Paul, however, continued to focus on the "adventure" part of his business and used his scientific background to learn and study the mysteries of the jungle. That changed when he employed Dolores Arevalo in 1992.

"Dolly," as she prefers to be called, is a diminutive dynamo with strong interests in environmental and social issues. She has powerful management skills. Paul wisely married her in 1994 and a daughter, Stephanie, was born a year later. Working together, the couple developed their adventure travel business, based in two lodges along the river. Paul concentrated on expanding the business and Dolly helped manage operations. They created a unique blend of comfort and accessibility to the wonders of the green paradise along the Amazon River.

Paul Beaver was the successful owner of the internationally renowned Amazonia Expeditions organization. The company offered its intimate jungle experience to visitors from around the world. After arriving in Iquitos, a motorboat carried them to a lodge located in the Tamshiyacu-Tahuayo Reserve, on a tributary to the Amazon. The original lodge now contained fifteen cabins of various sizes, many with modern bathrooms. Another lodge designated as an "ARC" – Amazon Research Center – was recently constructed. There major universities carried out primate research during the summer months.

In both lodges, kerosene lamps had given way to LED illumination powered by solar panels and, amazingly, a satellite wi-fi connection was sporadically available in the heart of the jungle four hours away from Iquitos. Both Wylie and Paul believed these locations would provide an excellent base to explore the remote areas of the jungle in search of Anne's super plants.

A factor in the success of the Amazonia enterprise was that the people Paul and Dolly employed shared their dedication to providing an appreciation of their green world. The principal guide whom Paul selected for Wylie's group was one of his most knowledgeable, at home in both the hustle and bustle of Iquitos and the silent and dangerous ways of the jungle.

Edson Montechristo Gonzales-Moro lived half his life in Esperanza, a village not far from one of the lodges operated by the Beavers. His early years were ragamuffin wild, running through the dirt streets of Iquitos with a band of other children, causing mischief and challenging mother love. When his father died, his mother could not work and care for all three children. As the youngest, Edson was chosen to return to Esperanza, the village where his mother's family lived. There he played with his many cousins and learned all the crafts and secrets of his surroundings. He attended the little school there but returned to Iquitos to rejoin his mother when it became time to begin high school.

He thrived in high school, especially in the introductory earth sciences courses. He grew tall and slenderer than most of his friends and dominated the field in football, Peruvian soccer. Girls liked him well. Perhaps too well, his mother thought, but Edson thirsted for learning more than easy conquests. He matriculated at Universidad Nacional de la Amazonia Peruana and learned more about the river, its flora and fauna, and the history of the green paradise that surrounded him. He studied abroad for six months, in Florida, where he learned English and the habits of the Florida manatee.

He graduated with honors and accepted a position as caretaker and assistant director at a government-sponsored manatee orphanage and research station in the outskirts of Iquitos. That was where Paul met him and persuaded him to join his growing adventure tourism business. Within a few years, Edson established himself as an expert guide and friend to the many visitors to his jungle. At the time Wylie and his group arrived, Edson was twenty-five years old.

Close association with Emma softened Mavis' desire to do away with her. Mavis succumbed to the soft and trusting eyes, the loving nudges, the eagerness to please that Emma offered to a human companion. The dog's behavior was not enough to forge a bond between them, but it served to insulate her from further thoughts of poisoning on Mavis' part. As promised, Mavis dutifully visited Wylie's condominium the first two mornings after he left for Peru to collect Emma and lead her on a walk through nearby roads. On the second morning it was cold and blustery, and Emma became unruly after sighting what she thought was a rabbit. After being dragged along an ice encrusted macadam surface and almost losing her balance, Mavis reconsidered her agreement to walk the dog. The next day she enticed Emma onto the back seat of her car and drove four miles to an enclosed dog run area sponsored by the township.

After navigating two steel mesh doors leading into the run, Emma, for the first time, entered a new three-acre world of canine excitement. Perhaps twenty-five other dogs of different sizes, ancestral persuasion and temperament raced over the snow-dusted field socializing in classic canine fashion. In an ecstasy of indecision as to where to begin, Emma raced from dog to dog, sniffing back and front to catalog characteristics only another dog would understand. She conferred briefly with one or two dogs about her size, then continued to explore the possibilities of the enclosure.

Mavis pulled her fur collar close around her neck, decided that Emma required no further supervision, and returned to the warmth of her car. She tapped the button to begin playing her Sinatra CD and returned to the fifties for a few minutes. Emma continued to play with other dogs, front legs stretched forward and head down before leaping up and crowding their faces. A large Airedale offered to play in a new way, mounting her with front legs locked around her middle. Emma thought little of it and pulled away quickly, racing ahead of male dogs that developed a sudden interest.

When Mavis returned to call for her, Emma was happily exhausted and gratefully retook her place in the back of the car.

Mavis glanced at the panting dog.

"Good girl. We'll do this again tomorrow."

Except for the times when snow conditions made it impossible to navigate the rural roads, Emma went to the dog run daily while Wylie was away. There would be interesting repercussions.

A wall of heat and humidity physically restrained the passengers stepping from the air-conditioned interior of the airplane onto the steps leading to the runway in Iquitos. Portia, the first off, recoiled as she entered the equatorial atmosphere of the Peruvian jungle. Grover, just behind her, said "Uuuf" as he encountered the dramatic contrast in the air. The only one in their group who did not react to the sudden change was Sunny Weschler, who had joined them during their layover in Lima. He had visited Iquitos numerous times and was accustomed to the abrupt change in atmosphere that occurred on entering the Amazon basin.

"You probably won't believe it, but you get used to the change quickly. In a few hours the body will adjust. You will be fine by evening," he offered.

Anne Proctor agreed. This was her forth visit to Iquitos, and she welcomed the tropical air. It was certainly more pleasant than the ice and cold of Middletown.

Fritz Gumbach preceded Wylie down the metal stairway, and the group made its way across the shimmering pavement to the small baggage area, waiting for the handlers to deliver their bags to the rickety conveyor belt. Edson stood beside the conveyor holding a clipboard emblazoned with "CYPHER." The board was superfluous as there was no question about the identity of the Cypher group. Edson wore the Amazonia Expeditions logo emblazoned with the distinctive image of the hoatzin bird, so his identity was not in doubt either. Wylie walked toward him, and they shook hands.

"Welcome to Iquitos. I hope you had a good flight."

"Fine. No problem. It's good to be here. Paul said your name is 'Edson.' Right?"

"That is how they call me."

"Please call me Wylie."

"Yes, Mister Wylie."

Pointing to waiting attendants, Edson said, "These porters will collect your bags and bring them to the van, and we will move to our office in town. Paul wants to meet you, and then we will have lunch before taking the boat to the lodge."

"Did Paul tell you about our mission here? About looking for those special plants."

"Yes. I 've been talking with other guides and people we know from villages along the river. There is some talk about special plants but, you know, many plants we grow here are different from those in the States. In any case, we know where most of the farms are and we will take you to them. Now, let's get your things together and go to our office."

Two rickety vans were needed for the journey into the center of Iquitos. Since the city was reachable only by plane or boat, cars and vans arrived by barge on the river, and the vehicles tended to be driven well past the point of exhaustion. Wylie, Anne and Fritz piled into one van while the younger members of the group rode in another. Their creaky caravan sped off past the airport and on toward the center of town, past shanty buildings, "almacens," little factories and shops. When they reached broader streets, three-wheeled motor taxis, scooters and carts that shifted and turned like schools of sardines in a bright ocean surrounded them. Glimpses of the green-encrusted river were visible between buildings. The vans stopped in front of a glass-walled office building from which two grizzled porters emerged to help with their luggage. The hoatzin bird logo showed on one of the doors.

Spying the wide expanse of the river through a corridor in the building, Grover and Portia walked to a balcony facing the little port of Iquitos. Grover raised his ever-present camera and began recording the boats cutting through the green aquatic plants solidly covering the inlet. Wakes of brown water followed the boats, soon to be engulfed by the green pennywort. The patchwork channels leading to the great expanse of the river beyond resembled ever-moving footpaths cut across a green lawn. Portia was enthralled.

"Green and wide and moving fast! This is fabulous. This is what I imagined it should look like," said Portia.

"Um," offered Grover, focusing in on a multi-hued motorboat loaded with firewood.

Edson checked all the bags to be sure nothing had gone astray and directed the porters to load them onto the speedboat that would take them to the lodge.

As they shouldered the bags, Paul Beaver appeared from an office down the corridor and approached Wylie.

"You must be the gentleman Señor Weschler told me about. Mr. Cypher?"

Wylie confessed that he was.

"It is an honor to host your group. Our people will do all they can to make your visit enjoyable and productive. I need to be in town for a few days and then I have business in the States, but I promise you that Edson will take excellent care of you. And, incidentally, Dolly is at the lodge for a few days, checking on supplies and working with the staff. I know she is looking forward to visiting with you."

Wylie thanked him and introduced the other members of the group. With that, Paul guided them down the street to a restaurant overlooking the harbor. He recommended a specialty – fresh fish from the river. There was lively and excited chatter. Anne sat next to Fritz, and they compared notes about their travels. Fritz, it appeared, was a widower and somewhat withdrawn. He was also very serious about his role on the expedition and joined Wylie and Paul as they discussed plans for exploration after lunch. Fritz came prepared with a topographical map of the region and made little notes on it as Paul pointed to promising areas. Paul relied on his extensive travels throughout the area, although he advised Wylie that he had never come across the plants he was looking for.

Sunny Wechsler was not a typical Peruvian aristocrat. His curly copper hair, bright smile and jet-black eyebrows confirmed his European ancestry. He and Grover were the same age, but that did not imply instant camaraderie. Sunny had flirted with Portia almost from the time they met at the airport in Lima, and Portia, charmed by his accent and good looks, seemed to enjoy it. His easy command of two languages and his stories about mineral and petroleum exploration in the Amazon basin interested Portia. Grover, not as much.

There were last minute words of instruction from Paul Beaver and wishes that they would have good fortune. Edson led them to a concrete staircase that deposited them on a dock where a cigar shaped boat was moored. Their luggage and supplies for the lodges were stowed in the stern. The captain, dark and rotund, offered to help the passengers find their places on the two-seater benches. Grover was occupied photographing close-up views of little boats cutting through the green vegetation, so Sunny handed Portia into the boat and took the seat next to her. Grover quickly stowed his camera but found himself sitting next to Fritz, in front of Portia and Sunny.

A sturdy roof covered the boat and transparent plastic sheets were rolled up at the sides, ready to be unfurled in case of rain. Paul had reminded them that heavy rains could occur at any time along the river, although the peak of the rainy season was in March and April. With all passengers in place, the captain started the engines and guided the boat from the dock toward the middle of the river at very slow speed. Edson sat in front, next to the captain. He found the microphone secured under the dash.

"Just settle in for about a four-hour ride to the lodge. When we get to the main channel of the river, Captain Jorge will open up our twin motors and you will not be able to hear me for a while. So, before it becomes too noisy, let me tell you something about the Amazon".

Edson gestured toward a point beyond the spit of land they were crossing to the broad expanse of the river.

"There is more water in this river than in any other river in the world, more than the Mississippi, the Nile and the Yangtze combined. Every second it pours more than fifty-five million gallons of water into the Atlantic Ocean. It begins as a little waterfall in our Andes Mountains and gets to be as much as forty kilometers wide in the wet season – at a place in Brazil many kilometers west of where it meets the Atlantic. Where we are right now is over thirty-seven hundred kilometers from the Atlantic. That's about twenty-three hundred miles. If you want to paddle there, at least you would be going down stream."

Jorge pushed the throttle forward and the twin engines roared, raising the bow of the boat a meter in the air. The boat skimmed over the water, creating a rooster tail wake. The group observed the passing drama on the riverbanks. Shipyards spewed fountains of sparks as welders repaired worn metal. Peruvian navy patrol boats painted battleship gray nosed toward the center of the river. A few residences with thatched roofs appeared, soon followed by banana trees, then the blurred emerald fronds of cultivated rain forest. Jorge swept close to the bank to avoid a flotsam of large floating trees and vines determined to snag propeller blades. Except for clouds squatting over the horizon, the sky was bright and clear. Wylie and Anne uncased sunglasses to reduce the glare on the river.

The roar of the engines and the sound of the hull slicing through the brown water had a calming effect on all the passengers except Grover. Anne dozed off for a few moments and rested her head on Wylie's shoulder. Fritz had never been in South America before, much less on the Amazon River, so the sights along the way fascinated him. As little children waved from tire swings suspended over the water, he was sure it was just for him. He waved back. The sound of the engines made it impossible for Grover to join in the sporadic conversation Portia and Sunny were having, so he pointed his camera toward the banks of the river to photograph passing scenery.

After about two hours, Edson pointed out that they were leaving the river and joining the tributary on which the lodges were located. The captain throttled back a bit to avoid swamping smaller boats and dugout canoes that appeared with greater frequency near the riverbanks.

Soon they arrived at a village located high on the bank of the river and a dock with steps leading to an official looking frame building. The boat pulled up to the dock.

"Police office. I need to show them the copies of your passports we made in Iquitos. Should only take a few minutes," said Edson.

Brown cherubs in shorts and tattered t-shirts climbed on the front deck to stare at the novel species in the boat. They smiled and called "Hola, "Gringo" and "Gringas" and pushed their faces against the glass windscreen. The captain handed out little candies and shooed them away as Edson returned.

Within the hour, they arrived at the lodge, raised high on stilts above the riverbank. A floating dock extended into the river and broad steps carried the passengers to the walkway that connected the cabins, dining hall, kitchen and outbuildings.

Dolly Beaver greeted them as one of the staff members handed out drinks made with jungle fruits. She was both gracious and efficient, welcoming the guests warmly and assigning rooms. Wylie received a single room with bath, and the two women shared a room with bath. The three other men were together in a large dormitory-like room adjacent to the common bathrooms.

The sun was already low on the horizon and dinner would be at six, at sunset. The travelers agreed to meet in the spacious dining room for cocktails at half past five and hastened to unpack their bags. Wylie, experienced in traveling light, was first to arrive in the dining area and discovered a refrigerator chest filled with large bottles of beer and soft drinks. Unfamiliar with either Cristal or Imperial beer, he decided to try them both. He was beginning his second bottle when the other travelers wandered in.

Under Dolly's tutelage, meals at the lodges were healthful, nutritious and made the most of jungle fare. They dined on fresh fish, plantain, beets, rice and something that resembled butternut squash. Desert was a chocolate cake prepared specially for Wylie's group. Other visitors joined in and there were friendly exchanges of information among all the guests. Later, as the LED lights blinked on to brighten the dining room, Edson and Dolly met with the Wylie Group to review the next day's activities. Dolly spoke first.

"For the first day's activities, we usually offer an early morning bird walk or trip on the river, and a walk in the jungle or trip to our zip line after breakfast. However, Paul explained that you are eager to locate specific types of plants, so Edson and I have begun to map out trips to areas that have farming activity. All are located near villages along the river."

Edson shone his headlamp on the wall map behind him. It showed a hundred-kilometer square grid with the lodge approximately at its center. He pointed to locations on the map.

"We have much area to cover, so we will split up into two groups each morning. Each group will have a boatman and guide – and I will be going with Mister Wylie."

As the two most familiar with the plants in question, Anne and Wylie would be in separate boats and, for the first morning, Grover and Portia would be with Wylie. Fritz and Sunny rode with Anne. That decided, they felt ready for bed. The clock in the room showed it was a little after nine in the evening.

As early morning mists huddled over the water by the lodge, two small boats with big motors awaited the Wylie group. Its members covered themselves with the latest brands of insect repellent, sunscreen and UV ray protective clothing.

Wylie wore a battered safari hat to help his few remaining hairs protect his scalp. Bottled water was secured in the boats and cushions fashioned from life jackets covered hardwood seats. They shoved off at eight in the morning. The boats traveled together for a while and then Anne's boat veered off to follow the left fork of the river.

Within half an hour Anne's boat pulled up to a single large home raised high on stilts and situated a hundred meters in from the river's edge. Like other places she had seen, the house was constructed completely from building materials taken from the jungle. Poles and narrow logs constituted the frame and flooring while different types of palm fronds created roof and siding. A verandah surrounded the home and a flock of chickens pecked busily under and around the home. Anne could see two pigs resting in a large pen behind the house and, beyond that, a sizeable cultivated area. She recognized banana leaves rising above the many green things growing behind the house.

Two small children with eyes like ebony saucers stared down at the peculiar people with the odd clothes stepping from the boat. Their mother appeared at the doorway and smiled at them, and a muscular man wearing faded blue jeans and rubber boots came toward them holding a machete. Sunny stepped forward to greet the man and they exchanged a handshake. Sunny introduced Anne and Fritz and the man gave each a little bow. Sunny seemed to be speaking about the weather and the condition of the river. Then he pulled two ballpoint pens from his pocket and pointed to the little children. The man grinned and accepted the pens. Sunny gestured toward the cultivated area and asked some questions that Anne vaguely understood as inquiring about the nature of his vegetables. Sunny spoke very rapid Spanish.

"He says, sure he has big and beautiful plants. Very big. He says you should come up and see them."

Anne and Fritz accompanied Sunny and the Amazon farmer to his lush field. There were cabbages, corn, soybeans and various melon-like plants Anne could not identify. The rows between them were covered with weeds, except for the places the farmer had addressed with his machete. The plants were robust, but no more so than well-tended vegetation at Van Poppen farm. She knew this would have been too easy, but she was disappointed nonetheless, as she returned to the boat and thanked the farmer for letting her see his lovely garden. The farmer beamed and helped push the boat back on to the river.

A senior partner from the most revered bluestocking law firm in Middletown sat across the desk from Frank Jones, prosecuting attorney. He had requested an interview on behalf of an undisclosed client to discuss a matter of "mutual interest." Jones knew the attorney to be serious and honorable and arranged to see him the next day.

"It is my understanding that your office has an interest in matters pertaining to the Bemis International Group," he said.

"Correct."

"And that your interest relates not only to industrial property rights but also to issues of anti-trust and similar business improprieties."

Boy, thought Jones, this man is well informed. He focused all his attention on him.

"Frank, my client is a highly placed executive in the Bemis headquarters. She has come across very sensitive information that points toward ethically suspect and probably criminal behavior on the part of the Chief Executive Officer and others. She is thoroughly disgusted by what she has learned and wishes to cooperate with your office to bring these people to justice. However, she needs this to be done in a way that produces little or no damage to the company's reputation and, incidentally, stock value."

"Of course," said Jones, "that depends on the facts at hand. However, you know this office has a reputation for discretion and evenhandedness. I promise that we will honor your client's concern."

"Very well. Now, as to matters of immunity..."

The two lawyers continued their meeting for more than an hour, as the attorney representing Lavitra and Rayseen unfolded the nature of activities engaged in by Bemis' top managers. Toward the end of the meeting, after obtaining proper assurances, he disclosed his clients' identities. Jones confirmed he would assign the matter to his most seasoned attorneys. He decided Mary Smith would lead the investigative team. Smart, feisty and ambitious. Yes, Mary would be right for this assignment.

The very cold shower water that poured over Wylie after his first day on the river became, after the first chilling moments, refreshing. He and Anne experienced mutual disappointment in their search, although they had both seen remarkable animals and birds as they coursed over various tributaries in search of super plants. Portia and Grover were not as invested as the older couple in the search for the mystical plants, and they were thrilled by the experience of the river and rainforest.

A half-tame woolly monkey named Dorilla hopped through their boat during the afternoon and ate little bananas offered by Portia. Toucans clattered at them and spider monkeys hung over them in the tall trees along the river. Male two-toed sloths smiled at them through green frames and pink dolphins popped up their heads and beaks, only to disappear beneath the dark waters. Grover tried to capture much of what they saw with his camera, and he and Portia looked at the days' images as Wylie joined them in the dining area for dinner.

Wylie and Anne were disappointed but, as Wylie said, they still had another nine days for the search. After that, Portia and Grover had to return – for school and work. The large beers tasted especially good that evening, an appropriate beginning for another meal in the rain forest, this time featuring chicken as primary protein. Dolly and Edson again briefed them on the next day's exploratory excursions, and Dolly advised that she would be returning to Iquitos the next day.

Exploration continued for another four days. Fascinating forest creatures, black-necked hawks, tiny gray bats, pigmy marmosets, scarlet macaws, scores of sloths and red-faced (English) monkeys crossed their paths, but each promising view of gardens and farms in the jungle proved disappointing. Each day the search expanded into new territory, and each day Wylie and Anne swallowed their disappointment and hoped the next would bring success.

After five days of touring the rivers in small boats, the three younger members of the group decided that they would explore the jungle on foot, beginning with the zip line Paul had helped build less than an hour's walk from the main lodge.

Trees in the jungle easily reach heights of one hundred and thirty meters. A grove of such trees provided the foundation for a two-stage zip line. Portia,

Grover and Sunny looked up into the canopy from the platform under the first stage. The smooth gray bark of the tree rose skyward, and its leaves obscured the launching area above. Several ropes dangled down toward them. Peter, their guide for the day, supervised two other young men who showed the young people from the States how to put on their harnesses. Then Peter showed the group how to ascend the ropes with the help of hand and foot held tubes with ratchets that one pushed upward and held. The prospect of learning a new climbing technique excited Grover and he was eager to ascend. Peter, however, suggested Portia go first, and a safety rope, held high up in the tree by one of the helpers, was attached to her harness.

She clumsily began to climb the rope, rose about fifteen feet and lost her grip. She began to slip downward. Sunny, standing beside the rope, reached upward and grasped each of her buttocks to keep her from falling. Grover, silently seething since he first met Sunny in Lima, snapped.

"Take your hands off her!"

"Huh?"

"You heard me. Take your goddam hands off her."

Portia recovered and, not knowing or caring who had stopped her fall, concentrated on pulling herself up. She was unaware of the controversy below her.

Sunny was about seventy per cent innocent. Mostly he acted as a Good Samaritan, but there was a part of him that anticipated with pleasure the sudden opportunity to grasp her firm female posterior, fleeting as it might be. He played the innocence card.

"What are you talking about? I was just keeping her from falling."

"Bullshit!"

Grover poked Sunny in the chest with a stiffened finger.

Sunny poked back.

Grover pushed with both hands.

Young men in their middle twenties, of whatever background or nationality, do not tolerate poking or pushing with impunity. Testosterone, adrenalin and the peculiar psychochemical reactions generated by poking and pushing incline young men toward battle. Sunny took a half step backward and proceeded to unleash a powerful roundhouse right aimed directly at Grover's head, specifically just to the left of his nose. Grover ducked, and Sunny's momentum caused him to lose his footing on the slick ground. He reached down with his left hand to cushion the fall. Unfortunately, a large black bullet ant occupied the spot where he placed his hand.

The bullet ant is named for the impact of its powerful sting, which is like being shot with a bullet. A potent neurotoxin venom causes extreme pain that lasts about twenty-four hours. In Sunny's case, it would be even more painful. He happened to be very allergic to venom from wasps and similar insects.

The ant opened its retractable syringe-like lance and injected its venom into the flesh of Sunny's thumb. Seconds later Sunny felt as though his hand, then his entire arm, were on fire. The pain was so sharp it literally took his breath away. Peter recognized the symptoms immediately.

"We must go back right now. The Hormiga Veinticuatro stung him. It is thirty times more potent than a wasp sting. We have some medicine at the lodge, but he needs to go to the hospital in Iquitos, fast. This is very serious."

Sunny became faint and began to perspire as pain and nausea immobilized him. Peter and Grover supported him under each arm and half dragged him to the lodge. The other two guides collected Portia and the zip line gear and followed them.

One of the women who worked in the kitchen located an EpiPen and injected the epinephrine into Sunny's thigh, and a staff member hastily collected his belongings. At this point, groans and curses were his principal mode of communication, but he managed to say goodbye to Portia as they bundled him into their fastest boat. He seemed not to notice Grover who also offered a guilty goodbye. The boat disappeared around a bend in the river. Two days later, he managed to send an e-mail to the lodge saying he felt better and was returning to Lima. He hoped they found what they searched for.

This all happened while Wylie, Anne and Fritz were on another fruitless excursion. When they returned, Wylie was very upset that his old friend's grandson was suffering as a direct result of his generous desire to help them on this trip. He expected to have a long conversation with Sonny's father when he returned home. Fortunately for Grover, Portia was not aware of the argument that precipitated Sunny's accident. She believed he had slipped and fallen.

Grover's feeling of responsibility was not so strong as to explain the details of the accident to her. That evening Edson, Wylie and Anne completed plans for another foray into the jungle. Time was running out.

The founders of Malimsa gathered in Dick Geier's office for their monthly review of operations, and to discuss plans for the current quarter. Severe winter storms had delayed some shipments from a mid-Atlantic warehouse, but Home Warehouse took that in stride. Their optimistic projections for revenues were adjusted downward a bit, but remarkable profits continued to flow into Malimsa's offshore accounts. That, along with the generous year-end bonuses received from Bemis, put them all in a jubilant mood. Although it was before noon, Geier uncorked a bottle of very expensive aged bourbon and poured for three. With drinks in hand, they toasted a prosperous new year.

"Now, what about that tax problem? That thing about not withholding state taxes properly?" asked Geier.

"Magically evaporated," noted Edger. "The girl that was digging into that was let go almost a month ago. Far as I know, it's a dead issue."

"Yeah, well, not so fast," said Stirrup. "My girl says what's her name, Ray something, got a promotion and is working over in HR. Haven't seen her around, though."

"We need to check on that."

Geier made a note on the pad by his desk to ask Lavitra about that. The men's conversation turned to other matters: basketball, hockey, and vacations in the sun. The bourbon tasted especially fine in the warm office that protected them from the sharp wintry blasts just outside the windows.

Four more days passed as Wylie and Anne scoured an ever-widening area along the net-like tributaries and streams leading through the jungle. By Wylie's count, they had visited more than sixty farms near the river. All supported robust growth, but there were no super plants.

Since Sunny's departure, Wylie encouraged Portia and Grover to treat the trip more as a vacation, and they went their own way, in the jungle, to nearby villages and on self-propelled dugout canoes. Grover showed Fritz how to operate his camera, and Fritz became the official cinematographer. There was nothing to photograph, however.

The day before they were to return to Iquitos, Edson guided the three toward another farm a short distance from the river. As usual, it had rained the night before and the ground was slippery beneath their rubber boots. The path was lined on each side by thin palm stalks bristling with sharp slender thorns. Wylie pricked his hand on one. It felt like a mosquito bite. Edson confirmed the thorns contained a mild irritant. They were all wary of the plants after that.

The farmer greeted them, machete in hand, and proudly showed them his two hectares of growing produce. His farm was larger than most and he sent much of what he produced to villages along the river. He had no super plants, although he thought he had heard of them once upon a time. They were north, he thought, somewhere north. Not too far, he thought.

Somewhat discouraged, Wylie thought that was where the wild geese were too, up north.

Returning to the boat, Anne lost her footing and began to slide backward toward the thorny palms. Fritz was just behind her and reached out to steady her, causing them both to slide inexorably toward the thicket of thorns. Gallantly, Fritz moved his body to shield hers just as Edson grabbed them both and saved Anne from puncture. Fritz was not so lucky. Buttocks and right shoulder contacted the thorns. They penetrated his light clothing and induced a prickly sensation that quickly blossomed into feeling like a combination of road rash and a poison ivy attack. Edson hustled him to the boat, bent him over a wooden bench and began to extract thorn tips with his fingernails.

"He'll need attention when we return to the lodge," said Edson. "We have a salve there that soothes the itching, but those little bits of thorns need to come out too."

This accident ended the day's exploration, and the boat returned quickly to the lodge. Anne offered to help Fritz who, after all, had saved her. She found a pair of surgical tweezers in her travel kit, and Edson handed her a can of yellow salve. She helped the grimacing Fritz back to his room and ministered to him. Two hours spent extracting tiny bits of black thorn tips from a person's posterior form a unique bond between the extractor and extractee. Wylie and Portia noticed Fritz and Anne holding hands the next morning. Well, thought Wylie, not all excursions in the jungle end badly.

Unfortunately, their explorations in the Tamshiyacu-Tahuayo region were ending badly. Though they gained deeper knowledge of life along the great river and an appreciation of the wonders of the rain forest, they had not beaten the odds. There were no super plants. Glumly, Wylie watched the lodge recede as the long boat began the return trip to Iquitos. They were scheduled to take the early afternoon flight to Lima.

The office manager in Paul's office had bad news. The day's flights to and from Lima were cancelled. She was not sure whether the cancellation was caused by mechanical difficulties or bad weather, but she had secured rooms for the night in the fine hotel on the city square, the El Dorado Plaza, just across from the old Eifel opera house. They offered a very favorable rate. No doubt, they would be flying to Lima tomorrow. Or, certainly, the day after.

It was only a few blocks from the office to the hotel, and Edson was organizing transportation for them and their luggage. As bags were being moved to the back of a truck, a teenager on a motor bike pulled up to the curb next to Edson. They engaged in animated conversation for a few moments and the boy pulled away into the mainstream of traffic. Edson seemed lost in thought. He turned to Wylie.

"That boy, he says there are extra good plants in the finca of his father's cousin. He says it is not far from here, near where the Bora Indians live. That is only about forty-five minutes from here by boat."

Though discouraged, Wylie was prepared to grasp at a final straw. However, he was concerned about the others' reaction to this news. Portia spoke up.

"So, we have free time and my guidebook says the Bora Indians are well worth a visit. We could just look at the farm and then visit the Indians. They try to maintain their old customs and welcome all visitors."

She glanced impishly at Grover.

"And the girls all dance topless."

Anne, who overheard the conversation, suggested it would help round out the day. She certainly wouldn't mind another short trip on the great river.

Early afternoon found Edson and the Wylie group at water's edge near a large covered market area outside Iquitos. By a miracle of communication, the boy on the motor bike awaited Edson by a water taxi. Edson negotiated a price for the trip, and they descended into the boat. Within the predicted forty-five minutes, it had passed a sign announcing the location of the Bora Indians and sped onward to an inlet the boy pointed out. Drooping leaves obscured the narrow path through the weeds, and the driver poled the boat toward shore. A wide path carved by machetes led inland.

They followed the path as it sloped gradually upward and, after a ten-minute climb, came upon a well-tended grove of plantains. The forest opened wide beyond those trees, and the boy pointed to ordered rows of green plantings nearby. Wylie and Anne rushed up the slope for a closer look.

They could have been Anne's plants growing at Van Poppen farm in early August: evenly spaced, weed-free rows of lush soybeans and corn. She could see four or five ears protruding from each corn plant. She kneeled next to a row of soybeans. They were her super plants – they really were.

Wylie walked with Edson to visit with the farmer who appeared at the side of the field. He wore blue jeans, a cream shirt and, a New York Yankees baseball hat. He greeted Edson and Wylie, and Edson engaged him in conversation for a few minutes before gesturing to Wylie, saying the Señor had a pregunta or two.

After some careful questioning, it was clear that these plants came unaltered from the jungle and had for as long as the farmer and his grandfather could remember. Yes, there were similar farms in the north. But, ironically, the land in the area they had been searching was too low for these plants. Certainly, the farmer would be glad to make a gift of some of his plants. He had seeds they could take as well.

The farmer refused money, but sheepishly whispered to Edson that he greatly admired Wylie's wide-brimmed Tilley hat. He handed it to the farmer who was pleased with how well it fit. The farmer offered Wylie his hat in exchange, and Wylie became a Yankees fan for the afternoon.

Grover was photographing everything he could about the farm: its long rows of plantings, close ups of ears of corn, soybeans and all the other varieties growing beyond the first rise of the forty-hectare fields. Fritz busied himself taking measurements, snapping pictures with his little camera, and obtaining soil samples for future study. Anne and Portia helped where they could. Their investigations continued until the long shadows of evening crowded the fields. They stood together and Edson looked a question at them. They nodded in ascent. It was done. It was good. Hell, it was fabulous!

The plane flew to Lima the next morning. A jubilant Wylie drew Edson aside as they waited in the airport. He praised the young man for his excellent qualities as a guide and friend and thanked him profusely for his services during the past two weeks. Then he pressed his smart phone and ten crisp one-hundred-dollar bills into his hand.

"If you wish, I will arrange for you to visit us in the States. But not in the winter. Too cold."

"I thank you, Mr. Wylie. You are a good man. But, maybe winter, yes? I would like to see snow."

"Of course."

The old and young men embraced in proper Peruvian style, a strong abrazo.

The plane climbed swiftly toward the clouds, and the morning sun glinted off the river, giving it the appearance of gold flowing through wild green walls. At eighteen thousand feet, the jungle seemed a closely-knit mat of vegetation with little hint of human presence. What secrets do you still hold, thought Wylie. But we unlocked one of them. Yes, by God, we did.

Chapter 12

February

Middletown Courier-Times

Mastering your Garden

By Elizabeth Pendleton Crangle

We are now a month and a half past the shortest day of the year, and the days are growing longer. Now it is time to begin work on our garden!

Most of us by now have accumulated a little pile of seed packets, either in the mail or from the local garden center. Since many of you have experience in starting seeds, I'll make only a few comments about annual flowers you might start in February. Review the information on the packets about the proper conditions for germination. Some seeds require light, others darkness, and soaking in water or refrigeration could be involved.

The proper temperature for starting these seeds is between 65- and 75-degrees Fahrenheit. I use electric warming pads to maintain temperature, and always water from the bottom so as not to dislodge the seeds. In the past, I have been bothered with damping off (a fungus causes wilting at the base of the seedling), so I am extremely careful that all containers and tools are sterilized before planting. I use my faithful alcohol spray bottle.

The flowers I start in February are petunias, snapdragons, dahlias, impatiens and begonias. There are many others, as you can tell from seed packets, but these are my favorites. Remember that the seedlings derive their energy from food stored in the seed. Fertilizing them before transplanting makes them leggy and weak.

For our fruit growers, this is the month to prune peach, plum and cherry trees when temperatures are above freezing. If pruning is done close enough to normal bloom time, you can force the pruned branches to bloom indoors. Last year I was lucky enough to have cherry and forsythia branches blooming together on "leap" day.

For those concerned about intensive maintenance of fruit trees, don't forget the two fruits recommended by Master Gardeners in our area – blueberries and raspberries. So long as your soil is slightly acid and well drained these are easy and very productive plants, and there are wonderful varieties available. The berries called Early Blue are plump and ready for eating in June, and the orange raspberry varieties are sweet as honey in August. With a little planning, you can enjoy handfuls of berries every week all summer.

There is not much to do about lawns this month but be sure to service your mower (or deliver it to a professional service provider). There is nothing more frustrating than failing to start a balky mower when your grass is four inches high in April. Last year I experimented with "frost seeding" where I seeded bare spots early in February and waited for frost heaves to open the ground and let the seeds fall in. Weather conditions were just right, and I was rewarded with abundant new grass. That is a good, lazy approach to seeding, but lawn expert friends say I was just lucky. They prefer proper overseeding in the fall.

It is a good month to look at last year's garden pictures and remember, in dull February, how glorious June will be.

Yours for blissful gardening - Bitsy

Bitsy II

Randi Fochik was fully prepared for Dick Geier's next question and opened his PowerPoint presentation on the boardroom screen. A composite photograph of corn plants growing in a laboratory and in experimental fields in Florida filled the screen.

"In our continuing analysis of the 'Proctor Plants,' we used the meristem system to clone many different varieties and subjected them to tests in the lab and field. By way of background, you probably recall that wheat, like rice, pollinates itself so that their seeds breed true to the hybrid parent. Not so with corn. It is the slut of the vegetable world and breeds indiscriminately with whatever pollen first reaches the corn ears. The reason we include a 'doomsday' gene in our corn is to be sure that benefits of our genetic engineering do not disappear through indiscriminate breeding. With our wheat, of course, it is to require the purchase of new, and possibly better, seeds each year."

"All right, Randi, we get it," said Geier. "What's your point?"

A new series of slides and graphs appeared on the careen.

"We have been working for years to develop a corn plant that pollinates itself -- it is a process called apomixes. Our interest is to find quicker ways of creating new hybrid plants once the parent plants have been genetically engineered. The thing is, the Proctor Plants seem to have this quality already. The damn corn plants are self-cloning!"

That caught everyone's attention.

"You mean those plants reject pollen from other corn plants?"

"Exactly. The golden stuff we see on the plants probably has something to do with it. That stuff, incidentally, also seems to thwart interest by non-pollinating insects like borers and such. Seeds from those corn plants breed true."

A fresh cigarette glowed under Geier's nose.

"Jeesus, any other disasters to report?"

"Well, on a way, yes. Pollen from the Proctor Plants' tassels that migrates to other corn plants in the vicinity tends to imbue those plants with 'noble' characteristics. We haven't had enough time to explore that aspect thoroughly, but our computer models indicate that, over time, entire fields of ordinary corn all would take on the character of the Proctor Plants."

"So, unless we are able to stop this a whole aspect of our business is S.O.L. Right?"

"Well, Dick, it may not be that bleak. No matter what, it would take a long time for all that to happen. And Klobber would still be used in lots of other applications. I think that…"

"Listen, a-hole," Geiger bellowed, "don't put lipstick on this pig. What we have here is a plant with abundant yield, kills weeds, resists insects and duplicates itself freely. If the press ever gets hold of this, our stock goes in the crapper. Even more reason to cut them off at the knees, put on a full court legal press. Simon, what's new in our negotiations with the University?"

Simon Targle pushed on the sides of a stack of papers before him on the table. Uneasily he cleared his throat.

"It is interesting you would bring that up, Dick. Just yesterday afternoon I received a call from the University General Counsel, Andrea Popov, inviting me to a meeting with their patent counsel, a fellow named Fritz Gumbach from the Patent Office, and a small-time local lawyer named Wylie Cypher who represents Anne Proctor. She said she had new information that would help conclude this matter. I will see her next Monday. I plan to include our patent counsel and one of my assistants in the meeting."

"So, is that good news? Are they ready to settle?"

"Not sure. It may well be."

The talk turned to other matters, but a feeling of unease pervaded the room. Lavitra Gascoigne maintained her composure, disguising her concern that the just discovered qualities of the super plants and revelations about top management's chicanery would seriously wound her company.

Grover and Mary Smith met occasionally for coffee or a beer to talk shop. It was an opportunity for the two civil servants to exchange information about their respective projects, work on developing their growing friendship and gripe about the less desirable aspects of public employment to a fellow sufferer.

Grover was the first to arrive at the Do Drop Out Taverne, roughly equidistant from their offices, and ordered a rasher of warming liquor to combat the slushy cold still clinging to ears and neck. Mary soon arrived, stomping moisture from her fur topped boots. She ordered a large cream sherry before sitting down.

"So, world traveler, sorta different here than in the jungles of the Amazon," she said as she

placed her cold hand on his cheek before sitting across from him.

"That's an astute observation. Must be why you're such a crafty lawyer," said Grover.

Banter seemed to be required at this stage in their developing friendship. It was difficult for both to be comfortable in a purely friendly relationship. At their age, the beating wings of Eros sometimes kindled embers of lust – which they promptly ignored. Grover was thoroughly committed to Portia, and Mary pretended she was completely committed to her job. After a few more months, though, sexual tension between them disappeared.

Their routine, during occasional meetings, was to pass on jokes recently arrived from friends via the internet, talk about non-confidential developments at their workplaces, touch on personal matters and, perhaps after two drinks, wax philosophical or seek help with domestic issues.

This afternoon Mary was glowing from more than the cold and her drink. She explained to Grover how thrilling it had been to reconnect with her "real" mother and meet the many relatives who looked like her. It seemed to her a fine idea to introduce her birth mother to her adopted mother, which had occurred the day before.

At first, it seemed the meeting would not go well. Mrs. Smith appeared in what she called her "grown up lady" outfit that included pearls, silk blouse, her best gray suit and matching bag and shoes. Mary's mother, who had rushed to lunch from school, wore a blazer over what appeared to be a t-shirt, tracksuit pants and running shoes. The two women quickly took the measure of each other,

(Poor Mary, having to put up with this overdressed prig. She's probably a Republican.)

(Poor Mary. How disappointing to discover this slovenly person bore her. How sad.)

For Mary's sake, Irma and Barbara maintained their best behavior, and the atmosphere over their dining table clouded over with small talk. Mary anticipated the possibility of a frosty first meeting between her two mothers and came prepared with an icebreaker akin to a Russian nuclear-powered one -- an album of her baby pictures. Between cobb salad and BLT, she displayed the little book. Barbara immediately began to describe, in detail, the scenario of each photograph.

"Oh, here's where she was scowling because a tooth was coming in; this is her christening dress – how adorable; that's after her cousin bit her on the finger; here's where Joe was playing horsey with her..."

Irma moved to touch two of the pictures, as though that tactile sensation would bring her closer to a time she never shared with her baby daughter. Soon she and Barbara were fully absorbed in the photographs and the stories behind them. Irma sought to know who the others were in the pictures, filling in her knowledge of her daughter's upbringing. The two older women were now on a first name basis, and Barbara began to understand the awful pain Irma felt in losing a child and the sublime joy in finding her again. How difficult it had to be to share her with another mother. There were hugs as they left the restaurant, and the two older women promised to get together again – soon.

All this Mary conveyed to Grover in a gush of words that permitted him to understand the gist of the encounter and appreciate Mary's current joy in her newfound expanded family. He winked and raised his glass to her.

"Let's hear it for friendly Asian-American relations! I'm really glad for you, Mary."

"Thanks. But, listen, now that's out of the way, please tell me about your trip to the Amazon."

Grover had explained the purpose of the trip to Mary before his departure, so his narration mainly involved specifics about the sights they saw, the people they met and, finally, the successful discovery of the super plants under cultivation in the jungle. He punctuated his comments by showing her photographs of the expedition on his iPad. Some of them were quite spectacular -- multi-hued sunsets over the great river, pigmy marmosets glaring into the camera, a close-up of a tarantula, and Portia feeding bananas to a woolly monkey.

"Oh, that's got to be Portia! She is very attractive."

Grover agreed.

"So, now that you have brassbound confirmation of those super plants growing in nature, what is next?"

"Well, like most things, it is not that simple. We have proper documentation of their existence in ancestral farms in Peru. There are movies, photographs and a careful analysis and report by this guy named Fritz Gumbach from the government Patent Office. The minute we returned, we passed on sample seeds and actual plants to the plant scientists over at the University. I learned today that their preliminary findings indicate no evidence of genetic alteration. The plants and seeds appear normal in all respects. They just have spectacular innate characteristics."

"So, what does that mean?"

"Once we have unambiguous confirmation of their unaltered state in nature, Portia and her grandfather, Wylie, say he can use that to blow Bemis International Group out of the water."

"Did you say Bemis International?"

"That's right."

"You didn't mention them before."

"Well, I didn't know about the whole thing before we left. Mainly, it was an excuse to spend more quality time with Portia… and to explore that jungle."

Mary sipped the remnants of her sherry and looked thoughtfully at Grover.

"I guess, at this moment, I am at liberty to tell you something about my involvement with Bemis International."

Her tone of voice and the fact that she hunched forward across the table alerted Grover that something of interest was to be disclosed. He pressed closer to her.

"My office has just completed a months-long inquiry into certain activities by members of Bemis' top management. We received incontrovertible documentation of management's wrongdoing from a very persuasive whistle blower, as well as information about competitive practices that seem to violate Robinson-Patman and Justice regulations. Just this afternoon an indictment was handed down, and we issued arrest warrants along with a *Subpoena duces tecum…*"

"Whoa!" demanded Grover. "Robinson what? And a poker game subpoena?"

"Sorry. I sometimes get carried away. What I should say is that Bemis is suspected of anti-trust violations, and we sent the F.B.I. over to their offices to recover computers and search for documents, e-mails and other similar materials."

"Okay. I get it. Looks like Bemis is in deep doo-doo."

"As they say, the spam has hit the fan."

In February of each year, the Middletown Master Gardeners held their annual meeting at a local country club. The chef there was known for using locally produced comestibles and promoting healthful meals. He even persuaded the club's managers to set aside a garden plot near his kitchen to grow his own organic vegetables, exotic lettuce and similar items not usually found in local supermarkets.

He was especially fond of the Master Gardener organization and enjoyed preparing unusual but nourishing meals for their annual meeting. He even prepared detailed recipes for the items served for future use by his guests.

The annual meeting differed from the monthly meetings in that it provided a relaxed social setting for members to enjoy each other's company, have a mid-day cocktail and accept recognition for their volunteer services. In a tribute to American volunteerism, the Master Gardeners were recognized for the hours of service provided in numerous outreach programs during the year. Over time, those hours accumulated into the thousands, with some of the "old guard" logging over five thousand hours. A county auditor reckoned each hour of service was worth $25.72, so the accumulated efforts of the group provided a substantial and valuable benefit to the county.

Each member wore, pinned or on a lanyard around the neck, a plastic identity card with name and affiliation. The volunteers with longest service stood out. Their cards were gold. Wylie's card was white, but the gold cards reminded him of the strange golden hue of Anne's super plants. He observed the same to her, leaning closer to her chair to be heard above the hubbub. Anne smiled her agreement. She had earlier learned from Wylie that Andrea Popov confirmed the satisfactory completion of all tests and studies relating to the plants they discovered in Peru. Moreover, they were identical to Anne's plants grown at Van Poppen farm.

That the super plants were found freely in nature destroyed BIG AG's claim of infringement of industrial property rights. Wylie told her how eager he was to meet with the Bemis' general counsel the next day. He smelled retribution in the air. Anne was simply very happy that she would be vindicated. Their conservation ended as the president of the group tapped on a microphone and asked the audience to settle down. Special recognition was next on the agenda.

After announcing the number of hours various members had contributed through volunteerism, she said, "And now we come to the selection of Master Gardener of the Year. The person selected is chosen for professionalism, dedication and the contributions made to our organization. As always, the choice is difficult, given the number of outstanding volunteers. But we chose a person who not only provided invaluable gardening advice to the public at large but was willing to risk prison in pursuit of a lofty goal. By unanimous consent, we give you Master Gardener of the Year – Elizabeth Pendleton Crangle, better known to us all as Bitsy."

Everyone did know Bitsy. If they failed to read her monthly gardening column, it was impossible to miss the recent newspaper and local television coverage of her exploits in support of the monarch butterfly. She even enjoyed perhaps not quite fifteen minutes of fame after being interviewed by CNBC news. Unfortunately, the interviewer mispronounced "monarch" as "mo-nark."

Two hundred plus participants applauded loudly as her invited guest, Jerome, stood to help Bitsy leave her seat and walk toward the podium.

Had it been two years earlier, she probably would have stammered a polite "thank you" and hastened to her seat with the engraved crystal vase that was her prize. Now, however, she reminded the audience of the plight of the monarch butterfly and explained that its numbers were dwindling partly because its host plant, the milkweed, was being decimated by liberal use of chemicals like Klobber. She described the work of her compatriots, individually named, and the thrill of flying with Jerome in his little plane to release life-sustaining seeds. She mocked the inappropriate application of the Patriot Act, noting its attempt to deny basic civil liberties. She even made a joke about narrowly avoiding water boarding. Bitsy concluded her remarks by describing how pleased and proud she was to be a member of their organization and thanked them for her award.

The applause continued until she returned to her table. As she passed her crystal award to others at the table for their examination, she frowned.

"Damn. I forgot to mention that my hero, Jerome Hastings, and I would be getting married in April," she said.

Bitsy and her intended tapped their half-empty glasses of white wine together and drained them in unison. To the others at the table it seemed a sign of a happy future together.

The meeting was not going as Simon Targle had anticipated. Since becoming Bemis' General Counsel, he was accustomed to being treated as though he was representing the eight-hundred-pound gorilla in the room – deference tinged with a dash of fear. In contrast, today he had been bombarded by one unsavory fact after another, beginning with Andrea Popov's statement that the University would not accede to any of BIG AG's demands regarding Anne Proctor's super seeds. In fact, the University was planning to set aside a large area of Van Poppen farm to propagate tens of thousands of scions and make seeds from the super plants freely available to researchers and growers alike. New evidence caused the University and Anne Proctor's patent counsel to conclude that the claims raised by Bemis were completely without merit.

"That's a very dangerous position to take," Targle advised. "Surely, you are aware of Bemis' long held policy of pursuing any infringement of its industrial property rights to the highest available legal authority until its position is vindicated. That is what we intend to do in this case."

"That is, of course, your option," said Wylie. "However, we have incontrovertible and thoroughly documented evidence that the super plants you are challenging are found freely growing in nature, unaltered, unadulterated and untouched by genetic engineers. Even Bemis must realize naturally occurring growing things cannot be patented."

Tangle's patent counsel, seated next to him at the conference table, leaned forward and whispered confirmation into Targle's ear. He frowned.

"Your simply making this statement is not probative, of course. Any such findings are subject to review by a trier of the facts and law."

Fritz Gumbach, who had been introduced as a Patent Office official, suggested that the Bemis team spend a few moments considering the evidence relating to the super plants. Reluctantly, they agreed.

He plugged his laptop into a projector cable and began showing a movie of the Peruvian farmer displaying his crop of plants remarkably like Anne Proctor's super plants. This was followed by close-ups of various plants – corn, soybeans, sorghum, beans, wheat and rice – all placed next to rulers showing their size.

"In the folders in front of you are affidavits from the team of witnesses, including mine, attesting to time and place of the discovery of these plants," said Fritz, "and other documents showing how samples of these plants were transported to laboratories at the University and independent testing groups. Federal evidentiary standards regarding the chain of evidence were scrupulously followed."

Targle was beginning to feel just a bit queasy. The meeting was taking a nasty turn.

Wylie then began reading from various statements offered by independent experts who had examined the genome structure of the plants found in Peru and confirmed that:

1) They conformed exactly to the structure of the Proctor super plants,
2) Their structure differed only slightly (and within acceptable standards of deviation) from standard heirloom plants grown in the United States, and
3) There was absolutely no indication of amending their genetic structure.

Targle's patent attorney took careful notes, even though the documents were included with the packet in front of him.

"Fritz, does the Patent Office have any comment on these findings?" asked Andrea.

The question and answer had been rehearsed earlier.

"Well, since we now understand that certain plant characteristics, such as resistance to invasive weeds, are found in nature, it may call into question the patentability of similar characteristics supposedly developed through genetic engineering. Likewise, we are re-examining claims made by BIG AG about genetically altered changes in plant structure to resist the effects of Klobber. We have found similar resistance in ordinary plants that have been exposed to that chemical for several years."

Targle's Patent attorney challenged Fritz' last observation.

"Those are not mutually exclusive. You can have a validly patentable genetically engineered plant that is later duplicated in nature. Happens all the time."

"My point exactly," said Fritz. "The questions are whether the patents were granted prematurely and/or whether the patent rights should be withdrawn when evidence of natural occurrence is presented."

Targle raised his hand as though trying to stop an onrushing car. As far as he was concerned, the meeting was concluded. However, as was his practice, he cleared his throat, preparing to summarize the meeting's results. He had a reputation for keen, insightful analysis.

"So, essentially, Andrea, you're telling us to pound sand?"

"Accurately put."

"Well, that's your choice, and you are doing it at your own peril. I have heard nothing here to dissuade me from proceeding with the matter in Federal District Court. We will let a trier of the law and facts decide the matter."

"It's been very nice to see you again," Targle said with great insincerity.

The Bemis entourage picked up their briefcases and departed, pointedly leaving the packages of information about the super plants behind them.

After the meeting, Fritz went directly to the restaurant where Anne awaited. Since their return from Peru, Fritz had found it necessary to visit Middletown frequently. As it happened, there was always a reason to meet Anne during those visits. Anne, on her part, developed a fresh curiosity about Capitol architecture, in which Fritz had a strong interest. They were both fond of a room on the fourth floor of the Hay-Adams, with such excellent views of the capitol from the king-size bed. They chatted cozily while waiting for Wylie, who had remained with Andrea Popov for a few minutes to consider next steps.

Wylie decided it was cold enough to warrant a double Glen Morangie as he joined his traveling companions from Peru. Both men briefed Anne on the details of the "super plants" meeting, and Wylie smiled as he described the departure of Targle and company.

"Not exactly with their tails between their legs, but heartwarming nonetheless."

"Heartwarming? What do you mean?" asked Anne. "Those people from Bemis are still planning to take me to court, even after all the work we did to show the plants grow normally in the jungle."

"Anne, it's a bit like a choreographed dance. Targle knows how unlikely it is that Bemis will prevail considering this new evidence. But for him it is ego first and a need to uphold his lofty self-image. He's going to tell his boss how tough he is, and, after a while, after going through appropriate face-saving motions, this will just slip away. As though it never happened."

"But, Wylie, if he knows he can't win, why does he still pursue me? It doesn't seem right."

"Anne, dear, I am afraid right doesn't have a lot to do with it. Part of legal strategy is obfuscation and delay. Don't worry. You are going to be all right. Be glad your name isn't Jarndyce."

"What?"

Apparently, Anne was not a fan of Dickens.

"Never mind. What shall we order for lunch?"

Recalling Billy's advice about the healing powers of jewelry, Wylie visited the H. Stern store in Lima on his return stopover from Iquitos. There he discovered a necklace of light blue topaz that he thought might go well with Linda's eyes. He mentioned that to her as he handed her the package and she received both the sentiment and the necklace with deep pleasure. The harmony that existed between them since their trip to Florida was strengthened by topaz.

After his busy day with BIG AG and counseling Anne over lunch, Linda awaited him with a Glen Morangie and a sweet kiss. This was somewhat out of the ordinary. He stoutly resisted the impulse not to indulge twice in one day but accepted the glass of golden liquor, wondering what might be coming next.

"It's been a cold day. Sit down and get comfortable. There's something we need to share."

Wylie's antennae buzzed. "Share" was not a word Linda used frequently – and when she did, it often meant trouble. She had his attention.

"Relax," she said. "This is about another member of the family."

She handed him a glossy print of a wedge-shaped something, obscured with speckled dots and lines. Like a half-remembered dream, Wylie dimly recalled what the photograph represented.

"What is this? I'm trying to think. A sologram?"

"Honey, it's a soNOgram."

"So?"

"It's from Emma."

"Emma?"

"Do I detect an echo in here?"

"Emma?"

"Yes! I noticed she seemed a bit sluggish and her nipples were slightly enlarged…"

"A nurse thing, right?"

"Slightly enlarged, so I took her to the vet this morning. She did the sonogram and it shows Emma is pregnant."

"You're kidding. Pregnant? How the hell did that happen?"

"Well, the bee goes to the flower…"

"Stop that. I mean, when was there access? How could this happen. Dammit, I should have had her spayed!"

"Horse – barn door?"

"You're right."

Wylie reflected a moment.

"Mavis? Sure, Mavis. She took Emma for walks while we were gone. It didn't happen on your watch, right?"

"No Wylie. It did not."

"Mavis. Must be Mavis."

Meanwhile, the subject under consideration rested on her mat in the hallway, occasionally licking her slightly swollen nipples. She heard her own name several times amid the white noise but did not comment. However, when "Mavis" was pronounced with such vigor she suspected a visitor might be arriving, and she rose to stand in front of her beloved humans – just in case there might be trouble.

Wylie gazed into her soft eyes and absentmindedly caressed the hollow behind her ears.

"Knocked up are you, you trollop?"

There was no malice in his voice. Emma moved closer. Linda distracted Wylie.

"You can actually see the babies if you look close. See, right here."

She pointed to what seemed like white marbles clustered near a string.

"Looks like a little bunch of grapes."

"You can count six of them. Those are her gestational sacs. There's a pup in each one."

"And when does the vet say they are, I guess the word is, due?"

"Should be early in April."

Wylie her lifted the gray chin with his hand. Emma stared at him lovingly with her soft brown eyes.

"Yeah. Trollop."

Bitsy and Jerome were enjoying their first drinks of wine in the glassed-in third floor room of his apartment that he called his den. Floor to ceiling west-facing windows offered a full view of the setting sun and now, as it glowed below the horizon, fingers of neon pink clouds and contrails illuminated the darkening sky. Bitsy resisted turning on lights. She wanted to enjoy the full drama of twilight's last gleaming. The ruddy light from the sky fell on the opposite wall, highlighting Jerome's library and shining on the model motorcycles in glass cases mounted above the little fireplace.

They had not spoken for a while, comfortable in silence. When deep purple covered the view from the windows, Jerome reluctantly turned on the light between their chairs. He offered to refill her glass. She nodded approval.

"So, we have talked about arrangements for the wedding, but what about the honeymoon?" he asked.

"I don't know. I enjoy being here together. It's not as though we were a couple of kids getting to know each other".

"Of course. But I feel that, since we are beginning a new life together, we should do it in a spectacular way. Maybe take a first-class trip around the world – or a long cruise."

"But that would be so expensive," she said.

"Bitsy, you know that is not an issue. That is nothing you need worry about, my love."

"Well, it was for a long time. Don't expect me to change overnight."

"Fine, Jerome said. "But, really, is there something or someplace you would like to do or see?"

"It is probably a cliché, but Fred and I never went beyond the States. I have always dreamed of going to places like Paris, Rome and London."

Jerome leaned forward and rested his hands on the arm of her chair. He blinked as though clearing his vision.

"Pears, pears, pears," he said.

"Paris, you mean?"

Still holding the arm of her chair, he slowly sank to his knees, moving his head from side to side and blinking.

"Pup. Pup. Pup."

His mouth remained open and he looked bewildered, as though he had no idea who she was or why he was in this room. For a moment, Bitsy recoiled in fright, and then reached for Jerome as he tilted toward the floor, his face slack and devoid of expression. She knelt beside him and cushioned his head with her arm. He made faint puffing noises and looked at her imploringly. She pulled a cushion from her chair and placed it under his head, then crawled across the room to the telephone and called for help. She returned and Jerome's jaw was moving again. Words slowly formed.

"Bits...Bits...Bits...love you."

By the time they arrived at the Emergency Room, Jerome's confusion had diminished. He understood he was arriving at a hospital and had almost recovered from the weakness on his left side. He pressed Bitsy's hand and told her in a hushed voice how embarrassed he was, and that there was really no need to go to the hospital. He was feeling much better - they should just go back home.

The ER physician, who took his history and examined him thoroughly, did not agree.

"Well, sir, it looks like you may have had a TIA, a mini stroke. What probably happened is that blood flowing to part of your brain was blocked for a little while. The blockage usually breaks up and dissolves, so no actual brain damage occurs. But this is serious, and we need to observe you at least overnight."

Bitsy patiently waited while additional tests were performed. A few hours later, she was sitting beside Jerome's hospital bed, holding his hand.

"There's some juice here. Want some?" asked Jerome.

Jerome, her motorcycle warrior and lover, her hero, seemed diminished and pale under the fluorescent lights in the room. However, he smiled and squeezed her hand. He had made a few jokes as an attendant wheeled his bed into the room, and Bitsy was relieved that his spirits were high. In particular, he expressed a strong desire to get the hell out of this room.

"The doctor says tomorrow. I think you should rest. There are things he says you need to start doing to avoid another, uh, TIA or worse."

"Right. I've got a feeling that any idea of driving you cross country in the side car of the Indian for our honeymoon is probably…"

"Out of the question?"

"Yes."

Well, most of her Jerome was here, she thought. She was deeply thankful for that.

"Where did you find time to do this?" Portia asked a few minutes into the mixed media presentation Grover projected onto the white wall of his dining/living room.

He had combined still photographs and movies, taken while they were in the Amazon jungle, into a running video narrative that, not surprisingly, featured many pictures of Portia. The more than life-size images beckoned from the wall of this small room and delighted Portia. They constituted a pleasant reminder of two weeks in the exotic realm of the Amazon, and the successful conclusion to her grandfather's quixotic search for peculiar plants in the jungle.

The few photographs of handsome Sunny Weschler strangely directed her thoughts to Grover, not so handsome, but steadfast, bright and a very good lover. She glanced away from the glowing wall to watch him manipulate keys on his laptop. The light from the laptop screen was less than flattering, but she felt passion stirring, nonetheless.

"Oh, there are all sorts of apps you can download from the net that make creating slide shows a breeze. And, it's fun. I put this together in about two hours. The program even adds theme music automatically. If you have the nerve to do it, it will also upload the whole thing to YouTube – which I am not about to do. No need to share you with other horny guys."

"So, just for one horny guy?"

"That's not what I meant, and you know it."

After a moment of silence. Portia reacted to a picture of a woolly monkey.

"Oh, isn't that great! Look at Dorilla holding my hand. You were very quick to get that shot."

The slide show continued for another twenty minutes and, like many amateur presentations, ended with luminous photographs of sunset on the river that Grover had taken from their moving boat.

Grover turned on the lights and retrieved a bottle of chardonnay from the refrigerator. They sipped wine and relived some of their favorite experiences during the exploration along the great river. Portia focused on the wild beauty of the place and the novel flora and fauna that they had seen. Grover recalled physically active stuff: the zipline, slogging through muck in rubber boots, paddling a dugout canoe during a drenching rainstorm. Portia observed that there was such diversity there that it would not be difficult not to find something of interest for every visitor. Grover agreed.

"Would you want to go back there some time?"

"You mean, just us two?"

"Yes."

"I might be talked into it," she said. "Maybe in another season, when the water is lower. When thc forest isn't quite so wet."

"We could do that."

"Yes."

Grover paused, then changed the subject.

"You were telling me about job interviews at school. Anything promising?"

"Yes. as a matter of fact. I've had word from two possible employers."

"Fantastic!"

"Well, I don't know about that. The University has a program where, if you go into lower paying public service, some or all your student loans are forgiven. The Philadelphia Public Defender's office has offered me a job under that program. But also, a large Boston firm that's now called 'Flannigan' would like me as an associate, beginning in June. They offer an eighty-hour workweek and six figures to start."

"Six figures – really?" Apparently, thought Portia, he didn't think an eighty-hour work week was challenging.

"Yes, but I am still waiting to interview two federal judges offering clerkships."

"I guess that would be good too, right?"

"Yes," she said, then paused.

"I know it sounds phony, but I am really humbled that actual job offers are coming my way."

"That shouldn't surprise you. You are the best!"

Their talk continued, and Grover shared some of the inside knowledge, gleaned from his conversation with Mary Smith, of coming events in the corporate life of Bemis International Group. Both he and Portia were now familiar with that organization. Wylie and Anne Proctor had spoken often about BIG AG's claims against Anne's super plants during their exploration in the jungle. Their thoughts returned to the Amazon.

"So, you might want to go back there again – with me."

"I said I might be persuaded."

"I um, I was thinking, like maybe on a honeymoon?"

"A what?"

Flustered, Grover said, "You know, like on our honeymoon.".

Portia placed her wine glass on the table, clutched its edge and leaned toward Grover. Her eyes blazed.

"I've been telling you about job offers that let me capitalize on the years of training and education I have pursued, and here you come trying to sweep me off my feet with what sounds like a truly half-assed proposal of what – marriage? Sorry, Buster, not interested."

Grover suspected he might have handled the situation differently.

As a professional courtesy, Simon Targle was advised by the Attorney General's office that Bemis International Group and certain of its top officers were under investigation. He was cautioned that any travel plans contemplated by top officers, including him, and board members must be abandoned. Agents from the F.B.I. would soon visit to collect documents, computers and other electronic devices. The company's back-up computers in limestone caves along the Mississippi River had already been impounded.

Targle, often on the other side in such matters, blanched. This was an all-out, brass-knuckled campaign. Bemis could be in very serious trouble. He considered areas of legal weakness, corporate and personal. Perhaps Bemis had been overly aggressive in challenging some weaker competitors, and an acquisition or two crossed the lines of certain federal and state anti-trust regulations. Bemis certainly had not colluded with competitors; of that he was sure. No competitor trusted Dick Geier to uphold any illicit bargain that he agreed to.

Personally, well, perhaps he was guilty of rounding up an expense account number or two, and perhaps he should have paid for personal travel that he and his wife took on the corporate jet from time to time. Of course, there was no bright line distinguishing personal from corporate travel. Who was to say the trip to his son's graduation from college on the west coast was not for corporate entertainment purposes? He convinced himself that he, personally, was blameless.

Next, Targle wen to Dick Geier's office to tell him about the telephone call from the AG's Office and offer his thoughts about areas of vulnerability and the potential seriousness of the matter.

"No shit?" said Geier. "So how many times have we been challenged by the feds? Patent Office, Labor Department, Anti-Trust Division, those environmental sad sacks, the crybabies over at Commerce. We have put them all in their place. Don't you start going soft on me. Don't you start being a legal a-hole!"

"Dick, I'm just doing my job here. I think there is some sort of full court press in the works, and I don't understand what..."

Geier's assistant stood nervously at the doorway and raised a finger to interrupt.

"What. What?"

"Mr. Targle's assistant wants me to pass on an urgent message."

"So, what is it?"

"She says to tell you there are F.B.I agents in the lobby with carts and boxes, and they need to serve you some kind of legal paper."

Geier acknowledged Targle's questioning expression by moving his hand as though to shoo away a curious pigeon. His General Counsel moved quickly to the elevator bank, urgently pressing the down button.

Geier treated Targle's announcement as the overanxious of prattle of a professional worry wart. He'd been through entanglements with the government many times—all ending with settlements or admonishments that did not interfere with operations or cash flow. He was sure that this was just business as usual, though there had never been a squad of government agents mustered in his lobby.

Just before Targle entered, Geier had been planning to wander the plant and find his way to his Thursday afternoon assignation with Ms. Sudby. Targle had simply delayed his departure by a few minutes. You don't run a huge chemical operation without stepping on a few toes, bending a few noses out of joint he reminded himself. Only when he pulled open the steel door to the blending room did thoughts of Malimsa enter his mind.

There was that issue with the bookkeeper and the state tax thing. But, hadn't George taken care of that? Or, wait, was that the thing Frank talked about – that the stupid girl was still on the payroll. Over at HR? Dammit, he should have followed up on that. Be fun to tease Lavitra again. Anyway, George said it was covered, didn't he? He was reliable, right?

He climbed the metal stairs to the catwalk that was the shortcut to the cottage where Priscilla awaited him. Distracted by his thoughts, he reflexively placed a cigarette in the corner of his mouth and pulled his lighter engraved with the Bemis logo from his pocket. He had to spin the spark wheel twice to create a flame. That was just enough to ignite not only the butane in his lighter but also the myriad explosive particles concentrated in the hazy air above his place in an alcove on the catwalk, directly above one of the enormous vats where mixing blades the size of destroyer propellers lazily ground through silos of fertilizer.

The explosion began like the sound of distant thunder, a low, almost inaudible, rumble near his feet pushing upward through the metal grid. Then there was a bright orange flash that caromed off the wall of the alcove behind him and lifted him, in slow motion, fifteen or twenty feet into the air above the fertilizer vats. Geier's mouth was open in a scream that remained unheard above the sound of the crackling mini explosions above the catwalk. Suddenly, all explosive particles exhausted, there was silence, except for the cries of workers below, staring at Geier's soaring body. He rose from the catwalk through an orange sheet of flame and awkwardly descended into the opening of a huge vat.

He entered the surface of the fertilizer particles headfirst. The inexorable movement of the blades churned the gray granules into all Geier's available orifices, clogging mouth, nose and ears almost immediately. He tried to propel himself upwards, clawing through the yielding gray mass like one caught in quicksand. Involuntarily, he blinked his eyes, allowing the pellets to scratch and sting. Upended as he was, the downward current created by the huge propeller blades forced him toward the bottom. Panic-stricken, breathless, disoriented, believing he was about to die, Geier's feet began to disappear into the foul-smelling gray mass.

His life did not race before his burning eyes. Rather, it was the horrifying thought that his life would end in a grave of chicken shit.

Chapter 13

MARCH

Middletown Courier-Times

Mastering your Garden

By Elizabeth Pendleton Crangle

A flock of robins arrived today to harvest the remaining berries on our hawthorn trees. (Although this column appears in March, I'm writing it in late February, so these certainly are early birds.) Harbingers of spring indeed!

I have not referred to roses these past months because there is not much to do once they have been mulched against winter frosts. At the end of this month, however, it will be time to prune them, and I want to review proper practices. I was called to task for not doing so last year! First, don't prune climbers now. They bud from last year's growth and should be pruned after they bloom. On the other hand, all roses should have dead or diseased wood removed.

Proper pruning now assures a healthy and well-shaped plant during the summer months. Given the aggressive winter weather this year, you can be sure of significant die back in the canes. The center of dead canes is brown, while the living cane is white or cream colored. Dead canes should be removed. Before proceeding, check to see if any suckers are growing from below the graft. These would be from the rootstock, not the rose you want, and should be cut off as close to the stem as possible.

Hybrid teas are fussy. Cut all the canes to about two feet and select three or four healthy ones, cutting the others above the graft. Then prune to an outside bud on the remaining canes. That means cutting the cane about a quarter inch above the bud, forcing the future branch away from the center of the plant. You can find diagrams of the pruning process on my fiancé, Jerome Hastings' web site, www.hastingspudding.org. Bush and shrub roses are much easier to prune. Once the dead, crossing and diseased canes have been removed, cut out an old cane near the base to encourage new growth. If you have not tried one of the knockout rose varieties, do so this year. They really live up to their name!

I am guilty of carrying on about roses too long, but a little careful pruning in late March assures glorious blooms this summer.

By the end of this month, early daffodils, even tulips, will begin to emerge. Although these plants get most of their energy from the bulbs underground, it is helpful to fertilize them as the green leaves begin to show. 5-10-5 fertilizer sprinkled around the base is good, and water-soluble fertilizer may be used.

March is a good time to examine your trees for winter damage. The leaves are off, and cracks and broken limbs show clearly on bright days. I have found a few ornamentals that will require pruning. For those of you unfortunate enough to have Bradford pear trees with many broken limbs consider replacing them with Callery pears. They are much less brittle and withstand our tough winters better.

Finally, as you thin seedlings, why not pot some up for friends. Generosity is the hallmark of a good gardener!

Blissful Gardening – Bitsy

Dick II

It was time for tea in Senator Rowe's office, where Congresswoman Pert Pewtree and her senior staffer, Grover Merson, listened to him catalog the latest turn of events in the arcane world of inside-the-beltway politics and the weighty concerns of the "best Congress money can buy."

The current topic was the progress, or lack thereof, in maneuvering The Probity Act out of committee and onto the floor of the House for a vote. Senator Rowe had already arranged for passage of the bill in the Senate, but it required House attention soon, or it would die of inaction. At his boss's request, Grover devoted much of his time during the past month to promoting the legislation to his counterparts in the offices of influential representatives, while Pert lobbied her peers in the House. It was six months since the bill had been proposed, not an unusual length of time for nothing to happen in the House, but Pete Rowe was growing impatient. He looked at Grover.

"Tell me again why we can't move this thing forward over on your side."

"Well, Senator, although there is no overt opposition to legislation that would prohibit sexual liaisons between members of congress and lobbyists, two basic issues have been raised. One is political and the other relates to details. The political concern it that the voters in general could assume that the purpose of the legislation is to curtail rampant promiscuity on the Hill..."

"Hold on. Nobody's been calling rampant."

"Yes, sir, but that is the concern. Voters might wonder about congressional promiscuity in general, and it could encourage more thorough journalistic investigation of the issue. Of course, this is a completely hypothetical matter, but there is significant concern."

"On the other hand," offered Pert, "some members of Congress feel a new issue like this could divert attention from the inability of Congress to deal with national problems of joblessness, a plan to address long-term debt, repair our infrastructure, or to reverse the country's decline in areas of education, infant mortality, health care, and so forth. There's nothing like a juicy bit of sex-oriented legislation to take people's minds off important, but difficult, public issues."

The Senator nodded agreement. He was willing to accept crackpot logic if it furthered passage of pet legislation.

"Now, what are objections to the details? Lord knows we can always accommodate small changes if it moves the ball down the field."

"Yes. Details. You know how porous the rules are about who is and who isn't a lobbyist. Suppose someone who should have but didn't register as a lobbyist was involved. Would the law apply to him or her? There is also the issue of gender discrimination. Historically, most members of Congress involved both in illicit homo and heterosexual situations have been men. There is concern that the law would discriminate against male members of Congress, vis a vis female congressperson."

"Anything else?"

Grover replied.

"It isn't exactly clear which members of the administration would be included in the act. The language mentions appointed officials but doesn't define a cut-off level. For example, would it apply to an acting deputy assistant secretary? Nobody seems to know. Basic issues of fairness are involved. The legislators don't want to be degraded to the level of minor appointed administration officials, when they have spent hundreds of thousands of dollars to be elected. They feel that only high-level administration officials should be subject to the act – to maintain parity with their exalted position as members of Congress. It would be embarrassing to have a criminal law that applied equally across the social spectrum."

"Does that cover it?" the Senator asked.

"Pretty much."

"What do you think, Pert, is this worth pursuing?"

"I'm scheduled to discuss it with the Chairwoman of the Moral Principles Committee, which has its annual meeting next week. And my instincts say the act is worth pursuing. Do you agree, Grover?"

"It is definitely worth more effort."

The meeting continued as the legislators discussed other matters of common interest. Pert and her husband were planning a brief vacation to Baton Rouge, and Pete was helping them arrange private tours of plantations along the Mississippi.

Grover had been working so hard in the Capitol to promote the Probity Act that his contacts with Portia during the past few weeks were limited to texting and brief telephone conversations. His last comment to the legislators echoed in his mind. "Worth more effort" applied to Portia as well, especially after her clear rebuff of his artless proposal. He would have to be more persuasive.

Wylie noticed that Edson had sent an e-mail. The two corresponded every week or so since the discovery of the super plants near Iquitos. Affection had developed between them during the time along the river, and Wylie was already considering ways in which he could be Edson's host next winter – so Edson could experience snow. Probably ice, slush and freezing winter weather as well.

Wylie laughed. It's true. You must be careful what you wish for. The e-mail was addressed to "Mr. Wylie."

"I am good and hope you are too. Many thanks for your invite. I look to coming to your city with much taste and do not wait for so much time to go past. You are so good a man to gift me with airplane tickets. I send you a thousand thanks. This is now a poor time along the river. Snow in the mountains melts quicker than before and our river goes much higher. You remember Esperanza? Generator there is flooded, and people have moved away to higher ground. Never have I see water so high. People have died from the water. The lodge is OK, just some people have got wet feet. I was there tomorrow, and Dolly says hello? Do you come again? Best wishes to you and salutes to all you friends. Your friend, Edson M."

Wylie reread the note. So, it seems global warming has affected the great river. Edson's message about the flooding was no surprise. Since his recent visit to Peru, Wylie was more attuned to news from that region, and routinely visited web sites offering reports from that area. He had seen videos of people on the thatched roofs of their homes, and pigs and chickens being moved to high ground in dugout canoes. Helicopter views showed the Amazon stretching well beyond the borders he recalled near Iquitos. Huge trees uprooted and churning through the swiftly flowing waters hampered navigation. The scenes compared with flooding in the American Midwest, except not so many cars and trucks were involved. Edson was right. Nature is cruel and people die from the water.

Wylie composed a friendly note to his young protégé. It was very good to hear from him again, everything was fine with him and his family and he, too, was looking forward to Edson's visit in the winter. He closed the lid to his laptop and glanced at the time on his cell phone. He needed to hurry for the weekly meeting with his cronies.

"There he is! Wylie of the jungle! Must be pretty chilly swinging along those vines in your loin cloth. Better come in and warm up."

Billy had seized on this reference to early Tarzan movies when Wylie returned from his trip to Peru and had not yet tired of it. Wylie, Sy and Arnie had, but knew complaints would only prolong the juvenile teasing. Billy gave

Wylie a good-natured hug and motioned for him to join the two other men seated at the card table. In consideration of the cold weather, Billy's wife had prepared buttered rum to lubricate the evening's card game. Arnie judiciously sipped as Sy played with the glass in his hand. Wylie settled in his chair, and Billy began to deal cards.

The conversation, which followed a script developed over the years, resembled a corporate board meeting. First, old business to resolve any loose ends from the previous week's meeting (Sy's mother's pneumonia was better). Then new business (Wylie had some to be reviewed later), then gossip and, lubricated by rum, personal matters that even Billy would not repeat or employ in future teasing. Neither Wylie nor Sy had yet disclosed the news of their cancers during the most personal moments of the gathering. Some things would remain secret, even among the best of friends.

Vacation plans, focusing on condominiums in Ashville and Palm Beach Gardens, were announced, and adjustments made to the card game calendar. Billy promoted a four-man fishing trip during the summer and suggested a private lodge on a lake in Maine. Sy was not enthusiastic.

"There are only two good weeks to be in Maine. Winter is too cold; Spring is just mud; black flies come in May followed by mosquitoes that have been known to carry off chipmunks. There are two good weeks in mid-August before winter comes again. Can we arrange the trip for mid-August?"

Billy frowned.

"Turns out that time is always already booked."

"See," said Sy.

Arnie, who had conferred with Wylie about the patent infringement matter, turned to his classmate.

"Strange goings on over at Bemis International. I hear their CEO is missing in action and there's a huge shake-up in management. I was advised to unload their stock a while ago. I should have listened! It lost about twenty percent in value in just a week. How about you?"

"I've never been attracted to chemical stocks" said Wylie, "especially since I began looking into Bemis in connection with Anne Proctor's plants. But whatever precipitated the management changes there, it has been good for the possible litigation involving Anne's super plants. You remember I told you about the crap I got from their General Counsel even after we demonstrated that the plants were not genetically engineered?"

"Yes. But it seemed to me he was just being lawyerly. Delay can be a helpful strategy."

"Maybe in litigation, but not so much in business. In any event, the Honorable Simon Targle is no longer Bemis' General Counsel. His number two now has that job. He called Andrea Popov to advise that he inherited a massive backlog of cases and was weeding out what he considered non-starters. Long story short, Bemis has withdrawn its demands regarding the super plants. Tomorrow, Andrea and I will be looking over an agreement with Bemis that absolves the University and Anne Proctor of liability for their use and promotion."

"That's a good result."

"I agree, and Anne Proctor thinks so too."

Billy chafed at the conversation that ignored him and focused on legal matters in which he had no interest.

"So, are we playing cards, or what?"

They played. Sy continued to mutter about black flies in Maine.

It was not long after the F.B.I. raid on Bemis International Group and the hasty hospitalization of Dick Geier that the company's board of directors, many handpicked by Geier himself, met in emergency session. They evaluated suddenly disclosed problems, initiated damage control and positioned themselves to avoid responsibility for their lax oversight of the business. Lavitra Gascoigne, a member of senior management who appeared blameless, aided them.

As Chief Human Resources officer, she arranged for the hasty departure of George Stirrup and Frank Edger, even before all details of their involvement with Malimsa came to light. Unknown to them, the decision was taken not to prosecute them for their malfeasance since their employment agreements required the company to pay for their legal expenses – even if the company sued them.

Lavitra kept that decision to herself and promised not to prosecute the former executives in exchange for help in unraveling the tangled corporate maze that obscured the location of the funds they had liberated from Bemis. They agreed to let Lavitra claw back the ill-gotten gains and void the "golden parachute" terms of their employment agreements. They also agreed to turn in their company cars and forgo other customary executive retirement benefits, such as golf club memberships and use of the corporate jets.

Manfred Balducci, Bemis' Vice President of Marketing, journeyed to Home Warehouse's headquarters to undertake the difficult task of explaining how their second source for Klobber was a sham. He carefully avoided any implication that, God forbid, anyone at Bemis was aware of Malimsa's unholy provenance. The chief executive of Home Warehouse was understanding, especially when Manfred offered house brand packaging of Klobber at a deep discount. In that way, Bemis would continue to be first and second source supplier, but all income would flow to Bemis. Board members agreed that Manfred achieved a win-win, turned lemons into lemonade. He had dodged the bullet. He would not, at that point, be among those who were frog-marched out the door into corporate oblivion.

Considering the size of the corporation and the potential magnitude of malfeasance under investigation by outside sources, two independent auditing teams scoured the company books, interviewed employees at all levels, and tallied inventories. Forensic accountants sniffed along trails of flowing money, and corporate attorneys examined deals promoted, promulgated or pursued by the company's top managers. Instances of corporate overreaching in areas of antitrust and price fixing emerged. Manfred Balducci's quarterly golf outings with marketing executives of other chemical companies followed by staggered price increases in certain commodities were reviewed. Coincidence was ruled out. Soon after he salvaged the Home Warehouse business, Manfred had an unpleasant interview with an outplacement counselor hired by Lavitra. He left the company.

A comparison between top managers' expense reports and corporate policies uncovered irregularities. Investigators established an arbitrary amount of ten thousand dollars or less worth of irregularities a year as requiring no further investigation, that amount being of minor consequence. Unfortunately for

Simon Targle, he had underestimated the value of his personal use of corporate jets. Red flags festooned his expense account file, and he soon met with Lavitra's favorite outplacement counselor. He managed to find work with a lobbying firm in the Capitol that expected he would attract work from Bemis. He and his new firm were disappointed in that regard.

And so it went.

Discoveries were made and actions taken with enthusiasm unusual in Bemis' corporate culture. Rayseen Jackson, an assistant to Lavitra Gascoigne, provided valuable assistance to the various independent counselors, advisers and investigators. This young woman had an uncanny understanding of the inner workings of the company computer applications. She seemed to hold a big broom when it came to corporate house cleaning. The board of directors, now challenged to find replacements for senior staffers, including the absent chief executive, noted her capabilities.

Dick Geier was in suspended animation while his company was besieged by hordes of investigators and examiners.

After watching him carom through the air in the blending facility and land headfirst in the huge fertilizer vat, a team of workers scrambled up the ladder attached to the vat and looked vainly for a sign of their chief executive in the churning grains of nitrogen, phosphorus and potassium. The huge paddle slowly stirring the mixture created a depression and Geier's feet briefly appeared. A heroic worker waited for the next turn of the paddle and grasped his feet, extracting the unconscious man and carrying him to the factory floor. An emergency vehicle soon arrived, and the medical team did its best to clear his breathing pathways. He remained alive but unresponsive on the way to the hospital. There more sophisticated medical techniques roused his vital signs. He had serious internal and external injuries, and doctors placed him in a medically induced coma in hopes that edema and bruising would soon subside. Now, in the second week of the month, he remained in a coma, scheduled to be awakened in a few days.

Meanwhile, the board decided to appoint their most trusted senior manager of the moment as chief executive officer. They named Lavitra Gascoigne acting CEO, responsible for diminishing the current chaos and stabilizing operations.

She would also oversee recruiting replacements for the recently departed, a daunting responsibility. The erstwhile whistleblower, Rayseen Jackson, was designated her chief of staff. With the announcement of Lavitra's appointment, pundits in the financial world breathed a sigh of relief. The value of Bemis shares rose by five and a half percent and remained on the upswing as Lavitra took the reins of BIG AG. She was so busy she almost forgot Dick Geier completely.

Relations between Myron and Winston Wu returned to their former, pleasant state after the brunch at Jerome Hastings' apartment. They were drawn together in their concern for Jerome and often traveled together to visit him, first in the hospital and then at his home. There Bitsy supervised his care and shepherded him to appointments with rehabilitation specialists. At his doctor's request, Jerome was losing weight, and they agreed he looked good. Now, about a month after his T.I.A., he was reforming his daily habits, walking, eating correctly and following the advice of his therapists. He felt no aftereffects of his brief instability and persuaded Bitsy that they should "tie the knot" as soon as possible. Since there seemed no need for delay, they initially agreed on a modest affair for the following month.

Myron and his wife welcomed Mary Smith whole-heartedly into their family circle, and frequent family gatherings were organized to include his newfound sister. The Irminator presided at most of those gatherings and, once the novelty of finding her new daughter began to fade, behaved more and more like a Vietnamese mother – that is, like any mother concerned for the interests of an unmarried daughter no longer on the sunny side of thirty.

Each March the family followed the tradition of celebrating the Vietnamese holiday of Hai Ba Trung and honored the Trung sisters who fought to liberate Vietnam from the Chinese overlords nearly two thousand years ago. Myron invited Winston Wu and his young son to the weekend festivity at the home of one of his cousins. The little boy blended in immediately with the other children, racing around the large yard and throwing himself to the walls and floor of a "bouncy house." A few grownups supervised the play, but most of the older relatives remained indoors since it was still a bit chilly.

Myron introduced Winston as his friend from the Master Gardener program, not wishing to stimulate discussion about the Middletown Four, as the eco-terrorist group was described in the Courier-Times.

Irma did not accept this limited description and examined her son's friend as if she intended to offer him a large loan. Within minutes, she learned he was a professor of biology, with tenure, at the University and that he had involved Myron in the notorious milkweed escapade. A few more innocent questions divulged that he was a widower, aged thirty-seven, the father of the spirited little boy racing around the back yard, and without a significant other. She liked his features.

Myron was now in another room, so Irma took Winston's arm.

"Come, let me introduce you to a few more relatives."

As she propelled Winston toward the large living room, she came upon her daughter, Mary Smith, engaged in animated conversation with a cousin. She paused there, patted her chest as though searching for breath.

"Mary, I'm feeling a little faint. Would you introduce Myron's friend to some of your uncles?"

The information about feeling faint surprised Mary. She believed her mother was the fittest sixty-year-old she had ever met. However, she would not argue with the Irminator, who withdrew quickly to another part of the room. Winston offered his hand.

"Hello, I'm Winston."

"Hi. I'm Mary. Nice to meet you."

"Yes."

He held her hand in his perhaps a bit too long, but Mary did not seem to mind.

The reporter for USA Today noticed the wire service report that the University was planning to offer samples of recently discovered seeds for testing to a select group of experimental farms throughout the country. The plants from the seeds had noble characteristics that included abundant crop yields, mild soil toxicity that thwarted weeds and a selective insect repellent. If the plants retained those qualities through subsequent generations, it was planned that seeds from the plants would be disseminated worldwide, initially to farmers in less developed countries.

The reporter checked her notes and made a call to Anne Proctor, whom she had interviewed the previous fall. Yes, this was a further development of the "super plants" she had reported on earlier and, yes, Anne Proctor would grant an interview about the broader use of the plants derived from her magic seeds.

The reporter pursued all aspects of the story diligently and did not fail to understand the tremendous impact the use of the plants would have on world agriculture. The search for the super plants along the Amazon made excellent copy, as did glowing predictions from experts at the University. Anne provided some of Grover's photographs of the expedition and soon a picture of Anne, Wylie, Portia and Fritz Gumbach, all smiling and seated in a battered aluminum boat, was featured in newspapers and web sites everywhere. Suddenly their telephones rang ceaselessly with reporters seeking interviews and asking questions. Wylie and Portia demurred, but Anne and Fritz (now retired) agreed to appear at some morning shows on television. They were an engaging couple, and agents for speakers bureaus sought to represent them and arrange tours of campuses and garden clubs. It was a heady time for them both.

A rainbow coalition of pundits argued about, extolled and denigrated the super plants. The personalities of the explorers were examined, and conclusions drawn about romantic entanglements and mysterious goings on in the jungle. Supermarket tabloids offered sensational stories about Wylie and his relationships with 1) Anne, 2) Portia, and 3) Fritz. Anne was surprised to learn that a pack of woolly monkeys had carried her off, and that she was romantically involved with Fritz, Wylie and one of the woolly monkeys. Paul Beaver was besieged with requests for reservations at the Amazonia lodges.

Public clamor eventually diminished. The fanciful reports about the individuals involved ceased and more thoughtful discussions arose about the most effective manner of testing, producing, and distributing the plants. Non-profit agencies, funded by governments, private individuals and foundations, were created to study the plants and further their development and use. In some areas, conflicts arose over which nation-state would be the first to receive the seeds, and international agencies were called upon to resolve disputes. Criminal organizations offered bogus seeds to the gullible and enrollment in state university agricultural programs skyrocketed.

Lavitra Gascoigne reported that BIG AG would devote its considerable resources to producing the super seeds (now generally known as "Proctors") and making them available to needy farmers almost at cost. Of course, Randi Fochik's team had a head start on this project, what with the clandestine plant production begun last fall. The value of Bemis' shares rose slightly on rumors that the company had the foresight to be months ahead of competitors in the production of Proctors.

Wylie's stature among Master Gardeners and his pinochle cronies rose as his involvement in locating Proctors in the Peruvian jungle became general knowledge. He accepted his notoriety with good grace. Portia also benefitted from her visit to the jungle, as prospective employers sought her out. Grover, however, was busy fending off demands from the "media" for more of his photographs and movies from the trip to the jungle. Between dealing with reporters and producers, supporting The Probity Act and managing the working of Representative Pewtree's office, his visits with Portia became less frequent. He felt as though the one he loved was slipping from his grasp.

Dick Geier had been released from his medically induced coma three days earlier. Although the severe bruises and abrasions all over his body were healing, they remained painful, and prolonged inactivity left him weak and lightheaded. Nicotine had long left his body, but an almost insane craving for a cigarette remained. He also worried about a peculiar numbness in his feet and crotch. His medical coverage as former chief executive of Bemis assured excellent care in a well-appointed, sunny private room with dedicated nursing care.

Chief of Medicine, Morris Minor M.D., was his primary physician, and he carefully monitored his progress since he woke from his coma. He spoke to Geier in generalities: he was a lucky man; no serious internal injuries; he was receiving the best possible care; we are going to see that you are good as new. His nurses assured him that all his friends at Bemis were concerned about him and called daily. Just look at all the flowers! Geier didn't give a crap about his friends at Bemis. And, he recalled the beginning of an F.B.I. raid on his office moments before his accident occurred. That made him feel uneasy.

Dr. Minor appeared and reviewed his chart. He walked to the bed and placed a reassuring hand on Geier's shoulder – gently, as the shoulder remained painful despite doses of Percocet.

"Looks good. Nice progress here. All parameters in normal range. Have you been doing those little exercises that the physical therapist showed you?"

"Yes. She got me over to that chair and back this morning."

"Good for you! That is very encouraging."

The doctor then listened to his chest and back and observed the multihued blotches still on his body. He asked his patient to move his arms and legs and pressed lightly on his shins.

"Yes, I see improvement every day. How about your spirits? Are you reasonably upbeat about your situation? You certainly should be, considering, um, the alternative."

"Well, I do have a lot on my mind, but I basically am looking forward to getting the hell out of here."

Doctor Minor showed a wan smile.

"There is one other thing we need to discuss. I wanted to wait until you were completely aware and in a positive frame of mind."

Geier pushed himself up in the bed as best he could. The doctor had his full attention.

"You may not recall it exactly, but you fell into a large tank of fertilizer that was activated by a large paddle – like a propeller. The brave man who rescued you had to wait for that paddle to make a couple of revolutions before he could pull you out. Unfortunately, the edge of the paddle struck you in several places. That is why your shoulder is so tender and your ribs are so painful."

"And the numbness in my feet and crotch?"

Doctor Minor sat down on the edge of the bed so their heads were on the same level. He looked sympathetically at his patient.

"The numbness in your feet is temporary. The numbness in your crotch, however..."

Dr. Minor looked away, searching for the right words. Geier, concerned, prompted him.

"Numbness in the crotch is what?"

Minor cleared his throat.

"Well, you know, that massive paddle, you know, struck you in numerous places, which accounted for your multiple injuries. One of those, uh, blows hit just below the base of your penis."

"You're not telling me something I don't know. I'm damn near useless down there!" said Geier. "What the fuck is going on?"

"Unfortunately, our best people say you've experienced inoperable and probably permanent nerve damage there. The long and short of it, I mean, the result of the blow, in lay terms, means you can't get an erection. You have erectile dysfunction."

Geier paled. With his white hair and eyebrows, he began to blend into his pillows.

His doctor hastened to add

"These days we have numerous procedures to correct E.D. It is certainly not the end of the world. Believe me there are millions of men with that problem who manage to have sex. And, let's not forget that other functions, like urination, still work."

Geier stared blankly at the doctor, the impact of what Morris had said pushing blotches of color on to his face. After a few moments he said, "So," but couldn't complete the thought. Trying again, he said, "So, what, what gets it to work again?"

"Look, I know this must be terribly difficult for you," said Morris. "Just understand that we will do everything medically possible to alleviate the problem and your concern. I have asked one of our nurses who specializes in this area to visit with you this afternoon and explain your options."

"A nurse?"

"A male nurse. He is very good at this. I think he has you scheduled for around two o'clock."

The doctor offered further words of assurance and comfort and left to continue his rounds. Geier lifted his gown, looking downward. It was like attending a memorial service for a revered old friend.

A few moments after two o'clock a small man carrying a black vinyl portfolio appeared at his doorway. He was dressed in oversized blue scrubs and had a military haircut – shaved sideburns and russet hair styled like a pencil eraser. He could have been designed by an ornithologist to resemble a chipping sparrow. He looked at Geier's chart to confirm that he was in the correct room and offered his hand to the patient. Geier accepted it grudgingly. The nurse pointed to his name tag that read "Shafto."

"I'm Arnold Shafto, your penile implant specialist, but you can call me 'Arnie'."

The patient mumbled an acknowledgment.

"So, doc tells me you have a little E.D. issue. Happens a lot these days. Like it's getting fashionable. He He."

Geier doubted that was the case.

"So, I'm here this afternoon to help you choose which implant is best for you. I'm saying implant here because the penis pump is so awkward, we just don't recommend it any more. Why drive a Chevy when you could have a Caddy? Right?"

Arnie opened the portfolio to illustrations of each brand of prosthesis and flipped through the pages as he explained their capabilities.

"Today I reviewed the measurements they made while you were asleep, the raw data you might say. You know, size, ratio between length to girth, relationship to size of scrotum, all that stuff. When I am done, I want your dingus to look as natural as possible. So, over here, see, we have the non-inflatable penile implant. You might just as well forget about that baby."

Geier wondered why.

"It's cheap and simple all right. But I'm guessing you're not worried about the cost. He. He. Bend it up when you need an erection. Bend it down when you're done. But the thing is, a lot of men never get used to having a constant hard on. And there's the social pressure, too. Naw, this won't be right for you."

He turned a page to show drawings and photographs under the bold headline, INFLATABLE.

"Now these are top of the line. If you are going to do it, I am convinced this is the only way to go. I look over your profile, Dick (can I call you "Dick"), and I see a man who is accustomed to the very best. Just skip over the two-piece and go right for the three-piece, multi-component inflatable penile implant. Look here, how easy it is to use. You or your partner just pump it up and press the release valve to deflate. Everything looks completely normal and it is totally concealed in the body. I tell you, man, this is so comfortable you almost forget it's there – until you need it, of course. I'm looking at a man who is going to need it, for sure. He. He."

Geier attempted a weak joke to try and overcome his rising nausea.

"That's quite a sales pitch. Do you get a commission on these?"

Arnie was offended and stoutly denied it, even though, in fact, there were little benefits offered by the detail man who hawked the inflatables.

"Now, I won't lie to you, there is one other device in the testing stage. They implant a tiny transmitter in the part of the brain that lights up when you get horny, and it sends a signal to a pump that runs off batteries like a pacemaker. You get a natural erection without having to manipulate anything. And it is supposed to go down when you are done. Trouble is that, occasionally, it pumps more than needed, which I hear can be really painful. Creates pressure atrophy. They're working on that, of course, but it's best to go with tried and true."

Geier stared grimly at the pictures again. Arnie Shafto's cheerful sales pitch failed to lighten his mood. He stared at the open page of the portfolio.

"Show me again how this three-piece thing works," he said.

Arnie did, indicating the place where the pump reservoir was located and pointing out how natural it all looked. He emphasized that there was little pain post-operatively and less chance of atrophy. Were there any more questions?

Geier had many but chose not to ask them now.

"So, here's a little pamphlet that shows how it all works. Take your time to think about it. The doc will probably review it with you again tomorrow. Nice to see you. Have a good day."

The chipping sparrow flitted out the door. Geier remained in bed for a few minutes, and then painfully made his way to the chair by the window, monitoring his movements for signs of improvement. He settled in the chair and stared out the window at a row of blooming forsythias. A slender thread of tears fell from the corner of each eye.

Christ, he thought, I have got to get a second opinion.

Chapter 14

April

Middletown Courier-Times

Mastering your Garden

By Elizabeth Pendleton Crangle

In the "Waste Land" T.S. Eliot tells us "April is the cruellest month...stirring dull roots with spring rain." Except for the fact that we pay our taxes in April, I heartily disagree with the poet. April is the time between harsh winter and abundant summer when we glimpse the bright beginnings of a new season of growth. That is especially true for me this year. My dear friend, Jerome Hastings, and I are planning an April wedding. I am looking forward to a bouquet of early spring flowers.

Now it is time to get back to gardening. Looking at all those blooming daffodils, narcissi and tulips, I recall how worn they look as their foliage ripens and turns yellow, then brown. For years, I have planted them among daylilies that develop strong, large green leaves as the early spring flowers begin to fade. It's a happy combination. As our deer population expands, I am planting more daffodils and no tasty tulips. Deer, and rabbits also, seem to be repulsed by daffodils.

As you enjoy your spring crocuses, remember that there are wonderful varieties of fall blooming crocuses as well. The colchicums seem to grow larger each fall and the crocus sativus, blue with crimson stigmas, provides saffron spice. These plants are very popular now, so order them soon for August planting. They add a surprising touch of color to your borders in early fall.

One of my favorite springtime tasks is to select a flat or two of pansies. They can be planted in any sunny area and do especially well under deciduous trees.

They enjoy the sun shining through leafless branches, as well as shade later when the days become hot. I fill two large planters in front of the house with their happy faces, and they give a lift to passersby and me. For all their careless joy, it is important to remove all flowers and buds when planting pansies. That encourages root development and a stronger plant later in the season. Remove their faded blooms quickly, before they have a chance to go to seed and sap the plant's energy.

I favor raspberries and blueberries as reliable fruits in our local gardens, but strawberries, which come in late June, are also a desirable garden crop. Plant them in the middle of this month and be sure to add plenty of compost or organic material to the soil. And, as with the pansies, prune away all flower blossoms on the new plants. That assures robust growth in coming years. Hold off on fertilizing - strawberries do not need feeding until June.

On your lawn, grubs are at their hungriest now, feeding on tender grass roots before maturing into adult beetles. Unfortunately, no chemical control works to eliminate them at this stage. You need to wait until mid-July through August to apply proper control – and it is generally very effective then. Meanwhile, encourage flickers and blue birds to visit your garden. They love grubs!

You may be collecting heavy wet grass clippings when you mow. Add them to your compost pile to complement the autumn leaves. Eventually, you will harvest black gold to amend your garden soil.

Those of us who scratch our heads trying to identify the green shoots popping in our flower gardens should decide this year to use permanent markers. I use thin copper or white metal strips on which a ball point pen will leave a lasting mark. Some strips have their own legs. I attach mine to galvanized nails from the local hardware store.

Finally, mid-April is the time for the first application of fertilizer for roses. The slow release granules for roses work especially well. You don't need to fertilize again till late June.

So, until the Merry Month of May, blissful gardening – Bitsy

All

Grover stood waiting as Congresswoman Pert Pewtree entered her office. One glance at him confirmed that he was not the bearer of good news. He offered her a container of coffee and said, "It's not good news. The Probity Act isn't going to make it out of committee this session and, even if it did, the Speaker pledged it would never come to a vote. There are so many objections that he doesn't want to be embarrassed by failing to pass the bill, I thought it was a no-brainer. High moral principles and all. I am surprised."

Although Pert invested her support for the bill as an accommodation to Senator Pete Rowe, it was not of critical importance to her. "Well," she said," that's unfortunate. But it did create an interesting diversion for a while. The pundits found it a lot sexier than the debate about allowing the line item veto for the president.'

"Let's move on," she said, putting the matter to rest. "So, what is on tap for today?"

Grover pressed a button on his laptop, and a daily agenda appeared. Pert glanced at it and Grover added some background information about expected visitors. Next, Pert quickly reviewed the dozens of e-mails that had passed the review of one of her assistants. Grover had the same information in front of him. He took notes as Pert commented on the digital messages.

"The gun lobby is never satisfied," she said. "They have successfully promoted carrying concealed guns in churches and on college campuses in places like Utah, Colorado and Texas, and 'stand your ground' laws in many other states. Now they are trying to amend federal gun control laws to permit full reciprocity among states. Wait, but what's this? Billy Simpkins from Colorado is promoting universal carry permits for students and teachers in grades one through twelve?"

"Well, he is exempting kindergarten."

"What's next? Concealed weapons on the floor of the House?"

"It has been considered, but then the State of the Union address would have to be televised from a remote location. The ceremonial interests won't stand for that."

Another hour or so passed as Pert and Grover strategized about responses and worked out scheduling for the remainder of the week. Grover did his best to minimize the constant pressure on the congresswoman, as on all members of the house, to raise campaign funds daily. Yet, she was obliged to leave her office to dial for dollars at least every other day. At about ten in the morning, an assistant entered the office to deliver more coffee. They relaxed for a few moments and avoided shoptalk.

"I haven't heard much about Portia lately. How is that going?"

Grover had been her principal assistant and confidant for almost four years. Their relationship was complicated - master and servant, mentor and protégé, trusted advisor, even strains of maternal interest in Grover's affairs. So, her personal question was not unusual, and Grover responded honestly.

"It is a little unbalanced. I stupidly blurted out a dumb proposal of marriage after we came back from the Amazon, and she told me 'no way.' She is working hard to finish law school with many extracurricular activities, and you know I have not been in Middletown much lately. I have not seen her for three weeks. Texting and phone calls provide cold comfort.'

Pert understood that A-type men did not always shine in the realm of romance. She sipped her coffee thoughtfully, and then off-handedly asked Grover if he would accept a little guidance in one of his slightly less than perfect realms of endeavor. If it meant dealing with Portia, he was all ears. After establishing the level of his commitment (complete!), she suggested what was, for him, an uncharacteristic way to woo. The situation did not involve competitive sports, pizza and a movie, or quiet evenings in the sack. Planning relied on the support of some of her friends. Over the next two days, she organized a romantic evening to help woo the reluctant Portia.

Wylie completed removing the winter covering on his roses and sat for a while on a wooden bench to absorb the soft promise of springtime. There had been showers that morning, but now the sun shone on his face, causing him to shield his eyes as he observed early spring bulbs in bloom in the border of his little garden. A robin fussily flicked aside bits of garden waste searching for tender morsels in the soil.

He still glowed from the congratulations he received from both Andrea Popov and Anne Proctor the previous day. The property rights matter with BIG AG was settled. Not only had the new company counsel agreed to their complete exoneration, but a liquidated damages fee was included as well. After deducting the University's share, he and Anne Proctor divided the balance.

Anne was faint with delight. She stared at a check that would fund expensive vacation trips for the next twenty years – even if she included Fritz Gumbach on each one – which was a distinct likelihood. Wylie, in no immediate need of a windfall, decided to take his time in allocating the money. How pleasant and rewarding it was to realize that, even as an ancient lawyer, he still had what he considered "the stuff." Past feelings of guilt and frustration at an ignoble retirement disappeared. He was in the game, functioning at a high level. Now, this was what retirement was supposed to be!

The local lawyer dismissed as insignificant by Simon Targle was besieged with tangible evidence that he did, indeed, have the right stuff. As the media became aware of the importance of the "Proctors," reporters focused on Anne Proctor as the one who originally found the seeds. However, Wylie soon became recognized as the person responsible for discovering the plants in the wild. His actions thwarted the insidious downward spiral of engineering novel chemicals and seeds to replace similar systems in nature.

At a higher level, international organizations assessed the worldwide potential of the Proctors for alleviating hunger. Even the most conservative projections showed remarkable benefits for traditionally impoverished third world countries

As he puttered in his garden, he considered how that the trip to the Amazon, undertaken out of stubbornness and a refusal to accept defeat at the hands of BIG AG, had such an unexpected and important result. He searched for a proper adjective. "Wonderful," he decided. He was looking forward to a lot of wonderful.

The opening of the back door interrupted Wylie's reverie. Portia, home from school, called to ask if he wanted a cup of tea. He did. She sat across from him at the little kitchen table and chattered on about current events at the law school. He let her voice become distant, thinking how much she resembled her mother and how much he loved them both. Thinking about how much he would miss her when she graduated and went on her way in the world.

"I'm sorry," he said, "What was that about the AG's office?"

"It is just that, with the notoriety about our trip in the jungle, I seem to have attracted more potential employers. I had one solid offer to clerk in the fifth district circuit court and one to associate with that New York law firm. But, today, I was called into the dean's office where she explained that my interview with the deputy Attorney General for Civil Rights (who is her good friend) had gone very well. Apparently, they play this little game down there in the capitol. They don't want to make an offer unless they are sure I will accept. She asked if she could pass on my answer."

"And did you do that?"

"I couldn't decide just then. I need to think about it. And, Wylie, I would love your counsel."

"Each one of those opportunities could lead to a different career path. Judiciary, private practice, or government service. Of course, those paths could well converge in the future. But, of the three, I believe you would have more immediate responsibility and important cases if you chose the Justice Department. Of course, there's a lot more money in private practice, at least initially. But you will work hard for it. However, consider the source. I would like it just fine if you worked in DC, which is an easy commute and where I have good friends."

Portia reached across the table and pressed Wylie's hand. He sensed she had made up her mind, although she would continue to deliberate on this important decision. They were silent for a minute. Then the door from the garage opened, and Linda bustled in, placed two grocery sacks on the counter, greeted Portia and kissed Wylie on his bald spot.

"Tea! What a good idea."

Doctor Oliver greeted Wylie warmly and ushered him to the chair beside his desk. Wylie saw him close a file folder as he entered the office. The doctor smiled.

"You are quite the intrepid adventurer. I read about your exploits in the paper. You have set the bar high for us older guys."

"Thanks," said Wylie, "but I think that the newspapers played it up just to sell more papers."

The doctor smiled, glanced away and reexamined the file he had just put aside.

"Your results are all good. No perceptible change in six months. How are you feeling?"

"I feel very well. Occasionally, I get a tense sensation down there, but I suspect that is just nerves. Yes, I feel quite well."

The doctor nodded approvingly. "There is a saying about this form of cancer: you don't die from it, you die with it. My best advice is to live your life fully. Horace said it best, I believe. He originated the idea of Carpe Diem – seize the day. But there's more. What he said was 'Seize the Day, putting as little trust as possible in the future.' That's good advice."

"Live for the moment. Right."

There was a long pause and both men, sensing an obligation to extend the consultation with small talk, rehashed Wylie's adventure on the Amazon, talked sports and weather. The doctor rose and shook Wylie's hand, saying he would see him again in about a year.

As Wylie walked to his car, he cataloged his feelings. Elation was an overstatement, although he felt both contented and relieved. What he noticed most was a significant reduction in anxiety. He sat in his car and watched windblown seeds catch the morning sun. Insects buzzed. Reluctantly, he let the moment pass and started the car. Linda was home this morning, and he wanted to share the good news. Damn right, he thought. Wonderful! Carpe Diem.

Mary and Winston enjoyed a traditional family outing, taking Winston's young son, David, to the Middletown zoological garden. The administrators of the zoo were guilty of stretching the truth a bit. The three-acre park was an enlarged petting zoo that, in addition to the usual farm animals, included a single camel, an almost toothless and very bored lion, a family of black bears, a group of mischievous capuchin monkeys and a concession stand. That, and a rickety collection of playground equipment, comprised the "zoological garden." but it was the only animal park in the vicinity. A colorful poster boasted that is was Middletown's finest. Accurate, but misleading, thought Mary as she held David's hand and permitted herself to be dragged toward the monkey cage.

Winston had summoned the courage to ask Mary to dinner after their first meeting. That date might have been a disaster. David developed an earache an hour before the time they were to meet, and Winston did not want to leave him in the hands of the teen-age babysitter. He called Mary to postpone dinner, and she offered to deliver take-out – not Chinese.

She arrived and unpacked macaroni, cheese and little hot dogs for the boy, lobster bisque and filet mignon ravioli with salad for them. Winston opened a bottle of red wine, and they picnicked on the floor of the apartment's living room. David and Mary were close friends by the time he went to bed.

This visit to the little zoo was the sixth time Mary and Winston had been together since the evening of the earache. Winston was pleased that Mary was so fond of his son; she was a fresh companion – smart and funny and creative. She had an unending supply of "knock-knock" jokes that never failed to enthrall David. She and Winston treated each other as friends and colleagues, exchanging glimpses of their professional work, and learning to be comfortable with each other's silence.

As they watched David propel himself on a merry go round, Mary responded to Winston's question about a current project that was taking much of her time.

"Yes, the Bemis thing. My team continues to follow the many leads discovered in the materials found by the F.B.I. You know there are some things I can't talk about, but we have already filed complaints, which are public knowledge, in two main areas. One of them relates to Myron's involvement with Bemis."

'Yeah, he confessed to that a while ago. Everyone makes mistakes, I guess.'

"Well, it turns out the company had a long-standing program of recruiting employees and Master Gardeners at every agricultural college or university in the country. Their effort was like a military intelligence operation – bits of information gathered through guile or bribery. Samples of this or that, all funneled to their headquarters for analysis by their technicians. They crossed many lines and, in the process, obtained information they had no legal rights to."

"You're not going to enumerate the acts and statutes they violated, are you? I can remember the Latin names of thousands of plants, but that legal stuff makes my head spin."

"Not at all. That's one line of inquiry. The other is almost the opposite of the first. Where, on the one hand, they were screwing their competitors, on the other they were conspiring with them to screw their mutual customers. It is as simple as that."

"Thank you, for putting it in terms even a Ph.D. in biology can understand."

They grinned at each other. For the first time they had been bold enough to engage in gentle teasing.

Mary added a bit more about the current Bemis litigation – the criminal and civil remedies sought, the names of individual executives indicted, and the fact that investigators continued to pour over the enormous amount of digital information residing on backup files.

"We are holding off on indicting the Bemis CEO, Dick Geier. He was injured in a freak accident at their plant and remains in guarded medical condition. As soon as he is well enough, though, we will arrest him. It still surprises me that highly placed people engage in such risky behavior. They must believe they are above the law."

"Hubris, right?"

"Yes. You're probably right."

David interrupted their talk, charging toward them and stopping short to demand ice cream. He reached for their hands and began pulling them toward the concession stand. He was their intermediary. He was the element that joined them together.

Anne Proctor and Fritz Gumbach sat comfortably on the couch by Wylie's desk in the room he called his study. He had just completed his review of the agency's proposed contract under which Anne would undertake a two-month speaking tour, describing the discovery of the "Proctors," their development at Van Poppen farm and her exciting foray into the Amazon jungle. Fritz, as her manager, was also mentioned in the agreement.

"I have made a few language changes and strengthened your authority in selecting the person to help you write the forthcoming book. The working title of "Master Gardener" is fine for now, but it doesn't show much imagination. I recommend that you find something less bland, something with more pizzazz. Like, uh, 'Proctors – mystery plants of the Amazon.' Well, maybe that isn't very good, but you get the idea."

"Wylie," said Anne, "Fritz and I can't thank you enough for the splendid work you have done – first in helping resolve that whole genetic engineering mess with BIG AG and then in guiding us through this deal with the agents. I am very grateful. And, about writing that book specified in the contract, I was hoping that you would be the one to help with that. You certainly know more about the whole thing than even I do. How splendid if you could help me write it."

That idea had not occurred to Wylie. He was comfortable with the written word, having authored voluminous briefs, agreements and legal articles. It had been, what, more than fifty years since he had written as a reporter. The prospect of helping Anne intrigued him.

"Let me give it some thought. I kind of like the idea."

Anne smiled.

She and Fritz had slipped easily into the roles of incipient celebrity and faithful manager. At first, Anne was confused and somewhat upset by the attention of agents, publicists, media people and hangers on after her glowing profile appeared in USA Today. Then, as awareness grew of the worldwide potential for her super plants, competition for her services developed among agents and potential managers, and she turned to Wylie to help her sort out various offers and proposals. Throughout, Anne and Fritz intensified their romantic relationship. They were the lucky couple that simultaneously strengthened their business and amorous bonds. As they sat across from Wylie, they appeared to be among the happier couples he had known. Give it another day or so, he thought, and they will be finishing each other's sentences.

Wylie turned from the contract to the planned times and places Anne was to speak, and suggested changes based on his travel experience. Anne was to be "booked" for university campuses, major garden clubs and Master Gardener groups. Her remuneration was agreeable, and all expenses would be covered.

She and Fritz considered it a two-month adventure.

Wylie was intrigued by the arrival of a stately 1962 Rolls Royce Silver Cloud III touring limousine that turned into his driveway and come to a stop inches away from the garage door. A silver haired man in a dark blue suit and cap opened the door, checked the street number over the garage and strode to the front entrance. The two-tone chimes rang.

"I am here to collect Miss Portia Venezia. Is she at home?"

Portia, at the top of the stairs making final adjustments to her dress, confirmed her presence and came toward the front door. Wylie interrupted her.

"Porrie, what is going on? There is a quarter-million-dollar car in my driveway!"

"Car? I don't know. Grover called to say he would be working a little late and that he asked one of the guys in the office to pick me up. We are going to dinner."

The driver, now waiting at the open door, confirmed, "Yes, Mr. Merson engaged me to provide transport. We will be motoring to the Peninsula House, as soon as you are ready, Mam."

Portia followed the driver and examined the beautiful vehicle with spotless maroon body and black top. The body seemed to stretch almost to the street. The driver opened the rear passenger door and ushered Portia into the creamy leather interior. As she settled into the luxurious surroundings, she noticed daffodils glowed from bud vases on each side of the compartment, and burled walnut paneling stretching along the back of the driver's partition. A cooler with bottled water rested in the center armrest.

The eight-cylinder engine purred quietly as the driver backed out and turned the vehicle toward the Middletown business area. Portia was thrilled to be in such luxury, but confused and suspicious as well. This was "one of the guys" picking her up? This guy who was "motoring" her to the Peninsula House?

The Peninsula House was Middletown's newest and most exclusive high-rise located next to a little marina on the Passaquick River. By coincidence, one of Pert Pewtree's major contributors was President of the unit's house committee and was always willing to help his congressional representative and friend. For that evening, he arranged for Grover to use part of his Merson fortune on a private room in the Peninsula restaurant located on the top floor.

Three large bouquets of flowers graced the banquettes in the room, and soft classical music played. Pert had vetoed a live classical quartet or violinist. A server and busboy stood by, waiting to light the many candles in the room.

The Rolls Royce did not come to a stop but gently cruised to rest. Grover stood on the sidewalk, waiting in the crisp April evening air. He opened the door for Portia who emerged with a puzzled expression. Grover spoke before she had a chance to ask her questions.

"Look, it's been almost four weeks since we saw each other, and I missed you very much. So, I just got my quarterly foundation check, and I thought, why not use some of that to treat you to a nice reunion dinner?"

He took her arm and kissed her lightly on the cheek. Portia murmured something he did not understand and as she walked with him toward the building lobby she was illuminated by interior lights.

"You look beautiful tonight. Absence must make the heart grow fonder."

Seeing Grover in the brightly lit lobby she decided he looked, well, very nice also. Had he bought a new suit? My God, was that a tailor-made suit from DC?

"I missed you too," she said.

The lobby attendant smiled broadly as he showed them to the top floor elevator. Portia suspected he knew something she did not. The car rose silently to the top floor where the manager greeted them and guided them to the private dining room. This was their first visit to the restaurant. The heavy drapes and hushed atmosphere, the large windows exposing the winking lights of the city, the unhurried demeanor of numerous attendants bespoke civility and wealth. I wonder, she thought, if I will ever not feel intimidated by this.

The waiter seated her and placed her napkin on her lap. He lit the candles and offered crystal glasses of Lillet aperitif. Golden candlelight flickered through the light amber liquid. She sipped the wine and spoke with Grover about recent events in the law school, and he brought her up to date on Capitol affairs. The wait staff stood discreetly in the shadows. Grover noticed her glance in their direction.

"I thought it would be cool to have the maître d' suggest the dinner," he said. "No menu. I confess that I am intimidated by all this fancy stuff and don't always understand words on the menu, I wanted something special and different. He promised it would be. We just let the waiter know if we don't like it. This is supposed to be an adventure. Is that okay.?"

"Of course."

This was the first time in her experience that Grover had voluntarily relinquished control of anything. And say he was intimidated by anything. She saw him in a new light.

On cue, the waiter served the first course, accompanied by a goblet of white wine.

"The chef offers you crispy duck with blackberry gastrique. Would you care for a bit of fresh pepper?"

Neither knew what "gastrique" was, but they boldly requested pepper. The waiter withdrew and they sampled the duck and decided it was delicious. The wine made it even better. The duck quickly disappeared, and the plates were whisked away, to be replaced by spring garden lettuces which, the waiter assured them, also included shallot dressing, shaved breakfast radish (from their own garden), cucumbers and avocados. New glasses and a different white wine arrived to complement the salad.

As they awaited the next course, Portia informed Grover that she had decided to accept a position with the Attorney General's office, beginning the first of August – so she would have enough time for the bar review course and to take bar exams for the District of Columbia and New Anglia. Grover was delighted.

"So, that means you would be working in the Capitol, right?"

"Yes, that's the plan."

"Wow!"

"Wow?"

"I mean, I'm so relieved," he said. "I was worried you might decide to work some place like New Orleans or the west coast. But this is wonderful. We will be in the same town. Like together."

"That's right."

"Yes. That is so… Yes."

The main course arrived. Thin slices of bison Wellington glowed under a glaze of red wine reduction, which was also drizzled on crisp French beans and cipolini onions. Goblets with three fingers of fine Borolo wine were served to accompany the bison.

When the great beast of the American plains had been dispatched and the Borolo was just a hint of red at the bottom of their glasses, Portia and Grover were in a state approaching bliss. They leaned across the table and touched their foreheads together.

"I really missed you too," she said.

"I'm pretty sure I missed you more."

They unclasped their hands as dessert arrived. The chef offered his specialty – warm Meyer lemon steamed pudding with huckleberry sauce, pippin apples and schlag. The presentation was so beautiful neither one wanted to disturb it with a fork. They smiled at each other, and Portia finally scooped up a bite of pudding and offered it to Grover. Eventually the last course was gone. An after-dinner liqueur was offered that, now fully contented and slightly tipsy, they refused.

Portia saw that he suddenly looked nervous. Anticipation hung in the air.

He reached into a pocket of his new suit jacket, pulled out two three-by-five cards, and turned them so they caught the light.

"Index cards? Index cards?"

"Oh, Portia, I screwed this up so badly before, I didn't want that to happen again. I desperately want this to go right, so I wrote down what I want to say."

He stared at the two cards on the table, looking at Portia with a mortified expression.

"And now I've had so much wine I can't make out some of the words."

She put a hand to her mouth to hide the beginnings of a broad smile.

"But I'm going to do it!"

As he pushed back his chair, preparing to drop to one knee, the chair fell over behind him. As he tried to right himself and the chair, the cards fell from his hand and floated to the table in front of Portia. By the time he recovered, Portia was reading the last sentence of the second card, the one that ended with two question marks.

She looked at her future husband and grinned.

"And? Is there anything else?"

He moved his chair closer to her, sat and extracted a little black box containing a solitaire diamond ring from a pocket. Awkwardly, he presented it to her. She placed the ring on the third finger of her left hand and stood to kiss Grover.

"You will?"

"Yes, I will."

Grover exhaled a great sign of relief, murmured something about how much he loved her, and almost collapsed into her arms.

Applause came from the corner of the room where the chef and servers observed the moment that would be embellished for decades as Portia and Grover explained to their descendants how it was that he almost fell over a chair to make her his wife.

After two nighttime visits to the bathroom, Wylie still managed to return to deep sleep. Half an hour after sunrise his slumbering brain misinterpreted peculiar sounds coming from the hallway and he experienced a flashback to summer days in Sorrento, Maine, where he, Mavis and their small children stayed for vacation. He saw himself on the beach, looking across Frenchman Bay at the islands of Acadia National Park. Sea gulls cried as they wheeled above the lapping waves and strutted along the shore searching for tidbits of food. The cries of seagulls. The cries of seagulls?

Wylie awoke hearing them in the hallway. He was confused. Seagulls in his hallway as the sun peeked over the horizon. It made no sense at all. He found his slippers and moved to the hall where he and Linda had placed Emma's "birthing box." The veterinarian suggested that a large cardboard box lined with towels would comfort the dog as she approached labor and would be an ideal place for the puppies after birth. Wylie realized the seagull sounds came from the box.

Five hamster-like creatures, slick with wetness and stumbling into each other, wriggled next to Emma in the box. She looked wearily at Wylie and licked one of the pups, sending it onto its back. More seagull sounds rose from the box as the babies squealed and grunted. Then, almost effortlessly, another pup appeared, partially wrapped in a shiny membrane that Emma licked off and swallowed. Wylie was amazed that there were only a few damp spots on the towels. Apparently, Emma was an excellent mother.

He called Linda and knelt to examine the creatures. Their eyes were swollen shut and they pushed into each other on stubby legs. I forgot, thought Wylie, that their eyes don't open for about two weeks. They really are helpless at this stage.

By the time Linda arrived, most of the pups found their mother's teats, and the swollen sack on Emma's belly began to loosen a bit. One of the babies confused Emma's thigh for a nipple and Linda gently moved it so it could suck.

Linda and Wylie praised Emma highly as she proudly displayed her brood. Weimaraners always look a bit doleful, but not Emma who seemed to smile. Wylie found some favorite treats that Emma gladly accepted

Emma settled on her side in the box and the puppies slept next to her, lined up like kernels on an ear of corn. As their fur dried, Linda and Wylie, now joined by Portia, noted that there were three pairs of pups: two with silver–gray fur, two colored like dark chocolate, and two light brown. They admired the tiny dogs pushing their stout noses into their mother's belly.

Five weeks later, the puppies resembled furry little fireplugs on bandy legs rushing around the pen Wylie placed near his little garden. The veterinarian offered her best guess to help solve the mystery of their fatherhood. In her experience they resembled nothing other than Labmaraner pups, and she confirmed Portia's suspicion that daddy was probably a chocolate Labrador. She said they would probably grow up to resemble oddly colored Weimaraners, with their bright gray eyes and floppy ears – but, then again, you never know. Wylie decided that he had learned about all he cared to know about genetic matters while pursuing the BIG AG issue. He was content to watch them grow and become whatever the fates determined.

Mavis refused to acknowledge playing any part in Emma's condition. Although she did not exactly say it must be an immaculate conception, she claimed she simply did not know how it happened. After she learned of the veterinarian's diagnosis, she confessed to herself that she did recall seeing a large chocolate colored dog prancing around Emma.

All such matters, however, were put out of mind as she tended to Studly II. He had the unfortunate habit of dissecting the backs of overstuffed chairs and eating their tasty stuffing. Despite her best efforts, Studly II succumbed to a huge stuffing ball lodged in his esophagus at the end of March. Thus, when she visited Portia and Linda at the end of April, she was bereft of animal companionship.

Linda gave each of the pups a name. Feisty, Sleepy, Spaz, Nuzzle, Harry and Frank. When creativity failed, she used the names of high school boy friends. As Mavis visited and watched the puppies gambol in their pen, precocious Harry attempted to establish ownership of the large human by urinating on her foot. Harry was immediately out of the running in the adoption derby.

Wylie had reservations about letting Mavis adopt one of the pups. After all, she had gone through two cats in the course of eight months. On the other hand, he believed she bore some responsibility for their existence. It was probably appropriate that she be given one to raise.

In late May, Nuzzle went home with Mavis. He thrived under her care, received high honors in obedience school and became her constant companion. He matured into a light brown, gray eyed, almost Weimaraner dog with a tendency to engage in goofy, Labrador-like behavior. The dog seemed to help soften Mavis' personality as she grew older, becoming less of a thorn in Wylie's side. He was grateful for that.

As warm weather arrived, the puppies were ready for adoption. Emma was the ideal proud mother of her little brood. She herded them, cleaned them and fed them until it was time for them to leave. Harry stayed with her. She shared Wylie with him.

Dick Geier left the hospital to recuperate at one of his homes, the one by the lake in North Carolina. His doctors were satisfied that he could convalesce there just as well as at a rehabilitation facility and ordered a regimen of therapy and visits from a home health aide. Other service people were on call as needed. Priscilla Sudby was not among them. She found other employment while he was hospitalized and sent him a cheery get-well note. Wife number two lived nearby and planned to visit once or twice a month.

The pain and soreness lessened, but he continued to need the cane. He watched television during the day and drank at night.

What Geier missed most were the authority of power and smoking. For example, he could no longer order someone nearby to buy a pack of cigarettes for him. Visiting therapists concentrated on telling him what to do. He believed his driver, Hector, had signed an oath in blood not to provide him with any outlawed substances like tobacco. His doctor allowed red wine, and Hector monitored his intake. In better days, Hector would have been replaced by a more pliable assistant. However, the person who would have managed that had taken his job at Bemis – and she refused to communicate with him.

His abrupt departure from Bemis, followed by prompt dismissal "to allow him to deal with unspecified medical issues" was, in his view, very inconsiderate. After all, he had agreed to assign all his holdings in Malimsa, and repatriate profits to Bemis. Now he had a pile of official letters from Bemis that referred in a particularly nasty way to other of his dealings and policies while managing the company. The Board decided to hold him accountable for the many management decisions he made without bothering to advise them. Simon Targle did not return his calls, and Frank Edger and George Stirrup failed to provide him with their new unlisted numbers. His only recent contact with a person from Bemis was his former assistant, who made the long trip to his home to hand over bankers boxes containing personal items from his office. She hoped he would be fully healed soon and left quickly to beat the afternoon traffic rush.

Geier summoned his personal attorney, Charles Foible Esq., to review the noxious papers and assist in negotiating his termination package with Bemis. Chuck prepared his original employment contract that, as he recalled, had a generous payout in case of early termination or if his position was affected by any merger or acquisition. Chuck sat across from him at the dining room table on which he had carefully organized little piles of paper.

"Dick, you're looking a lot better than when I saw you in the hospital. Color's good. Any estimate of how long it will be before you lose the cane?" asked Foible.

"Do you have a cigarette?" was the response.

"Sorry. You know I don't smoke."

"Shit."

Geier reached across to the pile of sharpened pencils at Foible's elbow and began to chew on an eraser. Foible cleared his throat.

"You realize, Dick, that the Bemis Board is totally in C.Y.A. mode. They are taking serious heat from major shareholders and Wall Street, what with the abrupt drop in share prices and sharp scrutiny from the feds. They and the investors are unsure about the company's prospects, although they take it as a positive sign that this Lavitra Gascoigne is beginning to pull things together. One item they have made abundantly clear to me is that they must shake you off their fingers faster than a mouse turd in flour."

Geier always found Foible's similes obscure, although the meaning was clear.

"Now, this Malimsa thing, that's the crotch binder. Your employment contract includes a provision in the boilerplate sections that voids payment on termination in case you are fired for cause. That's a nice legal weasel concept that I usually never worry about. Nobody knows exactly what it means. However, this Malimsa thing is seriously close to cause. You'll pardon my saying so, but some might characterize it as stealing from the company, acting in bad faith and failing to perform your fiduciary duties. That is about as close as you can get to cause."

Pushing aside the masticated pencil eraser, Geier asked, "Assume for the moment that I accept that interpretation, what's the fallout?"

"I won't lie to you, Dick. It's not pretty. The Board will not prosecute you and will do its best to obscure the details of the Malimsa matter-- in exchange for a clean break between you and the company."

"A clean break?"

"That means absolutely no further payment of any kind, no perks, no retaining any shares put aside for your retirement. None of that. They did agree not to claw back past remuneration."

"That's a load of crap! After all those years of faithful service? "

"That's what I said! They finally offered a sweetener. They will pay for legal fees in connection with any charges brought by any government agency or agencies. And that could amount to a lot."

Either Foible's last comment or a flash of physical pain from his injuries caused Geier to grimace and sigh mightily.

"Jeez, Chuck, I expected better. I hired most of those ungrateful assholes. I'll have to get back to you on that."

"Of course."

Foible pushed one set of papers aside and selected another.

"This refers to your Bemis medical insurance. They wanted me to assure you that they are not heartless bastards and will fund your insurance until you become eligible for Medicare."

"Well, at least that's something."

"Of course. However, there is one small matter. Unfortunately, that insurance does not cover the, um, implant thing, which is elective surgery. Apparently, they are not inclined to cover that outside of the standard policy. The HR person I spoke with was emphatic that Bemis did not intend to fund a procedure that would permit you, and I paraphrase here, to screw anyone else."

Geier shook his head in disbelief. A month ago, he had overseen the entire operation, and now some pussy was denying him critical elective surgery.

"That's bullshit, Chuck. How petty can they get?"

The attorney chose to ignore that cri de Coeur. There were numerous other items to cover before he left. He selected a file in a bright red folder and resisted the impulse to lick his thumb as he opened it.

"Now, here is what's going on with Ms. Sudby's demand for palimony."

Geier sank into his chair and sighed.

Just north of Lancaster, Pennsylvania a flock of robins, their russet breasts bold against green shards of meadow grass, fossicked among decaying fall leaves. Worms and sluggish insects were their early morning fare. As they scratched and kicked their way along the field, they dislodged dead grass, soil and bits of winter debris. In their wake, a careful eye could see stubby green shoots pushing through the soil, like a child's fingers reaching for a toy. They were the beginnings of asclepias, native American milkweed, as propagated at Van Poppen farm. Growing conditions were excellent that spring, and the meadow would offer a blizzard of new seeds in late August. That would be after thousands of monarch butterfly caterpillars fed on their leaves, formed their jade green cocoons and released a new generation of brilliant flyers. The orange and black dancers filled fields and meadows along the eastern flyways in numbers not seen for years. As Jerome predicted, it was a very good year for mariposas.

During the weeks after Jerome's mini stroke, he and Bitsy concentrated on three things: following doctor's orders to help Jerome make a full recovery, deciding on the details of an open-air wedding ceremony at Van Poppen farm, and selecting invitees to the gala affair. Jerome managed to obtain use of the farm for that purpose, and Bitsy anticipated that the many fruit trees at Van Poppen farm would be in full bloom, providing a billowy and colorful backdrop for the celebration of their wedding.

As plans progressed, it became clear that the wedding would not be the modest affair they originally expected.

The large lawn in front of the main Van Poppen farm building was to be transformed for the wedding. Bitsy arranged for the installation of tiers of flowering azaleas beside a path leading to large white tents intended for dining and dancing. Jerome ordered the temporary installation of a covered platform on which they would exchange vows.

The chef from the Peninsula House was hired to supervise catering for the event. A splendid meal was planned, and a portable kitchen was installed behind the tents. One tent held a forty-foot bar with a brass rail. A disk jockey who promised to play songs that included distinguishable words and actual melodies was hired. In short, it would be the biggest, brassiest, blowout Van Poppen farm had ever seen.

The guest list began to take on a life of its own. Bitsy began with the fellow members of the milkweed project and their "significant others," and Jerome intended to invite members of his staff and a select number of motorcycling friends. Then Bitsy thought of Clem Gatz, Esq. and his team of law students, which reminded her that she should invite certain helpline companions and a few other Master Gardeners, including Wylie. Jerome felt that it would be appropriate to include friends and acquaintances who contributed to his business empire. And so it went.

Jerome's assistant asked if there were any last-minute changes as she prepared to mail the invitations. Bitsy said there were none.

"So, how many does that make, now?" asked Jerome.

"Three hundred and twenty-four."

"I guess it's like eating peanuts. Sounds like it will be a good party."

The day for the wedding dawned bright and clear. Temperatures would be warm for April, in the mid-seventies. Morning dew steamed from the great white tents as scores of attendants, cooks, servers and helpers arrived to prepare. The ceremony was scheduled for four in the afternoon, and guests, having heard of the massive preparations, began arriving at three. The parking area in an adjacent field began to fill with vehicles. The distinctive sound of Harley exhausts rumbled along the country roads as members of Jerome's group arrived. Immediate friendships were established at the bar with the brass rail. The covered platform where vows were to be exchanged was garlanded with flowers provided by Van Poppen Master Gardeners. Everything looked splendid. It was a perfect day for a wedding.

Bitsy drove to the wedding event next to Jerome in the sidecar to his Indian. Its deep blue hull was so highly polished one could lose a finger in its depths, but Bitsy outshone the cab in her ecru wedding dress and aviator goggles. She seemed only slightly less incongruous than Jerome did, in white tie and tails, as he pressed down on the starter to begin the trip to Van Poppen farm. Two close friends rode their Indians as escort, and the cortege cruised down the azalea-bordered lane to the white tents at exactly four in the afternoon. Bitsy alighted from the sidecar, retrieved her bouquet and took Jerome's arm to walk regally toward the platform. Guests cheered and waved as she and Jerome climbed the steps to the platform where the Reverend Annabeth Gimbel waited. The guests hushed as the ceremony began.

Bitsy and Jerome's wedding was a beautiful and flawless event. The guests long remembered the couple's nuptials as a perfect introduction to one of Middletown's most striking spring seasons – where every day was crystalline, and it rained only in the evening. Reverend Gimbel spoke briefly about God's grace that allowed two people to join together in their golden years. There was a quick exchange of vows, and Jerome bent down to kiss his new bride. The audience cheered and laughed, but there were few dry eyes as the couple navigated the steps and walked into the crowd of well-wishers.

Portia clasped Bitsy's hand, and Wylie kissed her cheek. Jerome hugged Portia and warmly acknowledged Wylie's handshake. Linda and Grover murmured their congratulations. The couple moved toward the milkweed group, greeting Winston (and meeting Mary Smith), Freddy C. (awkward in jacket and tie) and Myron. Freddy C. displayed his butterfly-shaped tie clip, and the men exchanged high fives and made little jokes about things known only to their little band. Then the newlywed couple moved to the large tent as the DJ reminded the assemblage that the bar remained open.

Later, Wylie delivered Ann Proctor's wedding gift, explaining that she was on her speaking tour and could not do it herself. It was a scrapbook containing all Bitsy's gardening columns and every newspaper article about the capture and disposition of the notorious "Middletown eco-terrorism group."

It was inscribed "To the most courageous Master Gardener I know! Jerome is a very lucky man. All the best – Anne Proctor." Bitsy was touched by Anne's thoughtful present and, as she gazed across the room toward Jerome, she thought that she was a very lucky woman as well.

Dinner was followed by dancing to what the DJ considered "golden oldies." Portia and Grover glided by, as did Winston and Mary, and Wylie asked Linda if she was ready for a spin and a dip. They executed the movement smoothly, and Linda grasped Wylie tightly once he righted her. Both were slightly flushed and held hands closely as they walked from the dance floor to their table. They watched the other dancers gyrating, swirling and turning, cooled by the evening breeze from the fields that would soon be alive with new growth.

Bitsy and Jerome managed to change from their formal clothes into riding gear and, as the music ceased and a full moon approached ten o'clock high, they returned to the Indian. The remaining guests showered them with birdseed as they boarded the motorcycle and, with a contented roar, sped down the moonlit lane to points undisclosed.

Portia and Grover stood with Wylie and Linda and watched the newly and happily married couple become lost in the folds of twilight.

"Well, that certainly was a fantastic event! Bitsy and Jerome have set an extremely high standard for a wedding. I think ours will be a bit less elaborate," said Grover.

Portia added, "Yes, we were thinking about using the University chapel."

Linda thought that would be a splendid location.

Wylie agreed, then thoughtfully added, "I don't think I could pull off a grand entrance on a motorcycle in any wedding of mine!"

Linda peered at him.

"What are you saying? Are you considering marriage?"

Wylie gave no quick answer. He gazed at Linda's face, soft and luminescent in the light of the rising moon. How could I not, he thought?

He took Linda's hand and pressed it to his lips, then whispered confirmation in her ear. After a long embrace, they joined the younger couple as they walked into the meadow under a night sky abundant with light and promise.

Linda would be at Wylie's side for many years to come.

Epilogue

Edson Montechristo Gonzales-Moro enjoyed the sensation of primitive freedom as he paddled the little dugout canoe along the shady side of the river, hearing bird calls and watching fish snatch crumbs from the surface, creating expanding ripples on the muddy water. He was back in the deep jungle, to the place he loved as he grew up, far from the noise and bustle of Iquitos.

However, he had mixed feelings about visiting his grandmother in the little village of Esperanza situated on the curve in the river near the Amazonia Expeditions lodge. On his last visit, the growth on his grandmother's face was worse. The grayish black crust engulfed the side of her nose and extended to the top of her lip. The deformed mouth seemed to draw the lip upward, exposing the teeth on the left side of her face. It hurt him to see her try to smile. Edson feared her condition would be even worse on this visit, and his heart sank as he approached the landing.

Younger cousins noted his approach and jumped into the water to offer splashy greetings on his arrival. They managed to soak him thoroughly as he pulled his canoe onto the grassy swale beside the communal building. As always, he brought trinkets for the younger children, who clamored around him demanding gifts. Pens, barrettes, bubble gum and plastic action figures tumbled from his pack, and the children clung to his hands and clothing as he made his way to his grandmother's house.

He walked across the open area in the center of the village and scattered some white ducks before reaching the short steps leading to her hut. Like all the other huts, it rose a few feet above the ground on stilts and had a verandah on which his grandmother waited. She had been busy preparing vegetables for the evening meal but paused when she saw Edson come across the field. She stood and opened her arms to him in greeting.

He searched her face and discovered the dark growth had disappeared, replaced by proud pink flesh. Her bright smile showed strong white teeth. There was no gap as before. She wrapped him in her arms and kissed his cheek, which was wet with tears.

Maria stood at the table in the front room of her house and examined the kitchen utensils Edson had brought for her from Iquitos. There was an assortment of plastic storage containers, basins, knives and, what she especially liked, a nutmeg grinder for reducing medicinal and edible tree bark. Only after she was sure she had learned all the latest family gossip and happenings in Iquitos did she explain how it was her lesion had disappeared.

Moises Torres, the one who joined the Army and returned to be a tourist guide before he decided to become a medicine man, had recently established a little farm not far from Esperanza. He came to the village for petrol, supplies and to use the internet when the generator was working. He had known Maria since they were children and was sorry to see that she was afflicted with the black growth. He told her he would try to help the next time he came to the village.

He did. He delivered an orange paste in a small gourd and told Maria to rub it on the dark spot twice a day. He said it would sting and itch, but that only meant it was working. After about two weeks, the black crust began flaking off, revealing bright red flesh beneath. The shrunken area of her lip slowly filled in during the next two weeks and the red color began to fade toward pink. Moises returned and promised the skin would eventually regain its original dusky hue. Maria rejoiced and thanked God every day in the little chapel behind the general store.

Edson recalled how excited Wylie had been when they discovered the bean plants growing in cleared areas near Iquitos and how well he was rewarded. Perhaps Moises would share some of his knowledge about the orange paste. It certainly would not hurt to ask.

Maria pointed to the cleared area along the river and the patch of land planted with bananas, plantains and other things Edson did not recognize. Moises came to the river's edge and helped Maria from the canoe as Edson secured it to some shrubs. Moises seemed ageless to Edson – tall, muscular and colored a burnished mahogany. Only his white hair and the wrinkles around his neck belied his age. The old man was glad to visit with Maria and proudly showed them both the results of his labors on the farm. He offered refreshment of acai juice and sweet plantains. Edson waited patiently as his grandmother and the grizzled ex-soldier lounged on wooden chairs under the palm frond lanai and spoke of other days.

"Yes," he told Edson, "it would give me pleasure to show you the plant that I used to make the salve for your grandmother."

He motioned Edson toward a path leading from the lanai into the jungle. On the path, they both used their machetes to clear new growth and soon arrived at a wet, low area devoid of large trees or shrubs. Clumps of stalks resembling cattails rose from the marshy area, and Edson noticed knobby ivory roots protruding slightly above the wet soil. He had never seen this plant before. Moises carefully maneuvered to one of the plants, reached down and pulled up a wet hand full of ivory roots and bits of the stalk. He snapped a root and showed Edson how its interior was bright orange. His machete nicked the stalk and a white latex bead formed.

"You grind the root the way you make yucca paste and add the white blood to thicken it," he said. After a few hours, it hardens a bit, like petroleum jelly, and it is easy to rub on sore areas. I use it on cuts, blisters and those black patches like Maria had. Most of the time it works. The medicine is good."

He had no objection to Edson collecting some of the plants and wrapping them in palm fronds and moss. Edson placed them in the bow of his little dugout and rejoined his elders. They included him in their talk and offered him beer. He listened attentively but was eager to return to Esperanza. It was not his place to suggest an early departure from Moises' home but, in the back of his mind, he hoped the generator would still be running when he and Maria returned to Esperanza.

He wanted to send an e-mail to his friend, Mister Wylie, about another remarkable plant in his jungle.

Afterword

Thank you for reading Master Gardener. I hope you enjoyed this novel.

If you are interested in learning about other books I've written, please visit my website – https://www.frogworks.com

And if you have a moment, please review Master Gardener on Amazon or the store where you bought it. That will help other readers find the novel and support an independent author. Reviews are so important these days.

Enjoy the read!

Rolf

www.ingramcontent.com/pod-product-compliance
Lightning Source LLC
Chambersburg PA
CBHW031314160426
43196CB00007B/531
9780988231115